THE INTERNATIONAL LEGAL REGIME OF
ARTIFICIAL ISLANDS

SIJTHOFF PUBLICATIONS ON OCEAN DEVELOPMENT,
VOLUME 2

*A series of studies on the international, legal, institutional
and policy aspects of the ocean development.*

General editor: Shigeru Oda

THE INTERNATIONAL LEGAL REGIME OF ARTIFICIAL ISLANDS

N. Papadakis

LL.B., Dip. Shipping Law, LL.M., Ph.D.

Sijthoff — Leyden — 1977

ISBN 90 286 0127 9

Printed in The Netherlands

To my parents

ACKNOWLEDGEMENTS

I wish to express my deeply felt gratitude to my teacher and friend, Professor E.D. Brown, for his encouragement and support in helping me develop my ideas over the past four years.

I am indebted to Miss M.M. Sibthorp, Director of the David Davies Memorial Institute of International Studies, and Professor K.R. Simmonds, who recommended the publication of this book, and also to Dr. T.S. Busha of IMCO for assisting me in keeping abreast of current developments in the field of ODAS.

I would like to acknowledge the patient assistance of Mr. P. Dijkstra in facilitating the appearance of the manuscript in print.

For their courteous co-operation my thanks are due to the library staffs of the Watson Library, University College, the Institute of Advanced Legal Studies, IMCO, and the United Nations Information Centre in London. I am also grateful to Mrs. E. Weston for her conscientious and accurate typing of this difficult manuscript.

My greatest debt is to my Wife, Martha, who in countless ways has made possible the completion of this study, while at the same time containing my unconscious within manageable bounds.

N.P.

LONDON
OCTOBER 1976

CONTENTS

Acknowledgements
Table of Cases
Table of Treaties
Abbreviations
Introduction   1

                        PART ONE

1. TYPES OF ARTIFICIAL ISLANDS   11
          I - Sea Cities   16
         II - Artificial Islands for Economic Use   17
        III - Transportation and Communications   25
         IV - Scientific Investigation and Weather
                 Forecasting   31
          V - Recreation   32
         VI - Military Installations   33
        VII - Other Uses of Artificial Islands   35
       VIII - Feasibility and Implications of Seaward
                 Advancement   37

2. THE RIGHT TO CONSTRUCT ARTIFICIAL ISLANDS   51
          I - Internal Waters   51
         II - Territorial Sea   52
        III - Contiguous Zone   54
         IV - High Seas   54
          V - Continental Shelf   66
         VI - Exclusive Economic Zone   76
              Conclusions   78

3. JURIDICAL STATUS OF ARTIFICIAL ISLANDS   89
        Introduction   89
      I - Natural Islands   91
     II - Ships and Artificial Islands   97
    III - A Proposal for the Legal Status of
            Artificial Islands   103

4. JURISDICTION OVER ARTIFICIAL ISLANDS   123
      I - State Jurisdiction Under International
            Customary Law   124
     II - Jurisdiction Over Artificial Islands
            Constructed on the High Seas   124
    III - Jurisdiction Over Artificial Islands
            Constructed on the Continental Shelf   144
     IV - Jurisdiction over Artificial Islands
            Constructed in the Exclusive Economic
            Zone   151
        Conclusions   151

                      PART TWO

5. INSTALLATIONS FOR THE EXPLORATION AND
    EXPLOITATION OF THE NATURAL RESOURCES
    OF THE CONTINENTAL SHELF UNDER THE
    GENEVA CONVENTION, 1958   161
      I - Resources and Technology   161
     II - The Outer Limit of the Continental Shelf   168
    III - Rights of the Coastal State Over its
            Continental Shelf   168
     IV - Legal Status of Installations and Other
            Devices   174
      V - Jurisdiction of the Coastal State Over
            Installations or Devices and
            Safety Zones   178

6. OCEAN DATA ACQUISITION SYSTEMS, AIDS AND
    DEVICES (ODAS)   193
        Introduction   193
      I - The Work by IOC/IMCO on the Legal Status
            of, and the Preparatory Conference on,
            ODAS (1972)   195
     II - The Preliminary Draft Convention:
            Defining the ODAS   198

7. DEPLOYMENT OF ODAS   205
        Introduction   205
      I - Maritime Zones   207
     II - Deployment of ODAS by International
            Organizations   221

III - International Co-operation in the
Deployment of ODAS and Exchange of
Scientific Data   222

8.   JURISDICTIONAL MATTERS CONCERNING ODAS   227
     I - Recovery and Return of ODAS Found
          in Maritime Zones Under the
          Jurisdiction of a Foreign State   227
     II - Registration of ODAS   229
     III - Jurisdiction Over ODAS   232
     IV - Liability for Unauthorized Interference
          with ODAS   235

9.   SAFETY RULES COVERING ODAS: ACCOMMODATION
     OF CONFLICTING USES   257
          Introduction   257
     I - Notification   259
     II - Marking and Signals   259
     III - ODAS Used as Aids to Navigation   260
     IV - Construction Arrangements and
          Other Safety Provisions   261
     V - Requirements in Matters of Safety
          of Deployment   262

Index of Persons   267

Subject Index   271

TABLE OF CASES

American Banana Co. v. United Fruit Co. (1909-U.S.) ... 153
Anna, The (1805-U.S.) 69
Award of His Majesty the King of Italy with regard
    to the Boundary Between the Colony of British
    Guiana and the United States of Brasil,
    (1904-G.B.-Brasil) 120

Behring Sea Arbitration (1893-G.B.-U.S.) 89

Cargo ex Sarpedon (1877-U.K.) 253
Cheerful, The (1885-U.K.) 253
Continental Oil Co. v. M.S. Glenville (1962-U.S.) ... 249
Cox v. The Army Council (1963-U.K.) 190

Dundee, The (1823-U.K.) 244

Fisheries Jurisdiction Case (1972-I.C.J.) 86
Ford v. United States (1927-U.S.) 153

Gas-Float Whitton, The (1895-U.K.) 243
Harlow, The (1922-U.K.) 118

Lotus, The S.S. (1927-P.C.I.J.) 97,128,153

Mac, The (1882-U.K.) 118
Marguerite Molinos, The (1903-U.K.) 253
Matson Navigation Co. and Union Oil Co. of Calif.
    v. United States (1956-U.S.) 157
Medina, The (1876-U.K.) 253
Melanie S.S. v. S.S. San Onofre (1925-U.K.) 253

Merchants Marine Insurance Co. v. North of England
    P. and I. Association (1926-U.K.).   117
Ministre d'Etat Charge de la Defençe Nationale et
    Ministre de l'Equipment et du Logement v. Starr
    et British Commonwealth Insurance Co. (1970-France).. 84

Naim Molvan v. Attorney General for Palestine (the Asya)
    (1948-U.K.)   126,138
North Sea Continental Shelf Cases (1969-I.C.J.)   119
Nottebohm Case, Second Phase (1955-I.C.J.)   251

Palmas,Island Of, Case (1928-P.C.A.)   130
Placid Oil Company v. S.S. Willowpool (1963-U.S.)   ...   249

Renpor, The (1883-U.K.)   253
Reparations for Injuries Suffered in the Service of
    the United Nations (1949-I.C.J.)   221
Rex v. Godfrey (1932-U.K.)   153

St. Machar, The (1939-U.K.)   118

Tarbert, The (1921-U.K.)...   253
Tolten, The (1946-U.K.)   254

United States v. Aluminium Co. of America (The Alcoa
    case) (1945-U.S.)   153
United States v. Ray (1969-U.S.)   7,74

Wells v. Gas Float Whitton (No.2) (Owners) 1897-U.K.) ... 118

Zabel v. Tabb (1970-U.S.)   111

TABLE OF TREATIES

1884   Convention for the Protection of
        Submarine Cables 188,241,252
          Articles 2, 4 241,252
          Articles 8-9 252
1910   Convention for the Unification of
        Certain Rules of Law Respecting
        Assistance and Salvage at Sea 241-242
          Articles 2-3 241
          Articles 8-11 242
          Article 14 242
        International Convention for the
        Unification of Certain Rules of
        Law in Regard to Collisions 246
          Articles 2-4 246
          Article 7 246
1933   Montevideo Convention on Rights and
        Duties of States 121
1952   International Convention on Certain Rules
        Concerning Civil Jurisdiction in
        Matters of Collision 246
          Articles 1-2 246
        International Convention for the
        Unification of Certain Rules
        Relating to Penal Jurisdiction in
        Matters of Collision or other Incidents
        of Navigation 246,247
          Articles 1-2 247
          Article 4 246
1954-1969 International Convention for the
        Prevention of Pollution of the
        Sea by Oil 102,117,252
          Article IX 252

1958 Geneva Convention on the Territorial
   Sea and the Contiguous Zone ... ...
    Article 1 ... ... 5, 79
    Article 2 ... ... 5,19, 79
    Article 4 52,224
    Article 5 ... ... 52, 79
    Article 8 11
    Article 10 ... ... 7,23,92,93, 96
    Article 11 96
    Articles 14-17 79
    Article 15 53,209
    Article 24 54,123,130,210
  Geneva Convention on the High Seas
    Article 2 ... 5, 55,57,58,125,174,211
        212
    Article 5 ... 125,233,250
    Article 6 125,189
    Article 7 140,226
    Articles 8-9, 13, 22-29 189
    Article 10 257
    Article 11 189,247
    Article 12 229
    Article 15 236
    Article 26 174
    Articles 26-29 174
    Articles 27-28 252
  Geneva Convention on the Continental Shelf
    Article 1 19,187
    Article 2 22,42,66,144,168,169,170
    Article 3 ... 54,67,68,70,144,145,168,
        176,179,210
    Article 5 ... 20,22,53,67,119,144,145,148,
        170,171,172,173,174,175,176,
        178,179,215,216,218,219,223
        235,263,264
    Article 7 175
  Geneva Convention on Fishing and Conservation
  of the Living Resources of the High Seas
    Article 13 19-20
1960 International Convention for the Safety
  of Life at Sea 178,257
  International Regulations for Preventing
  Collisions at Sea 117,257,260
1965 European Agreement for the Prevention
  of Broadcasts Transmitted from Stations
  Outside National Territories 35-36,135
    Articles 1-3 135
    Article 4 36,135

1967   Agreement on the Rescue of Astronauts, the
         Return of Astronauts and the Return
         of Objects Launched into Outer Space ...   228-229
               Articles 2, 4   228
               Article 5   229
         Treaty on Principles Governing the Activities
         of States in the Exploration and Use of
         Outer Space, Including the Moon and
         Other Celestial Bodies   250
1969   International Convention Relating to
         Intervention on the High Seas in Cases
         of Oil Pollution Casualties   102
         International Convention on Civil Liability
         for Oil Pollution   117
         International Telecommunication Union Radio
         Regulations   135
1972   Convention for the Prevention of Marine
         Pollution by Dumping from Ships and
         Aircraft (Oslo)   103
         IMCO Convention on the Prevention of
         Marine Pollution by Dumping of Wastes
         and Other Matter (London)   103

ABBREVIATIONS

ACMRR	Advisory Committee on Marine Resources Research
A.J.I.L.	American Journal of International Law
ASW .	Anti-Submarine Warfare
B.Y.I.L.	British Yearbook of International Law
CLB	Continuous Line Bucket System
C.L.P.	Current Legal Problems
Cmnd.	Command Papers (United Kingdom), 1965 -
COSPAR	Committee on Space Research
Declaration of Principles	Declaration of Principles Governing the Sea-Bed and the Ocean Floor and the Subsoil Thereof Beyond the Limits of National Jurisdiction, U.N. Gen. Ass. Res. 2749 (XXV), 17 December 1970
DOC. E/5650	U.N. ECOSOC DOC. E/5650, 30 April 1975: Marine Questions - Uses of the Sea, Study Prepared by the Secretary-General
DOC.SC-72/CONF.85/8	IOC/UNESCO, IMCO DOC.SC-72/CONF.85/8, Paris, 30 March 1972: Preparatory Conference of Governmental Experts to Formulate a Draft Convention on the Legal Status of Ocean Data Acquisition Systems (ODAS),(UNESCO, Paris, 31 January-11 February 1972)
d.w.t.	dead weight tonnage
ECOSOC	Economic and Social Council of the United Nations
EEZ	Exclusive Economic Zone
FAO	Food and Agricultural Organization
FLIP	Floating Instrumented Platform

GARP	Global Atmospheric Research Programme
ICAO	International Civil Aviation Organization
I.C.J.	International Court of Justice
I.C.L.Q.	International and Comparative Law Quarterly
ICSU	International Council of Scientific Unions
IDOE	International Decade of Ocean Exploration
I.F.R.B.	International Frequency Registration Board
IGOSS	Integrated Global Ocean Station System
ILC	International Law Commission
L.L.M.	International Legal Materials
I.L.Q.	International Law Quarterly
IMCO	Inter-Governmental Maritime Consultative Organization
Indian J.I.L.	Indian Journal of International Law
IOC	Intergovernmental Oceanographic Commission
IOC DRAFT 1965	IOC/UNESCO: Draft of a General Scientific Framework for World Ocean Study, 1965
IOC, Techn. Ser., No.5	IOC/UNESCO: Technical Series, No 5: Legal Problems Associated with Ocean Data Acquisition Systems (ODAS), 1969
I.T.U.	International Telecommunication Union
IUGG	International Union of Geodesy and Geophysics
LORAN	Long Range Aid to Navigation
Margue Report	Report on the Legal Status of Artificial Islands Built on the High Seas, Council of Europe, Consultative Assembly, DOC.3054, 9 December 1971
M.L.R.	Modern Law Review
M.S.A.	Merchant Shipping Act (U.K.)
NATO	North Atlantic Treaty Organization
OAU	Organization of African Unity
ODAS	Ocean Data Acquisition Systems, Aids and Devices
OTEC	Ocean Thermal Energy Conversion
P.C.I.J.	Permanent Court of International Justice
RECHTSGELEERDE ADVIEZEN	"Legal Opinions" on the International Legal Aspects of the R.E.M. Broadcasting Station, published by the R.E.M. in 1964
R.E.M.	Reclame Exploitatie Maatschappij
R.S.N.T.	Revised Single Negotiating Text: U.N. DOC.A/CONF.62/WP.8/Rev.1/Part I-III, 6 May 1976
SAR	Search and Rescue
SCOR	Scientific Committee on Ocean Research
Sea-Bed Committee	Committee on the Peaceful Uses of the Sea-Bed and the Ocean Floor Beyond the Limits of National Jurisdiction, established by the U.N. General Assembly Resolution 2467 A (XXIII) of 21 December 1968

S.I.	Statutory Instruments
SIPRI	Stockholm International Peace Research Institute
SKAMP	Station Keeping and Mobile Platform
SOLAS	Safety of Life at Sea
T.I.A.S.	United States, Treaties and Other International Acts Series
U.K.T.S.	United Kingdom Treaty Series
U.N.	United Nations
UNCLOS III	Third United Nations Conference on the Law of the Sea
UNESCO	United Nations Educational Scientific and Cultural Organization
U.N.T.S.	United Nations Treaty Series
VLCC's	Very Large Crude Carriers
WMO	World Meteorological Organization
WWW	World Weather Watch
Y.B.W.A.	Year Book of World Affairs

INTRODUCTION

"Barring a radical turn in the course of human events
industrial societies will advance seaward to the point that
eventual ocean-sited urban/industrial complexes of some size
may become commonplace" (1).   Indeed, the growing awareness of
the state of depletion of our terrestrial resources, of pollution and over-population creates the need for new uses of
the seas which modern technology is making possible.   The
construction of artificial islands and installations for exploration and exploitation of sea-bed resources, industrial, scientific, and many other purposes, are notable examples of this new
trend.   New sources of food, energy and land for housing and
industries will urgently be needed before a crisis point is
reached.   The sea, with its immense potential, is one of the
possible answers to these pressing problems.
    The oil and gas industry has been operating off-shore on
a large scale for many years.   The recovery of marine hydro-
carbons and hard minerals from the seas requires the construction
and deployment of off-shore installations and submerged
structures in deeper waters.   Fixed platforms are already
possible in 600 to 800 ft. of water under moderate weather conditions and Exxon Oil Company is currently testing a model of
a 24-well platform, with an overall height of about 1,800 ft, for
the 1,500 ft. deep waters of the stormy reaches of the northern
North Sea (2).   Today, the industry has the capability (equipment and technology) to drill in 4,000 to 6,000 ft. of water,
while the drilling ship Glomar Challenger recently bored to a
record depth of 1,412 metres in explorations being conducted on
the Atlantic continental shelf (3).   Furthermore, as the oil
industry moves deeper to the sea to find new petroleum reserves,
the installation of subsea production systems to extract the oil

from the ocean floor is becoming commonplace.   According to
one survey, there were more than 60 subsea production systems
operating around the world off-shore by the beginning of 1975 (4).

The idea of mining a submarine ore reserve through construction of an artificial island is also frequently mentioned
and its advantages and disadvantages are appreciated by mining
engineers.   In certain circumstances, the construction of
artificial islands for underground mining of submarine reserves
will occur in waters at least as deep as those found at the
edge of the continental shelf (5).

A number of artificial islands and installations for
various purposes are being built in the North Sea, off the
coasts of the United Kingdom, France, Belgium, the Netherlands
and West Germany.   The North Sea Island Group, representing
twenty-eight leading construction firms, banks and shipping
companies, has completed a study concerning the construction
of a multi-purpose artificial island about thirty miles off
the Dutch coast in the North Sea (6).   In the United States
a research programme has been initiated by the National Science
Foundation's Research Applied to National Needs Programme to
evaluate the economic, engineering, legal and environmental
feasibility of artificial multi-purpose islands to be located
off the U.S. Atlantic and Gulf coasts.   The study concluded
that an artificial industrial/port island is technically
feasible to construct ten to eleven nautical miles off either
the New Jersey or Virginia coasts (7).

At Kobe, in Japan, several artificial islands of rock
and earth construction, in approximately 40 metres of water
are already in use providing access to off-shore coal mines (8).

Deep-water ports to provide loading facilities for mammoth
tankers have been built in many places around the world, notably
the Persian Gulf.   Over a hundred such off-shore terminal
systems are known to have been installed world-wide since the
first was constructed in 1959 (9).

According to a report published by the United Kingdom
Ministry of Public Building and Works in 1970, aerodromes
constructed off-shore, including floating airports which could
be towed to different sites, are technically feasible and in
many ways superior to land-based sites.   Off the East African
coast near Kenya, there is an unusual off-shore complex structure known as the San Marco Launching Facility, which consists
of a control platform and nearby the launching pad itself.
Independent of the mainland using its own generators for power,
the facility, which is operated by Italy, has been used since
1967 to launch satellites into equatorial orbit (10).

Offshore structures are also being built for scientific
use.   A permanent construction attempt on Cobb Seamount in
1970 was reported to be an unqualified success (11).   The U.K.
Natural Environment Research Council published a report in
1972 including proposals for a network of automatic data-

gathering off-shore stations to be operated jointly with
Germany, the Netherlands and Belgium (12).   Much research work
has already considered the construction of underwater habitats
to be used initially as underwater laboratories.   This research
has mainly been carried out under the American Navy's Sealab
programme and the American Interior Department's undersea
research project in the Virgin Islands since 1970 - known as the
Tektite experiments (13).   Fundamental tests on divers working
at simulated depths of 1,000 ft. water were recently conducted
in the United Kingdom while the industry has already developed
an atmospheric diving suit for 1,500 ft. water (14).

The deployment of Ocean Data Acquisition Systems, Aids and
Devices (ODAS), creates a number of novel legal problems which
require a detailed examination due to the magnitude of the
problems involved.   A Preparatory Conference of Governmental
Experts to formulate a Draft Convention on the Legal Status of
ODAS was held in Paris under the auspices of UNESCO/IOC and
IMCO from 31 January to 11 February, 1972 (15).   A second
session of the Preparatory Conference is hoped to take place
after the Third United Nations Conference on the Law of the Sea,
while a full diplomatic Conference, originally planned for 1973,
is now hoped to be convened before the end of the present decade.

According to Dr. Hammond, giant nuclear power stations on
floating platforms could be reshaping the world by the end of
the century (16).

The Japanese Government has started developing "underwater
tourism".   They have already built buoys moored off-shore with
facilities for tourists to descend below sea-level and observe
the waterscape through heavy glass ports.   They have also
designated several underwater parks on the Pacific coast with
underwater observation towers.   One such tower is fixed 100
yards off-shore and is connected to land by motorail (17).

In the United Kingdom the Pilkington Glass Age Development
Committee have proposed a city designed as a glass-and-concrete
off-shore island to be built at sea, 15 miles from Great Yarmouth,
off the Norfolk coast.   The Sea-City could accommodate a
self-sufficient community of 30,000 and although 50 years ahead
of its time, the plan is practical because the required materials
and technology are presently in use.   The extra construction
cost of building at sea has proved no more than the cost of
purchasing dry land (18).   The Japanese have already built the
world's first floating "sea-city of tomorrow", called Aquapolis.
Aquapolis is anchored off the west coast of Okinawa and was the
Japanese Government's main exhibit at the International Ocean
Exposition of 1975 (19).

In the last few years Europe has experienced the phenomenon
of the so called "pirate" broadcasting stations, anchored outside the territorial sea limits to avoid State control.

The creation of artificial islands on the seas inevitably
raises considerable and complex legal problems.   International

Law, as a body of rules itself in evolution, cannot of course predict and control all likely developments which modern science and technology are constantly evolving. Undoubtedly, artificial islands and installations can be obstacles and even a serious danger to freedom of navigation and fishing. Their presence on the oceans will aggravate the problem of the conflicting uses of the seas. The presence of 6,000 oil and other platforms in the Gulf of Mexico forced the introduction of "Shipping Safety Fairways", marked on nautical charts. They can also become extremely dangerous sources of pollution and nuisance. In particular, neighbouring States will be sensitive to these dangers and to risk of infringement of their laws. Indeed, the establishment of artificial islands by natural persons and corporate bodies under municipal law, outside the territorial sea of a coastal State may be aimed at evading its laws. An example of this is the "pirate" radio stations broadcasting from the high seas to circumvent the monopoly of State radio and television services.

Ultimately, the founders' ambition may be to set up a new sovereign, independent State. Obviously, the founders of such 'States' could embark on such lucrative enterprises as the tax-dodging registration of companies and "flags of convenience", radio and T.V. stations, international lottery, casinos, and even the issue of their own passports, stamps and coinage, the conferring of titles, etc. Already attempts have been made, some more serious than others, to create new 'States' by erecting artificial islands on the high seas. One such case involved two rival companies wishing to construct artificial islands on reefs four and a half miles east of Elliot Kay, off the southeast coast of Florida, to be named "Atlantis, City of Gold", and "Grand Capri Republic" (20). In Italy an engineer, Signor Rosa, built an artificial island of steel and concrete off the Adriatic resort of Rimini, and in early 1968, declared it a sovereign State (21).

Seamounts in the deep oceans may already provide bases for artificial islands. Technology for such enterprises is available now and only the necessary economic motivation is required. Seamounts are already being utilised as bases for emplacing scientific equipment, and possibly as bases for military installations. Given the secrecy surrounding such military operations, naturally, data is not available. States possessing such artificial islands could conceivably claim control of large sea-bed areas with valuable resources and assert wide jurisdiction. These could eventually become centres of large underwater empires and, should we witness that phenomenon, "present mini-State problems would appear insignificant in the light of such developments" (22).

Among other legal problems which have to be considered with regard to artificial islands is that of the entitlement of such islands to a territorial sea, continental shelf and exclusive economic zone.

Does the doctrine of the freedom of the high seas comprise this "freedom", namely, the right to erect artificial islands on the high seas? Is this "freedom" one "... recognised by the general principles of international law", since it is omitted from the enumeration of such freedoms in Article 2 of the Geneva Convention on the High Seas, 1958?

The problem of the juridical status of artificial islands is one of primary importance and poses difficult questions. On the first impression, they are neither islands nor ships yet they possess common features and for legal purposes attempts have been made to assimilate them to islands or regard them as ships. This inevitably raises the problem of what is an island and a ship in international law.

It would be of considerable significance if artificial islands were to be assimilated to natural islands, since every island has its own territorial sea. It will also be remembered that "The sovereignty of a State extends, beyond its land territory and its internal waters, to a belt of sea adjacent to its coast, described as the territorial sea", and that "The sovereignty of a coastal State extends to the air space over the territorial sea as well as to its bed and subsoil" (23). Apart from the territorial sea, the importance of the definition of an island is considerable because, however small the island or the area of land or the artificial structure purporting to be an island might be, it inevitably involves the questions of the zones contiguous to it and the continental shelf.

Assuming that artificial islands can be assimilated neither to natural islands nor to ships, the question of the appropriate legal system remains unanswered. Which law is to regulate the life and activities of the inhabitants of artificial islands? The potential conflict between the neighbouring coastal nation and the national State of the founders or inhabitants can already be seen.

It has to be emphasized further that this study is con-concerned with artificial islands constructed on the seas only for peaceful purposes. Thus, the remarks which follow do not, unless expressly stated, refer to military installations, which, because of the magnitude of the problems involved, need a separate and detailed examination. The question of these installations is naturally closely connected to disarmament and arms control measures. One of the main problems to be faced is, of course, how far the Great Powers are willing to go in setting limitations on the military uses of the seas. The military and political aspects are of fundamental importance with significant legal consequences, but are outside the scope of the present study. However, in order to underline precisely the magnitude of military, political, ecological, legal and other problems created by the construction of military instal-lations, a brief description of those already built or planned

for the foreseeable future, will be attempted in Chapter I deal-
int with the types of artificial islands.

One final remark. Literally speaking, an artificial island
is a man-made alluvion formed by placing soil and/or rocks
in the sea which partakes thus of the "nature of territory".
It is a non-naturally formed structure, permanently attached to
the sea-bed and surrounded by water, which is above water at
high-tide (24). The term 'installations' on the other hand,
refers collectively to man-made structures constructed from such
other materials as concrete and steel, for example drilling
platforms. These structures, therefore, do not partake of the
"nature of territory" and do not possess the same degree of
permanence as the artificial islands. Yet for working purposes
the term 'artificial islands' which primarily refers to
structures of the first category, is often rather loosely used
throughout this study, as comprising all man-made structures,
installations and other devices on the seas, which prima facie
are neither islands nor ships in international law.

NOTES

1. "Experiments in Excellence", a Report of the Conference
on Seaward Advancement of Industrial Societies, held on
December 2-3, 1974 at the U.S. National Academy of Sciences
(hereafter cited as Experiments in Excellence); see in
Marine Technology Society Journal, Vol. 9, No. 3, March 1975
pp 4-28.
2. Ocean Industry, December 1975, Vol. 10, No. 12, at p.35
3. D.J. Skinner and D.S. Hamett, Sedco 445 - Drilling
without Anchors in 2,000 ft.-plus water depth, in 1975 Offshore
Technology Conference, May 5-8, Houston-Texas, Proceedings,
Vol. I, p.9; San Diego Law Review, Vol.13, 1976, p.656.
4. U.N. ECOSOC DOC. E/5650, 30 April 1975 "Uses of the
Sea", study prepared by the U.N. Secretary-General, at p.19
(hereafter cited as Doc. E/5650).
5. U.S. National Academy of Engineering, Toward Fulfilment
of a National Ocean Commitment, 1972 (hereafter cited as U.S.
National Academy of Engineering 1972), at p.97.
6. North Sea Island Group, a Firm Footing in the Sea, 1975,
Offshore Engineer, June 1975; p.36.
7. J. Bonasia, Evaluation of multi-purpose Industrial-Port
Islands: Sea Island Structure Engineering Research Study, in
1975 Offshore Technology Conference, May 5-8, Houston-Texas,
Proceedings, Vol. III, pp 9-21.
8. J.J. Pot, Industrial Islands in the North Sea - A
Useful and Feasible Alternative, in "Beta" - Journal for Technical

and Chemical Officials, No.2, February 6, 1970 (hereafter cited as J.J. Pot, Industrial Islands in the North Sea).

9. Doc. E/5650 at p.20

10. Ibid., at p.22

11. Oceanology International, October 1970, at p.14.

12. Report of the Natural Environment Research Council, House of Commons, Paper 411.

13. Science News, August 3, 1969, p.235, and October 3, 1970, p.283; National Geographic, Vol. 140, No. 2, August 1971, pp. 256-96.

14. Oilman, weekending January 31, 1976, at p. 4; Ocean Industry, Vol. 10, No. 12, December 1975, at p.40.

15. DOC. SC-72/CONF. 85/8, Paris 30 March, 1972.

16. THE GUARDIAN, December 31, 1968.

17. THE TIMES (London), May 21, 1969.

18. The Progress, The Unilever Quarterly, Vol. 52, No. 2, 1968. See also THE TIMES (London) Feb. 29, 1968, and THE SUNDAY TIMES, March 3, 1968.

19. NEWSWEEK, August 11, 1975, at p. 25.

20. United States v. Ray 161 N.Y.L.J. (1969); 63 A.J.I.L. (1969), at p. 642; 64 A.J.I.L. (1970), at p. 954.

21. THE TIMES (London), December 4, 1968.

22. F.M. Auburn, The International Sea-Bed Area, 20 I.C.L.Q. (1971), at p. 182.

23. Articles 1 and 2 of the Geneva Convention on the Territorial Sea and the Contiguous Zone, 1958, 516 U.N.T.S. 205; 1965 U.K.T.S.3; Cmnd 2511.

24. Compare this with Article 10 of the Geneva Convention on the Territorial Sea and the Contiguous Zone 1958, which provides that: "An island is a naturally-formed area of land, surrounded by water which is above water at high-tide".

Part one

Chapter 1

TYPES OF ARTIFICIAL ISLANDS

As has already been indicated the pressure of competitive, and often conflicting, needs for land use will inevitably lead to the development of what might be called 'sea land'. The possibilities of extending land into the sea, by landfill for instance, and the construction of artificial islands are a vast potential to cater for immediate and future needs.

It is thus the purpose of this chapter to examine the various artificial islands and installations already erected or planned for the near future, in view of the increasing pressure to utilise the ocean resources.

The phenomenon of extending artificially 'land' into the sea is already well-known and in certain cases, it has not escaped the attention of international law. The most notable example is that of ports where the artificial extension takes the form of technical improvements of already existing 'natural' port or harbour facilities. According to Gidel, the extent of the port is limited by its artificial works or if the port is a natural one, the low water line (1). At the 1930 Hague Codification Conference, the following text with regard to ports was produced by the Second Committee :

"In determining the breadth of the territorial sea, in front of ports the outermost permanent harbour works shall be regarded as forming part of the coast" (2).

Similarly, Article 8 of the Geneva Convention on the Territorial Sea and the Contiguous Zone 1958 provides that :

"For the purpose of delimiting the territorial sea, the outermost permanent harbour works which form an integral part of the harbour system shall be regarded as forming part of the coast".

The International Law Commission stated further in the

Commentary on Article 8 that permanent structures erected on
the coast and jutting out to sea, such as jetties and coast
protective works, are assimilated to harbour works (3).

The practical effect of Article 8 is that the baseline
for measuring the breadth of the territorial sea will move
seawards when taking into account the "outermost permanent
harbour works ..." However, it is acknowledged that the
language of Article 8 creates a few problems of interpretation
and application. The Article refers to "outermost permanent
harbour works which form an integral part of the harbour system",
but it says nothing about the location of such harbour works.
What will happen, for instance, in the case of an installation
which juts out to sea several miles from the coast? Already,
in 1954, the United Kingdom delegation commenting upon the
International Law Commission's draft stated that the Article
on ports should be modified in the light of some recent
developments, citing as an example, a pier 7 miles long under
construction in the Persian Gulf. It stated that it would
seem to be desirable that installations of such a type should
be treated on the same basis as artificial installations on the
continental shelf, in that they should be entitled to a relatively limited navigational safety zone rather than to a belt of
territorial sea (4). McDougal and Burke have also supported
a similar view : "... when such projections do reach excessive
length, there seems to be little justification for creating
a bulge in the territorial sea, and even less for creating an
area of internal waters, since coastal interests do not, by
reason of the object, become heightened in such a degree as to
require such a substantial increment of authority. Recognition
of limited authority for safety and maintenance purposes would
be fully adequate to meet coastal needs" (5).

Another matter for concern has been whether the phrase
"which form an integral part of the harbour system" is meant
to require physical contact between the harbour works and the
coast. According to McDougal and Burke, the purpose of this
phrase "may have been to emphasize that the works involved
must be physically connected with the coast in order to
affect delimitation" (6). Professor Riphagen, on the other
hand, interprets this phrase as apparently not requiring "a
physical contact between the "works" and the more or less
natural harbour, let alone (again) a physical contact above
water. Off-shore terminals connected with the main harbour
by underwater cables and pipelines would seem to be included;
such terminals may be located at a considerable distance from
the coast" (7). Article 8 does not further require that the
harbour works are installations which are above water - either
at high tide or only at low tide - and it does not make any
distinction between fixed and floating harbour installations.
It would appear, however, that within the context of Article 8,
and more generally within the context of Section II of the

Territorial Sea Convention which deals with the delimitation
of the territorial sea, only harbour works above water
at high tide (or at least at low-tide) are envisaged (8).
Article 10 in Part II of the Revised Single Negotiating Text,
presented by the Chairman of the Second Committee at the
end of the fourth (New York) session of the Third United
Nations Conference on the Law of the Sea, attempts to rectify
some of the deficiencies of Article 8 of the 1958 Territorial
Sea Convention. That Article, entitled "Ports", reads as
follows :

> "For the purpose of delimiting the territorial
> sea, the outermost permanent harbour works, which form an
> integral part of the harbour system are regarded as forming
> part of the coast. Offshore installations and artificial
> islands shall not be considered as permanent harbour works"
> (9).

Apart from the technical improvements of already existing
'natural' port or harbour facilities, artificial new harbours
are planned to be built in several countries through land
reclamation in sea-waters adjacent to the coast (10). Even
though these harbours would not appear to be covered by Article
8 of the Territorial Sea Convention, nevertheless such activities would seem to be of a similar character. It is further
assumed that land reclamation in sea-waters immediately
adjacent to the shore, wholly unrelated to harbour facilities
or other activities incidental to traditional uses of the sea,
is probably taking place in several places around the world (11).

The Geneva Convention on the Territorial Sea and the
Contiguous Zone 1958, is completely lacking of any provisions
as to the admissibility and effect, if any, of such land
reclamation, on the delimitation of the territorial sea.

The next step, after the artificial extension of land
into the sea, is the construction or emplacement of artificial
islands and installations far from the shore. As was indicated
earlier, seamounts in the deep oceans may already provide bases
for artificial islands. Technology for such enterprises is
available now and only the necessary economic motivation is
required.

Seamounts are underwater mountains formed by volcanic
activity. They are elevations rising from the ocean floor and
"are classified as such when their elevation reaches one kilometer
or more from the surrounding ocean floor" (12). It is
estimated that there exist in the Pacific alone some 10,000
seamounts, over 2,000 of which have already been discovered and
mapped (13). Other seamounts have been discovered and
explored in the Indian Ocean, the Caribbean, the South China
Sea and the Gulf of Alaska (14). These may be found at varying
depths below the surface, depending upon their age and the
conditions to which they have been subjected, but at least
several of them rise to within several meters of the ocean's

surface.   Of the seamounts now mapped in the Pacific, which
are outside the territorial sea of any nation, seventy rise
to within 200 metres of the surface (15).   The largest known
seamount which is located northwest of Midway and lies 1500
feet below the surface, is approximately seventy miles
long and forty-five miles wide, rising some 15,000 feet from
the ocean floor (16).   The Cobb Seamount lies within 122
feet of the surface and some 270 miles west of Washington State
(17).   The summit of the recently discovered Vema Seamount,
500 miles off the coast of Southwest Africa, is 30 to 40
fathoms below the ocean surface, and its small peak rises
to 14 fathoms below the surface (18).   It is further estimated
that "approximately 430 seamounts in the inter-tropical belt
are capped by atolls, which are coral rings that grew upon
volcanic mountains during their slow subsidence"(19).
     The preceding short analysis makes it clear that "the
common characteristics which all seamounts possess and which
makes them of immediate concern and value is their elevation
above the sea floor, and their relative proximity to the
ocean's surface.   Those which rise very close to the surface
may provide a base for above water operations;   while those
which rise thousands of feet above the deepest parts of the
ocean may be used, when technology permits, as stepping stones
from the surface to the abyssal depths" (20).   It is precisely
this proximity of seamounts to the ocean surface which will
permit the construction of installations and artificial islands
in the very deep seas.   The uses will be many and varied,
practically limitless, including the construction of installations protruding above sea surface, completely submersible
installations and systems, and ultimately the possible construction and establishment of large artificial cities.   Perhaps the
economic, political and military significance of seamounts is
best summarised in the following extracts by E.W. Seabrook
Hull (21) :
     "It is this last category, seamounts rising from the
     deep sea-bed to within a few feet of the surface, where
     we feel the first activity of economic/political/military
     significance will occur, and which, therefore, is most
     demanding of a suitable international legal regime ...
          There are four basic areas in which certain conditions
     must be met before a given activity will be initiated on
     the deep sea-bed.   They are: (1) Motive;   (2) Technology;
     (3) Resource; and (4) Investment...
          The motives, or reasons, for doing something on the
     bottom of the non-sovereign ocean break down into
     (a) economic.... (b) extension of existing national sover-
     eignty;   (c) the establishment of new sovereign entities;
     (d) military, such as the installation of either offensive
     or defensive manned or unmanned bases, and the deployment
     of weapons, detection gear, counter measures equipment, etc;

and (e) "other" which might include secure Mafia retreats,
an escape for a wealthy recluse, etc."
... "The United States Naval Civil Engineering Laboratory
at Port Hueneme, Calif., has a project underway to
establish a manned base at a depth of 6;000 feet, which puts
it clearly within the upper depth limits of both the Mid-
Atlantic Ridge and countless seamounts and guyots (table-
mounts) in both the Atlantic and Pacific Oceans.   There
is no cost-effective reason currently for private individuals
to wish to establish manned habitats at these depths.   It
can be done, but it is too costly.   There are, however,
in excess of 70 readily identifiable seamounts in the
Atlantic, Pacific and Indian oceans (a) which are
clearly beyond anyone's sovereign jurisdiction and
(b) which rise to within 100 fathoms (600 feet) of the
ocean's surface.   An appreciable number are within 200 feet
of the surface, and several are within 30 feet.
      These seamounts are clearly within the depth limits of
current technology.   At least one is being examined and is
shortly to be occupied for scientific purposes - Cobb
Seamount off the United States northwest coast.   At least
one more has been extensively fished for lobsters - indeed
fished out.   That is Vema Seamount off the southwest coast
of Africa.
      In terms of profit-orientated criteria, these seamounts
are already in the "gray area" - that is, there are a
variety of things that are now or soon will be possible to
do on these seamounts for a profit.   They are so imminent
that precise forecasting is no longer possible.
      Obviously, then, the technology exists for anyone who
cares to occupy one or more of these seamounts for purposes
of extending sovereignty or establishing new sovereignty.
Land-locked nations may thereby become maritime nations.
And, there is nothing short of the use of force that can
prevent anyone who wishes and has the wherewithal from
setting up one or more entirely new nations.   It would
be expensive to set up and maintain, but it can be done;
and the cost is not so high as to put such an event beyond
the realm of imminent possibility.   Not only can habitats
be emplaced on such seamounts, but artificial islands can
be built and extensive complexes bored out of the seamount
itself...
      The technology, the motive, the resource (the seamounts)
and the necessary investment are all currently available.
In point of fact, it only remains for the realisation to
sink in that it can indeed be done for the occupation of
the seamounts for non-military purposes to begin.   Then,
international law will have to reckon with an established
fact - a fact for which present international law does
not provide.   As for military bases on the seamounts, in

the sense of unmanned detection gear many seamounts are
already occupied.   Under the cloak of secrecy, the establishment of manned military bases may also have already begun..."

I.   SEA CITIES

The twenty-first century is going to be, by all accounts,
a critical century for mankind owing to the population explosion
and its pressure on land.

Many experts are predicting that the sea-cities could be
one answer to the United Nations' warning that the world will
double its population within the next 40 years.   Indeed, it
appears that there are quite a few good reasons to support such
a prediction:
(a) The oceans cover 71 per cent of the surface of the globe and
    the sea cities, as they are envisaged at present, could be
    constructed in any of the shoal waters that exist over 10
    per cent of the surface of the ocean.
(b) Major centres of population in the world are either by or
    very close to the sea and they have enormous industrial
    expansion, growing with the development of water-borne
    communication.
(c) Bearing in mind the shortage of land for building sites, the
    construction of new cities at sea would relieve the pressure
    of taking vital agricultural land for urban development.
(d) Building at sea avoids gross costs of land acquisition, and
    as the Pilkington Committee has pointed out in the United
    Kingdom, the cost of building a sea-city could be much the
    same as for a similar city on land.

Sea-cities may be either fixed on the sea-bed or floating:

1.   Sea Cities Fixed on the Sea-Bed

It is common knowledge that real villages have been erected
on piles in the sea off the coast of South-East Asia, particularly
off the coast of Indonesia (22).   Such villages often were
bases for drug traffickers, smugglers and pirates.

In Japan, Mitsubishi was reported as long ago as 1967 to
have plans for a coal mining artificial island with a population
of 5,000 people and all services, including hospitals and schools
(23).

In the United Kingdom, as has already been noted, the
Pilkington Glass Age Development Committee have proposed a city
designed as a glass-and-concrete off-shore island, to be built
at sea, 15 miles from Great Yarmouth, off the Norfolk coast.   The
sea-city could accommodate a self-sufficient community of 30,000
people, and although 50 years ahead of its time, the plan is
practical because the required materials and technology are presently in use.   The extra construction cost of building at sea
has proved no more than the cost of purchasing dry land (24).

2.   Floating Sea-Cities

A Japanese study of the economic evolution of ten South-
East Asia countries has resulted in the Project Kotair.   This
study comes up with the extraordinary proposal for a floating
sea-city in the year 2020 having a population of 30 millions (25).
It has also been reported that the University of Hawaii is
testing a 1 : 20 scale model of a floating city (26).
Another scale model concerns an entirely ocean-based
community, the 'Triton City' which is "a floating community that
would accommodate about 5,000 people and weigh 150,000 tons" (27).

II.   ARTIFICIAL ISLANDS FOR ECONOMIC USE

1.   Installations for the Exploration and Exploitation of Natural Resources. (See below Chapter 5).

2.   Industrial Artificial Islands

The conflicting goals of preservation of the environment
and rapid industrial growth, exacerbated by the lack of industrial
space, have prompted the experts - engineers, planners, environmentalists, etc. - to seek some solution to the seas through the
construction of artificial islands.   Industries, particularly
the heavily polluting ones, could be concentrated on man-made
islands remote from densely populated areas.
The advantages of these islands would appear to be:
prevention of irreparable damage to the environment; separation
of residential and industrial areas; they make it unnecessary
to invest money in attempts to update inadequate facilities;
and finally, they will be constructed under governmental supervision instead of being promoted by stricly private interests.
Furthermore "the very nature of an island brings important
advantages no industrial site on the mainland could equal:
there is always sufficient water for cooling purposes;... there
is almost always wind.   The air above the island circulates
so that no layer of polluted air can hang above the island;
smog, like that above cities such as Los Angeles and Tokyo, cannot
occur above the island, for there is no traffic there; acids,
dust, plaster, clay are all neutralized and absorbed in a
natural manner by the sea-water and the sea-bed " (28).
Thus, the North Sea Island Group, for example, has suggested
that the solution to the dilemma lies not with the slowing down
of economic growth, but with stricter demarcation between
residential and industrial areas.   Herein lies the importance
of artificial islands.   The Group recently completed a
feasibility study on the possibilities of a multi-purpose
artificial island for industrial development to be built some
thirty miles off the Dutch coast in the North Sea (29).

The island, which would cover an area of 4,000 to 12,500 acres
will be built, quite solidly on sand and it will be protected by
a sea-wall, made up of a dam, consisting of gravel, rocks and
concrete blocks, and possible breakwaters in addition.   It is
planned to accommodate port installations, steel enterprises,
chemical and petrochemical works, aluminium factories and blast
furnaces, tank storage facilities and a tanker cleaning plant.
In addition to these a residential area in the form of a motel
has been planned for the employees, who would work in shifts.

The Bos Kalis Westminster Dredging Group, which is the
leading firm of the North Sea Island Group, first proposed the
construction of artificial islands as a solution to the twin
problems of pollution and lack of industrial space, in a report
published in 1971.   The report considered three categories of
industrial artificial islands according to their size which
would be constructed in waters averaging a depth of 20 to 30
metres (30).

In conjunction with this study, Bos Kalis released a second
one dealing with the feasibility of locating a waste processing
facility on an artificial island that could eventually become
a huge 'pollution factory' for handling industrial and domestic
wastes from Britain, the Netherlands and other North Sea Countries.
This plan calls for a 120 acre island built up from dredged sand
and concrete blocks in about 65 feet of water, 50 miles off the
Dutch coast (31).

The idea that artificial islands could be an answer to the
environmental problem, so far as the polluting industries are
concerned, may also be seen in the plan submitted to the
United Kingdom Government by Professor A.A.L. Baker and his
colleagues of Imperial College, London.   This plan is connected
with the Channel Tunnel Project.   It involves turning the
submerged mid-channel sandbanks of Varne and Le Colbart into
artificial islands, which should be no more dangerous to shipping
than the existing shallow waters of the banks.   These islands
could be a valuable base for industrial development and could
also provide a mid-channel port for deep-draught carrier ships.
The large corporations are extremely interested in the idea.
They want land for industrial development that cannot be conveniently located on increasingly scarce mainland sites (32).

Finally, a London consulting engineering firm, Bernard L.
Clark and Partners, have recently proposed the construction of
two industrial islands, 'Sealand' and 'Shipwash', some 11
kilometres east of the Naze - just above the River Blackwater on
the Essex coast.   Bernard Clark estimates that Sealand would
cost £15 million to build and Shipwash £35 million (33).

3.   Fisheries and Fish-farming

Since time immemorial fish has been the staple sea resource
used by man, yielding high food protein.   The world fish catch

increased by over 250 per cent during the period 1948-1970 (34).
At present, between 11 and 15 per cent of the world's total
protein supply comes from the sea (35).   Technology has
been one of the major catalysts - more powerful and larger ships
and nets, fish detection by electronic devices and use of earth
satellites.   This has been accompanied by the expansion of
long-distance fishing fleets, particularly by the Soviet Union
and Japan (36).   Fishing, along with navigation, has naturally
been one of the first freedoms of the seas to be recognised and
consolidated by customary law, and is expressly referred to in
Article 2 of the High Seas Convention 1958.
    This tremendous technological expansion has, however,
led to over-exploitation of many traditional fishing grounds,
and, furthermore, it clearly threatens the balance of the marine
ecosystem.   Indeed, "permanent imbalance results if too much
exploitation takes place: overfishing, like some varieties of
pollution, is a permanent imbalance, changing a resource from
a renewable into a non-renewable one" (37).   The necessity
for fisheries management, both in terms of conservation and
allocation of fishery resources, has now come to be recognized
as a current problem in nearly all parts of the world.
FAO statistics show a decline in marine catches from over 60
million tons in 1970-71 to 56 million tons in 1972 and an
estimated 54 million tons in 1973, due mainly to a dramatic
decline in the catch of Peruvian anchoveta (38).   However,
apart from resorting to energetic conservation measures and to
fish farming in a systematic way, the fishing industry may also
have to turn to new areas of the high seas for survival (39).

(a)   Sedentary Fisheries

    Prior to the Continental Shelf Convention (1958), sedentary
fisheries on the high seas beyond the territorial sea, were
regarded in principle as part of the freedom of fishing on the
high seas.   However, exclusive State rights, which have been
generally recognised, could be established on the legal basis
of "prescription" or "occupation" (40).   Today, this holds true
only for the high seas beyond the limits of the continental
shelf, as the latter is defined in Article 1 of the Continental
Shelf Convention 1958.   The Geneva Conference of 1958 decided
to include sedentary fisheries (41) among the natural resources
of the continental shelf and thus they became subject to the
exclusive sovereign rights of the relevant coastal State (42).

(b)   Fisheries Conducted by Means of Equipment
        Embedded in the Sea Floor.

    According to Article 13, para 2, of the Geneva Convention
on Fishing and Conservation of the Living Resources of the High
Seas 1958, the expression "fisheries conducted by means of

equipment embedded in the floor of the sea" means "those fisheries using gear with supporting members embedded in the sea-floor, constructed on a site and left there to operate permanently, or, if removed, restored each season on the same site."

These fisheries remain subject to the principle of the freedom of fishing on the high seas. It makes no difference if the equipment used in these fisheries is embedded in the continental shelf, as they are not included in the natural resources of the shelf upon which the coastal State exercises sovereign rights. Similarly, the Convention on Fishing and Conservation of the Living Resources of the High Seas, does not accord to a coastal State the right to regulate a fishery of this kind in areas of the high seas adjacent to its territorial sea so as to exclude foreign nationals, "except in areas where such fisheries have by long usage been exclusively enjoyed" by its own nationals (Article 13, para. 1).

It follows that installations embedded in the sea-bed of the continental shelf for fisheries of this kind do not fall under Article 5 of the Continental Shelf Convention which accords to a coastal State the right "to construct and maintain or operate on the continental shelf installations and other devices necessary for its exploration and the exploitation of its natural resources, and to establish safety zones around such installations and devices and to take in these zones measures necessary for their protection" (para 2).

Fish traps, therefore, are not regulated by the Continental Shelf Convention, when embedded in the sea-bed of a continental shelf, and their legal status is not assimilated to that of the installations for the exploitation of the natural resources of the continental shelf, by virtue of their site.

(c)   Ocean Fish Traps

It appears that these could not be embedded in the deep sea floor in the foreseeable future. Such an enterprise is not yet feasible either technologically or economically. It is, nevertheless, considered possible that these could be embedded in the seamounts in the deep ocean (43).

(d)   Fish-Farming (or Aquaculture)

Many recent studies indicate that the expected total yield from the seas may not be adequate to meet the expanding world demand for food fish (44). In this respect the potential which fish farming or aquaculture presents is now an actuality. For example, it is considered very unlikely that any major increase in the production of certain fisheries, such as molluscs and shrimps, can be achieved otherwise than through fish farming.

The idea of farming the sea has received much publicity

recently, even though in some places, the cultivators of mussels, and especially oysters, have been known for generations (45).

Aquaculture has been defined as "the rearing of aquatic organisms under controlled conditions using the techniques of agriculture and animal husbandry" (46).

Fish farming on a world-wide scale is restricted largely to the cultivation of shellfish and, in particular, oysters (for both foods and pearls) and mussels. The only other marine species to be farmed on any scale are yellow-tail shrimps and prawns. Although it is generally agreed that at present aquaculture accounts for about 5 per cent of the total world catch, opinions vary as to the future role of fish farming in increasing the yield of food from the sea. Few doubt, however, the potential, particularly in the protected waters of estuaries, bays and sounds (47). It is also considered that in view of the fact that unpolluted areas must be sought out and utilised for aquaculture, seamounts might prove highly desirable for such an enterprise, since they are abundant in the high seas, and relatively unpolluted.

Fish farming inevitably involves the construction of artificial structures in the seas. It is well known by fishermen that permanent fish concentrations are always structures of some kind: natural reefs and lodges, artificial but accidentally or incidentally sited man-made objects such as shipwrecks, sea forts and piers; and artificial reefs deliberately designed and sited so as to provide homes for fish (48).

Floating culture involves further the use of anchored rafts (49). This method of floating cultivation involves the suspension of ropes from rafts floating on wooden buoyancy chambers which are coated with cement as protection against the teredo. By 1964, there were 1,500 special rafts at Gallicia, in Spain, built for farming mussels (50).

The erection of artificial structures in the seas for fish farming will inevitably lead to a conflict of interests between fish farmers and other uses of the seas, notably navigation. Large artificial reefs constructed in open areas may create obstruction and/or damage to boats, trawlers, or fishing nets and so forth. Conflict with recreational activities such as yachting and boating may further be envisaged (51).

4. Installations for the Exploitation of Non-Natural Resources

Non-natural resources would appear to include archaeological relics, sunken ships, or other lost objects lying on the sea-bed. Can they be considered as part of the sea-bed resources where no clear claim of ownership by any particular natural or legal person, or State exists? This problem was tackled by the U.N. Secretary-General in his Report on the study of the International Machinery submitted to the Sea-Bed Committee in 1970, in connection with these 'resources' lying on the international sea-bed area (52).

The Report points out that, assuming that the recovery of
such objects is regarded as another use of the sea-bed, they may
fall under the jurisdiction of the International Machinery -
provided, of course, that they lie on the international sea-bed
area. The Secretary-General observed that perhaps such objects
cannot be considered 'resources', or at least not 'natural
resources'.

Draft Article 19 of the Revised Single Negotiating Text,
Part I, entitled "Archaeological and Historial Objects", provides
that (53). "All objects of an archaeological and historical
nature found in the Area shall be preserved or disposed of for
the benefit of the international community as a whole, particular
regard being paid to the preferential rights of the state or
country of origin, or the state of cultural origin, or the
state of historical and archaeological origin."

In this context, we may also recall the ILC's Commentary
to Article 2 of the Continental Shelf Convention which in para. 1
lays down that "The coastal State exercises over the continental
shelf sovereign rights for the purpose of exploring it and
exploiting its natural resources." In that Commentary, the
ILC stated that : "It is clearly understood that the rights
in question do not cover objects such as wrecked ships and
their cargoes (including bullion) lying on the sea-bed or covered
by the sand of the subsoil" (54).

It is clear, therefore, that an artificial structure
erected on the continental shelf near a wrecked ship to facilitate the salvage of its cargo, will not be placed under the jurisdiction of the coastal State as falling under Article 5 of the
Continental Shelf Convention. That Article limits the coastal
State's rights of jurisdiction to installations connected with
the exploration and exploitation of the continental shelf resources.
It is, also, equally clear that the legal status of such installations is not assimilated to that of the installations for the
exploration and exploitation of the shelf resources, by virtue of
their site.

5.   Power Stations

Ocean tides, waves, currents and temperature gradients
may all be harnessed to generate energy, although opportunities
for their use are generally limited and methods are still largely
in the early stages of development. Furthermore, ocean space
may well offer advantages over land-based sites for the location
of energy production facilities, either fixed on the sea-bed or
as floating platforms.

The principle of tidal power, for example, has been understood
since the use of tide mills in the late Middle Ages, but so far
only a few tidal power stations are known to be operational.
The French have constructed a large-scale tidal plant on the

estuary of the River Rance with 240 megawatts of installed capacity (55). Another scheme for building a huge tidal power
station off the coast of Brittany to generate a large proportion
of the electricity used in France is currently examined by
engineers and energy specialists (56). A small experimental
station with a generating capacity of 400 kilowatts is in operation near Murmansk in the USSR, while it is well known that the
People's Republic of China has built a large number of small,
low-cost tidal power stations (57). However, the potential
of tidal energy appears to be rather limited in view of the
fact that only about 20 sites in the world have the requisite
combination of tidal range over eight metres, large basins
area and short barrage length (58).

Wave power would appear to constitute another potential
source of energy. In the United Kingdom the Department of
Energy has already undertaken a £1 million two-year feasibility
study which will assess possibilities of extracting energy
on a large scale from sea waves (59).

Another proposal for tapping ocean energy that has
received serious consideration in the last few years envisages
harnessing the Florida current, a major component of the Gulf
Stream, by emplacing windmill-like turbines in the upper layers
of the current, which may reach speeds in excess of five miles
per hour. Proposals have also been put forward for harnessing
ocean waves which, via the transmitting agency of winds, are
manifestations of solar energy (60).

One other source of energy from the oceans which appears
to be promising, and in recent years has increasingly attracted
attention and widespread research, is the ocean thermal gradient,
usually called Ocean Thermal Energy Conversion (OTEC). OTEC units
consisting of floating platforms in the ocean use the difference
in temperature between cold water at great depths and the sun-
heated water at the surface to generate electricity. Many
believe that ocean thermal energy may be a viable alternative to
plutonium breeder reactors and indeed OTEC has been developed
in response to widespread concern regarding hazards of nuclear
power. Costs and energy output considerations have also
played an important role in OTEC development. TRW systems, a
U.S.-based engineering firm, estimates research and development
costs of between $500 million and $1 billion, whereas the
plutonium breeder's research and development costs are estimated
at $10 billion. Estimated electrical output of OTEC is expected
to be 30,000 megawatts by 1990, with a resource potential of
700,000 megawatts in the U.S. Gulf Coast area alone (61).
Moreover, recent experiments indicate that the operations of an
OTEC plant could profitably be combined with aquaculture to help
provide power and food for countries near tropical seas, which
as a whole receive some 45 per cent of total incoming solar
radiation and constitute a vast heat reservoir. The nutrient-
rich bottom water pumped up to the surface would be used to

support shellfish farming (62).

Other plans concerning utilization of ocean space for emplacing power-generating stations which do not rely on the oceans as the energy source, include floating arrays of solar collectors based on platforms that could orient themselves automatically to the sun's changing position, and floating windmills (63).

Of immediate application, however, appears to be a proposal, by the above-mentioned TRW engineering firm, for the construction of a $250 million power plant in the Pacific off the coast of California, to be fuelled by Alaskan coal (64).

Finally, very close to realization as commercial energy sources are floating nuclear plants in the seas, despite the great controversy surrounding nuclear power hazards. Offshore Power Systems, a joint venture of two U.S. firms, Westinghouse Electric and Tenneco Inc., has already built a facility at Jacksonville, Florida, for the production of such plants. The first of the floating nuclear plants, which will be a third larger than the biggest aircraft carrier, is scheduled to be emplaced in 1979 behind a breakwater of 2.8 miles off the New Jersey coast in the United States. A second plant is to be installed in 1980 (65). Belgium is also planning the establishment of an off-shore artificial island on which a nuclear power station for desalination of sea-water would be constructed (66).

It is evident that important problems will arise following the establishment of power stations in the seas. Apart from the problems of legal status, jurisdiction and control, and so on, possibly the most important problem would be the protection of marine ecology. For example, OTEC plants "intended for emplacement in the Gulf Stream would... have to be scrutinized for their global environmental impact in view of the critical role of the warm waters of the Gulf Stream in ameliorating European climate" (67). The establishment of nuclear stations in the seas could further create immense pollution problems, such as possible radio-activity, heat, pollution, irreparable losses to the quality of the area's animal and plant life, etc.

However, as the U.N. Secretary-General has observed: "Though few of the proposals now being discussed have progressed beyond the drawing board, a combination of factors, environmental considerations, high and increasing energy costs and foreseen scarcities of conventional energy sources, increasing land values as land-based activities continue to proliferate and intensify, and advances in technology, point to a trend of increasing attention to the oceans both as a source of energy and as a source of space for energy-generating facilities" (68).

III. TRANSPORTATION AND COMMUNICATIONS

1. Off-Shore Terminals

The economics of mining demand the most efficient transportation system available since the latter constitutes a major
portion of mining costs. At sea, this results to an ever
increasing dependence on giant ore and oil carriers - the largest
vessel built to date is 477,000 d.w.t. with a draft of 117 feet,
while tankers of 1,000,000 d.w.t. are already in the planning
stage.
One of the attendant problems of the increased size of
tankers and other vessels is that of the port facilities. The
greatly increased draft of the supertankers forbids entrance to
many existing ports. World-wide there are only nine ports
which can accommodate fully laden 200,000-ton ships (69).
There would appear to be several alternatives to meet the demands
created by the giant vessels. Among such alternatives are the
partial unloading in nearby deeper waters of supercarriers
before their entry into port, the deepening and widening of
existing ports, and the undertaking of research programmes
to develop a shallow-draft supercarrier fleet (70). However,
the alternative now receiving predominant consideration world-
wide is the off-shore terminal and deep draft port facility (71).
The problems created by large tankers and carriers, and more
intense traffic, clearly encourage the development of off-shore
tanker terminals, deep-water port facilities and off-shore
storage tanks linked to the coast by submarine pipelines.
Various designs have been proposed for deep draft port
facilities according to the type of cargo they are designed to
accommodate - mainly oil and bulk cargo. There are at present
two main designs: the buoy mooring terminals and the deep-water
port facilities in the form of structures fixed or securely
anchored to the sea-bed.
The buoy type mooring system, designed to accommodate large
tankers, consists of a large floating buoy terminal well-anchored
to the sea-bed, floating and underbuoy hoses, terminal moorings
and submarine pipelines. Two types of such buoy systems have
been developed: the single buoy mooring terminal (72) and the
multiple buoy system (73). There were 106 off-shore terminal
systems known to have been installed throughout the world as of
December 1972 (74).
Norwegian contractors and consultancy firms have also
developed a new system, called Norbuoy, for the loading of oil
into tankers on off-shore fields. Three different types of
buoys have been studied on the Norbuoy system, which essentially
consists of a weight-stable floating body in pre-stressed
concrete and is kept on location by eight chains anchoring it to
the sea-bed. It carries a super-structure consisting of four
decks above the sea and flexible risers connect the sea-bed with

the buoy.   A permanent crew of nine will operate the system
which has been designed for continuous loading into tankers at
sea, even in very rough weather (75).

Designs for the handling of bulk cargo are more costly,
"and would probably be constructed at a later stage of off-shore
port development.   A stable platform and a modular semi-
submerged platform are the two most distinct possibilities for
the handling of bulk cargo.   The stable platform would consist
of a structure supported by steel or concrete pilings driven
into the sea-bed.   The modular system would be composed of a
platform resting upon submerged pre-fabricated modules
approximately one acre in area, secured to the sea-bed by a system
of mass anchors" (76).

While further research will undoubtedly result in other
approaches to the deep water port facilities, a brief reference
will be made to a significant number of existing projects for
off-shore port development, on a world scale.

In Europe, we already have a significant number of such
projects.   An artificial island-harbour (I'll du Parfond) to
accommodate tankers of up to 500,000 d.w.t. was completed in
1970, 17 miles off Le Havre, i.e. outside the French territorial
sea.   The French are also planning a second artificial harbour
on the Out-Ruytingen Bank, 8 miles off Calais, to accommodate
tankers of up to 500,000 d.w.t.   In Belgium, several private
companies and a Government Commission have developed plans for
off-shore artificial harbours.   These plans provide for a sea
city in front of the Belgian coast at Zeebrugge (harbour and
6,000 acres industrial area), for a tanker terminal 10 miles off
the coast, and for an artificial harbour on Thornton Bank, 17
miles off the coast, to accommodate tankers of up to 250,000 –
300,000 d.w.t.   The Dutch have already built the Maasvlakte,
a considerable reclaimed sea area in the vicinity of the Hook
of Holland and they also plan an outer harbour at Ymuiden and
artificial islands off-shore the resort city of Scheveningen.
Germany is planning an artificial island harbour off Wilhelmshafen,
a deep sea harbour and industrial island to be built in the Elbe
estuary, and a harbour facility 37.5 miles at sea off Heligoland
(77).

Several deep water loading terminals are in operation in the
Persian Gulf, and Japan has also constructed a number of off-shore
terminal facilities, largely to help reduce channel congestion
(78).

Canada has plans for a fifty-acre deep water port (79),
while in the United States three large off-shore terminals, now
in advanced planning stages, may be operational by mid-1978 (80).
These three terminals, by servicing less than ten supertankers,
would be able to handle approximately half of the U.S. daily crude
oil requirements.

An interesting case of an off-shore terminal facility is the
artificial island, to be used as a salt terminal, built by

Brazil 11 miles off the coast of Rio Grande do Norte. Cargo ships of up to 100,000 tons will be able to moor at the highly automated island, which will serve as a stockpiling facility for up to 90,000 tons of salt (81).

It has further been suggested that seamounts relatively close to the coast would make ideal locations for port facilities to handle petroleum products, which could then be piped to the mainland, and also other cargoes, which could be loaded onto barges when brought to or from offshore freighter ports. This could avoid the risk of the giant vessels approaching shallow waters (82).

Another important feature of modern marine technology is the development of submarine and sea-bed transportation systems prompted by the exploitation of oceanic minerals. Thus, many experts foresee the use of underwater cargo vessels for the transportation of these minerals and other cargoes. Such underwater vessels would avoid the problems of wind, tide and wave action, and presumably afford a greater degree of safety from detection or destruction by an enemy power. Utilisation of these underwater transportation systems will be faced with the same operational requirements as any present military submarine fleets; ports and bases to service, facilities to load and unload, and resupply of the craft without the necessity of surfacing. Such bases and facilities could be conveniently located on seamounts, particularly if mining or drilling operations were situated nearby (83).

However, the proliferation of off-shore terminal facilities has already led to major controversy, centering basically around their impact on the marine environment. Indeed, once again the problem of pollution is perhaps the most important one to be faced. Apart from the supertankers and pipelines, off-shore oil terminals, in particular, may prove extremely dangerous polluting centres.

Oil-spillages resulting from these are known to have occurred in many places around the world, despite the fact that they are well guarded information by the big oil companies (84).

Proposals for deep water ports in Delaware and Main, in the United States, have already met very determined public opposition. New Jersey rejected in 1973 as "unacceptable" a proposal to build off-shore terminals off its coast, when it met similar opposition. State officials concluded that the "environmental and social implications outweigh the benefits" in view of potential oil spills which could prove disastrous to the State's wetlands. Another proposal to build a terminal and oil refining complex off the coast of Puerto Rico has met stiff opposition from environmentalists and pro-independence groups. This opposition culminated in a political protest to the U.N. in 1973 when leaders of the Puerto Rican independence movement asked the U.N. Committee on Decolonization to help stop the project (85).

As a result, President Ford signed into law, on January 3 1975, the Deepwater Port Act of 1974 (86), designed to regulate deep-water facilities located off United States shores, beyond the territorial sea limits. Under this Act the Secretary of Transportation, who controls licensing of deep water ports, may not issue such a licence without first determining that the construction and operation of the port is in the best interests of the nation and that the facility does not interfere with adjacent States' coastal management plans. The Act grants each significantly affected coastal State a veto over the licence. Applicants are required to utilize the "best available technology" to minimize environmental impact and further to provide data on oil-spill prevention measures, clean-up capability requirements, construction standards and operational constraints. Licences may be issued for up to 20 years, with renewal periods not exceeding 10 years each, but should a threat to the environment arise, the Secretary of Transportation may order port operations suspended immediately; should he fail to take action in such a situation, a citizen suit may be brought to enforce suspension. When oil spills do occur, liability without fault, backed by a Deepwater Port Liability Fund, is imposed, while failure to report promptly the discharge can result in maximum fines of $10,000 or one year's imprisonment, or both.

In short, as one commentator has noted, "the Deepwater Port Act reflects the growth of environmental consciousness since 1953, when the Outer Continental Shelf Lands Act was passed" (87).

2. Off-shore Storage Facilities

The need for off-shore storage facilities, combined with off-shore terminals, is growing rapidly as mining moves into deeper waters and farther away from coastal facilities, and as tankers continue to increase in size. Oil is now being stored in huge floating tanks firmly anchored to the sea-floor and several underwater storage tanks constructed on the sea-bed have been developed for the Persian Gulf and North Sea.

The underwater storage system at the Fateh off-shore field consists of three giant steel tanks - each tank has a 500,000 barrel capacity - submerged at the bottom of the Persian Gulf in 158 ft. of water, 60 miles off the Dubai coast. The entire system is completely self-contained and remote controlled (88). A one million-barrel concrete storage tank has been installed in the Ecofisk field, 320 km. off the Norwegian coast (just within the Norwegian sector of the continental shelf). It is a huge concrete island over 90 metres in diameter and 90 metres tall, rising 70 feet above the waves, and it will be used not only as a storage tank, but also as a platform for production equipment when oil-gas pipelines come into operation. A £50 m. plan to build a large artificial island seven miles off Norwich to store Britain's North Sea oil and gas has also been suggested. The

island could be built off the main shipping lanes but surrounded
by deep water suitable for tankers of up to a million tons, and
it could store about 50 million tons of crude oil, or 200
million tons annually. The island could also accommodate up
to 10,000 people, a golf course, market gardening facilities,
and even a small airstrip (89).

Submerged storage tanks have also been designed for a
variety of sea-bed conditions in water depths up to 365 metres,
including systems for storing liquid natural gas (90). The
main advantage of off-shore storage is that it will make it
possible to unify the storage and delivery processes, and
thus eliminate the double handling involved when oil produced
off-shore is pumped through pipelines to shore and then back
out again to a tanker loading terminal.

In addition to the concrete or steel structures designed for
construction on the sea-bed, there are also plans for using
nuclear explosives to create storage caverns under the continental
shelf. According to a Russian scientist peaceful nuclear
explosions have already been used in the Soviet Union to increase
oil and gas fields and to blast huge underground reservoirs for
storing gas (91). The idea of eventually storing goods in the
sea is further being discussed. "Since the range of temperatures in the ocean is narrower than on land, the sea has great
possibilities both in its temperate and frigid zones as a giant
storage room for perishable materials; the Antarctic has some
additional advantages as a freezing compartment" (92).

With regard to oil and gas storage tanks constructed in the
seas once again the problem of pollution and liability will
perhaps be the most important to be dealt with. A mere
accident at the storage tank site might prove to have disastrous
pollution effects, given the quantity of the oil stored therein
(93).

3.   Floating Docks

The shipping industries significantly improve their
repair facilities by the addition of floating docks. Their
number is expected, therefore, to increase considerably in the
future.

A floating dock, 174 metres long, for ships up to 25,000
d.w.t. is now fully operational at Hong Kong, while another one
250 metres long, with a 100,000 d.w.t. capacity is operational at
Yokohama, Japan (94). A 400-ft floating dock that can take
aboard two nuclear submarines at once and is designed to reduce
the amount of time the submarines have to spend "off station" for
repairs, is one of the latest additions to the Soviet Navy (95).

4.   Off-shore Floating Airports

Aerodromes constructed off-shore, including floating airports

which could be towed to different sites, are technically feasible
and possess many advantages over land-based sites.' These are
the conclusions of a Report published by the United Kingdom
Ministry of Public Building and Works in 1970 (96).

According to the Report reclaimed land and platforms built
on the sea-bed are likely to be more economical and attractive
to engineers for off-shore airports at all locations except those
in deep waters (97). In those waters fully floating aerodromes
would be needed. Fully floating platforms are now possible
although there are still certain difficulties to overcome.

Studies on the feasibility of floating airports have also
been completed in the United States. A recent study has
recommended seven possible sites for an off-shore airport for
San Diego (98). A floating airport located about 35 miles from
the coast has been suggested as a supplement to J.F. Kennedy
Airport in New York. This project, known as the New York
Offshore Airport Feasibility Study, was sponsored by the
Federal Aviation Administration and, in addition to the airport
facilities, it would include a breakwater, a deep water terminal,
fuel storage and a utilities plant. The entire complex would
spread over an ocean area of about fifty square miles (99).

5.   Communications

Navigation has always been, together with fishing, the
most important use of the oceans, and the sea is still the
major highway for the long distance carriage of goods despite
the increasing use of the airplane. Improvement in the aids
to navigation is thus, always, highly desirable. Communication
stations, both civilian and military, constructed on the high
seas might well be used both to aid in the navigation of surface
and subsurface vessels (100), and to provide a link in the
global communications system made possible by the use of
orbital satellites. Seamounts in the open seas would appear
to offer ideal locations for such permanent communication stations.
The United States Coast Guard, for example currently operates
Long Range Aid to Navigation (LORAN) stations, built on atolls
or small islands, but much of the ocean area is not yet covered
to the extent which might be considered desirable. It has,
therefore, been suggested that "use of seamounts would permit
the completion of a network of these stations, thus reducing
the chance of vessel loss, and increasing the possibility of
recovery in case of accident by permitting accurate and
continuous monitoring of vessel location" (101). It has further
been confidently predicted that :

    "The use of complex detection and communication systems
    will eventually replace the traditional methods of
    navigation.....Submarine buoys will mark out waterways
    under the surface with traffic stacked in layers like air

traffic today. Eventually, no doubt, navigation will
become automatic with traffic passing from buoy to buoy
like guided missiles. At this stage, submarine ships
would be able to dispense with expensive inertial navigation equipment. Communications will be organised through
a system of fixed stations in the sea, satellites in
space, or a combination of the two' (102).

IV. SCIENTIFIC INVESTIGATION AND WEATHER
FORECASTING

With the advancement of technology, scientific
research is already moving from land and ship based operations
to installations located in or on the high seas. A great
variety of structures, platforms, installations, buoys and
other devices, as well as ships, airplanes and satellites are
being used for the collection of scientific data on the oceans.
Manned installations in the high seas, unaffected by
winds and current would probably permit more detailed studies
than research vessels which have limited range and maintenance
capabilities. Seamounts are already being used as bases for
emplacing scientific equipment. The first permanent construction attempt on Cobb seamount in 1970 proved an unqualified
success. As a result of the experiment, construction of a tower
looked feasible. Indeed, a long-term aim of the Sea Use
Programme, which is co-ordinated by the Oceanographic Commission
of Washington for scientific exploration of the Cobb seamount,
is construction of an instrumented tower or mast (103).
Scripps Institute of Oceanography has been reported to have
plans for the construction of an artificial island in the
ocean for observation and research (104).
Underwater installations would permit the study of every
aspect of the marine environment, including marine life, currents,
seamounts, the sea-bed and subsoil, and so forth. The exploitation of the ocean's resources would thus greatly benefit, once
its technical and economical feasibility has been established.
Much experimental work has already been accomplished as regards
the construction of underwater habitats to be used initially as
underwater laboratories. Such work has been carried out under
the American Navy's Sealab programme, and the American Interior
Department's undersea research project in the Virgin islands
since 1970 - known as the Tektite experiments (105). These
latter experiments have proved that scientists could live and
work safely for extended periods of time at depths of up to 100
feet below sea level. As a result of the Tektite experiments
on habitats, scientists in the United States Virgin Islands,
were planning a permanent ocean-floor laboratory in Great
Lameshur Bay, St. John, to provide a low-cost method of charting
"the untracked jungles" of the world oceans (106). It has
further been reported that the University of Hawaii is also

considering construction of undersea research stations (107).

Moreover, the increasing importance of the Ocean Data
Acquisition Systems (ODAS) should also be emphasised in the
present context. However, due to the complex and particularly
difficult legal problems which they pose and considering their
immediate importance in terms of present uses of the seas, these
will be examined in a separate chapter (108).

With regard to weather prediction a great number of buoys,
ships, airplanes, satellites and land-based observation stations
are already in use (109). However, advances in weather forecasting are expected to come from more extensive use of artificial satellites and from stations at sea. Immediate improvements can be made in short-range forecasting and although
"long-range forecasting is still in its infancy.... present
developments in space, marine and computer technology would
permit the continuous collection of data on a worldwide basis
resulting in accurate fourteen-day forecasts " (110). Thus,
installations constructed on the high seas could be beneficially
employed in weather prediction. Seamounts in the open seas
would appear to offer ideal locations for such permanent
installations, which "would afford a greater degree of safety
than surface craft, while facilitating the evaluation and
analysis of weather phenomena created over the oceans " (111).
If and when, finally, weather control and modification becomes
a reality, "these installations on the high seas, where
scientists believe much of our weather originates through air-
water interaction, would permit the harnessing of otherwise
harmful conditions before population centres and agricultural
lands were affected. Similarly, such establishments would be
the logical place for the "creation" of desired weather
conditions" (112).

V.   RECREATION

Worldwide, major populations and large cities tend to
concentrate in coastal areas, and this movement of populations
around the world to coastal zones will probably continue (113).
The trend to create development-free zones as national marine
parks can be expected to increase in the future, and regional,
national and local authorities will probably establish nature
reserves in coastal areas (including coastal land, waters and
sea-floor) (114).

Surface recreation activities, such as boating, speedboat
racing, cruising and surfing, as well as underwater recreations,
may become increasingly popular with the spread of leisure and
of the popularity of scuba diving. In addition, the idea of
creating recreational communities and parks has already received
much attention, and plans have been drawn up for the construction
of both above water and undersea resort hotels and other
installations for recreational purposes (115).

The Japanese have already built buoys which are moored
off-shore and have facilities for tourists to descend below
sea-level and watch the surrounding waterscape through heavy
glass ports. They have also designated several underwater
parks for recreational purposes and they have developed underwater observation towers for these parks. They are thinking
further about underwater restaurants, and the country's
technical research institute is working on plans for a moving
underwater walkway within an artificial tunnel on the ocean
floor (116). Plans are under way for a floating residential
structure on the Delaware River in the United States and also
in Hawaii (117).

VI. MILITARY INSTALLATIONS

The seas are being used as a ground for many military
activities - naval military operations and manoeuvres, testing
of nuclear weapons, testing of rockets and missiles, operations
by conventional submarines and stationing of submarines armed
with nuclear missiles, mine laying, blockades and quarantines,
and in general exercise of "sea power" - predominantly by the
major Naval Powers.

Many experts support the view that a strategic shift to the
oceans has occurred over the last fifteen years. According
to SIPRI, for example, "over the last ten years the vast
undersea space has been subject to increasing militarization.
New technology is pushing the research frontiers forward,
allowing military systems to penetrate deeper into the ocean.
This applies both to traditional submarine systems and to new
forms of military uses, such as fixed submarine detection systems
and manned underwater stations. This development in undersea
technology is accelerated by changes in the strategic competition between the great powers. A most significant factor is
the increasing vulnerability of land-based military systems
caused by advances in surveillance techniques and missile
accuracy and the use of multiple warhead missiles. The result
is a gradual shift of the main arms race from the land-based
systems to submarine-based systems, which can make full use of
the protection afforded by the undersea environment" (118).

It is well-known further, that continental shelves are
already being used for the emplacement of military installations,
although these activities are well-guarded secrets (119).
On the sea-bed along the coastal zones of some countries, notably
the United States, many submarine listening posts - sonar systems
- have been deployed for as long as twenty years. The North
Sea and the Barrents Sea are littered with sonar devices
deployed by both NATO and the Soviet Union. These bottom-
based detection systems form an essential part of development
in anti-submarine warfare (ASW). The characteristic feature
of ASW lies in continuous dissemination in the ocean environment

of systems of detection, the first necessary step towards identification, localization and eventual destruction of enemy submarines.   The detection is carried out mainly by acoustic means
which may be mobile or fixed.   The best known of the sonar
systems is the 'Caesar' static passive sonar system, supplemented
by the 'Colossus' system (1964) and the 'Sea Sniper' system (120).
It has also been reported that the United States is considering
the design and construction of the largest undersea acoustic
system ever conceived – the suspended Array System – a project
which would cost $1 billion and would involve underwater
structures, accoustic transducers and electronic systems on an
extremely large scale (121).

However, apart from the ASW sonar systems, naval authorities
are looking forward to establishing permanent fixed submarine
maintenance facilities, repair works, scientific and communication stations, storage depots, manned and unmanned military
bases on the sea-bed, and so forth.   Missile systems, both
offensive and defensive, could also be established on the
continental shelf or on seamounts in the deep oceans with the
supreme advantage of improved concealment.

Manned underwater stations is another serious possibility
contemplated by the navies of certain countries, such as the
United States, the Soviet Union, France and Japan.   Various
types of underwater habitats, the so-called Sealabs, have
already been developed and several experiments have been
carried out at continental shelf depths, involving the use of
"saturated" divers.   Beyond continental shelf depths, the
main interest has been in constructing a manned underwater
station for use at a depth of 2,000 metres, for instance on a
seamount.   Concepts have also been developed for stations to
be installed at depths of 4,000 metres and 7,000 metres, which
would include the greater part of the deep ocean floor.   An
experimental concrete station, known as project Seacon, has been
built by the U.S. Navy at shallow depths off the coast of
California (122).   Furthermore, manned underwater stations may
also be built into the subsoil by using advanced drilling
techniques and lock-out facilities.

Other developments concern submersible systems, unmanned
underwater vehicles, nuclear mines, communicating facilities,
navigational aids anchored to the sea-bed, logistic support
installations, and so on (123).   In Summary:
"full military use of the continental shelf is already
possible with advanced diving techniques... Military activities on continental shelf depths are likely to include
installation and repair of submarine detection systems,
mine warfare, operations of attack divers and in the
future, possibly, service and support of submarine systems.
Beyond continental shelf depths, advanced submersibles...
permit an extension of the operations of existing nuclear
submarines.   Unmanned work systems already exist for

carrying out work on the deep ocean floor. Before the
end of this decade experimental one-atmosphere manned
stations may be installed at depths of about 2,000 metres,
probably on underwater ridges and isolated seamounts.
The future military functions of these stations would
primarily be ASW operations. Towards the end of the
century, technology may allow the deployment of underwater
stations to depths of 7,000 metres.
     The fact that a combination of military, economic and
scientific motives lies behind this technological drive
into the deep ocean may make it well-nigh irresistible.
The direct military applications which now can be discerned may not even be the most important. The military
are taking a new environment in possession for functions
which may be defined later when mankind has adapted itself
to work and life under the ocean on a grand scale" (124).

VII.   OTHER USES OF ARTIFICIAL ISLANDS

     Many so-called "pirate" broadcasting stations, moored or
installed outside the territorial sea of many countries, have
appeared in the last twenty years (125).
     The best known cases are, perhaps, those of Radio Veronica,
located on board a ship registered in Panama and anchored off
the Dutch territorial sea; Radio Caroline (2) located on board
a ship registered also in Panama and anchored off the English
coast; and Radio and T.V. Noordzee, operated from an artificial
island erected on the high seas beyond the Dutch territorial sea.
The station was the property of foreigners but it was operated
by a Dutch private company, the Reclame Exploitatie Maatschappij
(R.E.M.) (126).
     The interests of the States which are adversely affected by
the operation of such stations are: avoidance of taxation,
actual or potential harmful interference with other radio
stations and with communications with ships, etc.   These States
have contemplated and taken certain measures of protection.   In
taking these measures, States have been aware of the difficult
problems created in international law.   The crucial question,
of course, is to what extent a coastal State can assume jurisdiction and control over such activities on ships and artificial
islands operating on the high seas.   Certain States have been
reluctant to take any preventive action against these "pirate"
stations for the fear of interfering with the freedom of the
high seas.   The United Kingdom Government for instance, has
consistently refused to take unilateral action and insisted that
the problem can only be solved by an international agreement.
Such an agreement has now materialised under the auspices of the
Council of Europe (127).
     The Agreement is intended to prevent the operation of all
broadcasting stations on board ships, aircraft, or any other

floating or airborne objects, established outside national territories.   It also makes punishable the provision of supplies,
equipment, transport and programme material to these broadcasting
stations.   It will be noted that the Agreement does not cover
artificial islands or installations fixed on the sea-bed, but
Article 4 stipulates that nothing in the Agreement shall be
deemed to prevent a contracting Party from applying its provisions to such stations.   However, the question remains open in
relation to fixed installations since it is not at all clear
under what conditions action against such stations is allowed
under international law.

The R.E.M. station forced the Dutch Government to pass
legislation as a result of which the station ceased operating a
short period after it started (128).   Much controversy has
arisen by the legislation enacted by the Dutch Government which
lays down that it may exercise jurisdiction over all installations erected on its continental shelf, no matter for what purpose.

Artificial islands built on the high seas may further serve
more than purely economic purposes.   As has already been indicated,
ultimately the founders' ambition may be to set up new sovereign,
independent 'States'.   Already, attempts have been made to
create new 'States' by constructing artificial islands on the
high seas.   Thus the former owner of the Radio Essex pop 'pirate'
station occupied with his family in 1966 a disused naval wartime
fort standing in the sea seven miles off Harwich, at Essex in
the United Kingdom, officially known as Fort Roughs.   He then
raised his red, black and white flag of independence on September
2, 1967, and he even drafted a constitution for the "Independent
State of Sealand" (129).   A number of companies have also
attempted to found new sovereign 'island-states' on the United
States continental shelf.   Thus, a private company decided in
1966 to cap the Cortes Bank formation, a seamount rising close
to the sea surface some 50 miles south of San Clemente island
and 100 miles off San Diego, California, with cement and create
a new independent 'State' called "Abalonia".   The commercial
idea was that since that area was rich in abalone and lobster
and virtually unfished, they would put on their island a
processing plant and use divers to harvest abalone and lobster.
The plan, however, failed because the 'State' s' base, a
reinforced concrete ship sunk in deep waters, with some of its
proponents barely escaping with their lives, while the United
States Corps of Engineers quickly gave notice that the ship was
a hazard to navigation and the United States Government declared
the area to be part of the Outer Continental Shelf (130).

A more recent attempt to create a sovereign 'State' in the
South Pacific on the Minerva Reefs has been reported.   In January, 1972 the Ocean Life Foundation proclaimed the Republic
of Minerva "outside the Territorial Limits and Continental
Shelves of any existing nation".   The founders raised parts
of the low-tide elevations above sea level at high-tide, and the

development plan provided for 2,500 acres to be reclaimed, creating a new 'State' based upon a free enterprise philosophy conveniently intended to solicit the registration of vessels under its colours, and claiming a twelve-mile territorial sea. The creation of the First Provisional Government of Minerva was promptly announced accompanied by a Declaration of Sovereignty, January 19, 1972 (131).

It is thus clear that artificial islands may be used in the future either for the creation of wholly new independent 'States' or for expansion of territory and sovereignty by existing States in the open seas. In this respect it is worth mentioning the great potential value of artificial islands particularly to land-locked States. Perhaps, in this context, their position and the possibilities offered to them by the construction of artificial islands, have best been summarised as follows :

"The land-locked nations of the world have a great interest in the sea and their inaccessibility to coasts and ports may be a contributing factor as to why the majority of them are underdeveloped. Seamounts may offer opportunities to the land-locked nations, possibly permitting the extension of sovereignty through the construction and maintenance of facilities on the high seas. The effect would be to make available to these states the benefits which come from participation in world trade through one's own ports" (132).

VIII. FEASIBILITY AND IMPLICATIONS OF SEAWARD ADVANCEMENT

A successful seaward advancement will undoubtedly require the solution of many technical, economic, energy, pollution and other problems, if industrial societies are not to commit in the oceans the errors they have committed on land.

The technical problems, which would appear to refer mainly to safe construction, structure, anchorage and protection of artificial islands, seem to be no major obstacle to seaward advancement. With regard to the materials used, many of the early structures were of steel. Steel will continue to be used for special purpose structures but major industrial/urban complexes will require a different material such as concrete. Concrete drilling and production platforms are already under construction in the North Sea for water depths up to 500 ft. For deeper waters, floating structures of pre-stressed concrete will be used. According to the North Sea Group, on the other hand, the principal material in the construction of artificial islands will always be sand, while another company has suggested that oil platforms, power stations and other types of offshore structures, can be supported in water depths up to 660 ft. with a hydrostatically supported sand structure (133).

In relation to the economic aspects, further study is required despite the "basic premise... that seaward extension of many activities is already economical in all costs being considered" (134). According to the North Sea Group:

"the construction of an industrial site in the sea is naturally more expensive than the construction of such a site on the mainland... As far as can be seen at the moment, we must calculate on a basis of 180 guilders per square metre, if we contemplate an island of 12,500 acres" (135).

The sociological and biological problems arising out of the possible habitation of the oceans by human beings should also be studied. What will the effect of such habitation be upon mankind? (136).

Yet, amongst the more immediate problems to be resolved, the most important appear to be those of pollution and energy. It is imperative that artificial islands be studied and built free from all types of pollution, within, of course, the existing at the time technological and economic limits. Construction in the oceans should be planned, co-ordinated and executed with systematic consideration of its favourable and unfavourable impact on the ocean environment (137). It is self-evident that the establishment of industries on artificial islands may under no circumstances be considered as a licence for pollution. It has further been recognised by many agencies concerned with the preservation of the marine environment that potential ecological problems exist with the construction of off-shore islands from dredged spoil. Indiscriminate dumping of dredged spoil has a deleterious effect on both fish and marine life in general (138). The wanton discharge of chemical processing water and water at high temperatures may seriously alter or interfere with the natural marine environment. Oil leaks of a serious nature could eventually pose a problem both at the site and on beaches. This is particularly true for oil terminals and oil wells. Oil and gas blow-outs may be a major cause of pollution arising out of the exploitation of petroleum resources.

As regards energy, it may be possible either to generate power at the site or to bring it from the mainland. High tension submarine cables more than 20,000 feet long have been laid in depths of 720 feet of water (139). Perhaps in the long run solar power could be the main source of energy used on artificial islands. Nuclear energy could also be either an autonomous source of energy or a complementary one.

In short, the technology for ocean expansion is well developed and the remaining problems will undoubtedly be resolved given the necessary motive. The possibilities open to mankind by the vast oceans on our planet have been summarised as follows by Dr. J. Craven of the University of Hawaii:

"Marine animals could be domesticated for work and life-saving; man could live in the ocean at depths of 600-1,500 ft.

at pressure for extended periods; submersibles could be
docked beneath the surface, free from the forces of waves
and weather; low-cost, plastic submersibles could be
built to operate at depths of 1,000 feet or more; low-
cost structures could be built to carry equipment – and
possibly men – to depths of 20,000 feet; platforms stable
in the roughest water could be built on the sea; and
safe nuclear power plants could be deployed in the ocean"
(140).

NOTES

1. Gidel, Le Droit International Public de La Mer, Vol. II,
pp. 26-27.
2. Report of the Second Committee, Conference for the
Codification of International Law, The Hague, 1930, League of
Nations DOC. C.230. M. 117-1930, V., p. 12. The Report was
not voted on in Plenary Session.
3. II I.L.C. Yearbook (1956), p. 269.
4. Report of the International Law Commission covering
the work of its seventh session 2 May-8 July 1955, U.N. Gen.
Ass. Off. Records, 10th Session, Supp. No. 9 (A/2934), p. 44.
5. M.S. McDougal and W.T. Burke, The Public Order of
the Oceans, 1962, p.423.
6. Ibid., p.422; see also I ILC Yearbook (1954), p. 88.
" The outermost of certain permanent installations associated
with port facilities are construed as parts of baselines, and
the breadth of the territorial sea is measured from them. Piers
and breakwaters are the most common examples. They must be
connected with the shore itself or an installation on the
shore... Buoys, lights attached to underwater rocks, or
other devices for maritime safety do not affect the breadth
of the territorial sea...", G. Etsel Pearcy, Geographer,
Department of State, "Measurement of the United States Territorial Sea", XL Bulletin, Department of State, No. 1044, June 29,
1959, pp.963, 966-968, cited in IV Whiteman Digest of International Law, p. 263.
7. W. Riphagen, International Legal Aspects of Artificial
Islands, IV International Relations (1973), No. 4, pp. 327-347,
at p.328.
8. Professor Riphagen is also of the same opinion, ibid.
9. Revised Single Negotiating Text, U.N. Doc. A/CONF.
62/WP.8/ Rev. 1/Part II, 6 May 1976. See also the relevant
Article 7 of the Maltese Draft on the delimitation of coastal
State jurisdiction in ocean space, Doc. A/AC.138/SC.II/L.28
16 July 1973.
10. See, for instance, the Maplin Project in the United

Kingdom, which has now apparently been abandoned; see the
Special Report from the Select Committee on the Maplin
Development Bill, London, March 27, 1973.

11.   W. Riphagen, supra, at p.329; U.S. National Academy
of Engineering, 1972, p. 134, et seq. "Dredging is perhaps
the best known underwater activity at present. We are taking
some 11 million tons of gravel from a depth of 30-50 m. in the Channel and North Sea and this is increasing rapidly. Dredging is
very important in harbour works and land reclamation such as will
be involved in the Foulness project," United Kingdom Science
Research Council, Report on Marine Technology, 1973, p.4.

12.   S.K. Keaton and J. Judy,Seamounts and Guyots:
A Unique Resource, 10 San Diego Law Review (1973), pp. 599-637
at p. 601.

13.   Ibid.

14.   W. Friedman, The.Future of the Oceans, 1971, at pp.
12-13.

15.   Ocean Science News, Vol. 11, No. 18, 2 May, 1969,
cited in S.K. Keaton and J. Judy, supra,at p. 602.

16.   Ibid.

17.   Ibid.

18.   J. Andrassy, International Law and the Resources
of the Sea, 1970, at p. 12.

19.   A. Guilcher, The Seabed and the Ocean Floor: Geo-
physical Characteristics, in New Directions in the Law of the
Sea, edited by R. Churchill, K.R. Simmonds and J. Welch, 1973,
Vol. III, pp. 109-118, at p. 118.

20.   S.K. Keaton and J. Judy, supra, at p. 602.

21.   Legal Regime of the Non-Sovereign Ocean, for
Geography 271 - Marine Geography, October 1, 1969, at pp. 2-8.

22.   See, for instance, I I.L.C. Yearbook (1954),pp. 90-91.
For ancient models of sea based societies, going as far back as
the neolithic lake societies that existed some 2,500 years B.C.
in the regions of Austria and Switzerland, see J.P. Craven in
Experiments in Excellence, at pp. 6-7.

23.   "Japan: New D.R.V. a Symbol of Fresh Thinking?"
(Nov. 1967) 1 (1) Hydrospace 29, cited in F.M. Auburn, The
International Sea-Bed Area, 20 I.C.L.Q. (1971), at p. 181.

24.   The sea-city is designed as a 16-storey amphitheatre,
built on concrete stilts around a central lagoon warmed by waste
heat from the city's industries. The central lagoon contains
a cluster of floating islands where houses, schools and public
buildings are erected. Energy for the area is provided by
a local under-sea natural gas field. Fish farming will be
the chief industry. It is envisaged as a self-contained city,
providing modern amenities and is even capable of creating
its own climate. A fast helicopter and hovercraft link with the
mainland would enable the inhabitants to commute back and forth,
The Progress, The Unilever Quarterly, Vol. 52, No. 2, 1968.
See also THE TIMES,(London) February 29, 1968, and THE SUNDAY

TIMES, 3 March, 1968.

25.   J.P. Craven, United States Options in the Event of
Non-Agreement, in L.M. Alexander (ed.), The Law of the Sea:
A New Geneva Conference, 1972, pp. 46-50, at p. 49.

26.   14 Ocean Science News, 5 May, 1972, at p. 4.

27.   McQuade, Urban Expansion Takes to the Water, Fortune
Magazine, Sept. 1969, at p. 151.

28.   North Sea Island Group, A Firm Footing in the Sea, 1975,
at p. 4; see also J.J. Pot, Industrial Islands in the
North Sea.

29.   Ibid; Ports and Dredging and Oil Report, No. 86, 1975,
at p.24.

30.   Lloyd's List, 4 April, 1972.

31.   Ibid; THE OBSERVER 16 July 1972.

32.   THE GUARDIAN, 27 April 1973.

33.   Offshore Engineer, June 1975, at pp. 36-37.   There
are several reasons to suggest that seaward advancement, if it is
to be a good investment, will gradually move toward multiple use,
even though almost all existing off-shore structures so far are
essentially single purpose.   See Dr. Ira Dyer, Multiple Usage
of Offshore Platforms, In Experiments in Excellence, at pp.10-
11, and B. Yeich, Adapting Industrial Processes for Multi-
Purpose Industrial Port Islands, in Offshore Technology Conference, May 5-8, Houston-Texas, Proceedings, Vol. III, pp. 51-63.

34.   Doc. E/5650, at p. 4.

35.   U.N. ECOSOC Doc. E/5648, 8 May 1975, at p. 4.

36.   The Russian deep sea fleet now amounts to more than
5 million tons gross tonnage - five times larger than the
combined fleets of the United Kingdom, the United States, West
Germany, France and Norway.   The Japanese fleet amounts to
1.1 million tons, THE GUARDIAN, 26 July 1973.

37.   E. Young and P. Fricke (eds), Sea Use Planning, Fabian
Tract 437, 1975, at p.10.

38.   Third United Nations Conference on the Law of the
Sea (Caracas Session), Official Records, Vol. I,, N.Y., 1975, at
p.200.

39.   For the potential of seamounts in this respect, see
S.K. Keaton and J. Judy, supra, note 12, at p. 608: "High
sea installations on seamounts could play an important part in
the revitalisation of the fishing industry.   Bases located
far from home ports would be more accessible to national fishing fleets, permitting extended operations, and providing needed
support."   In addition, processing plants located at these
seamounts would make possible the immediate processing of the
catch, and the fish could then be shipped directly to the
consumer countries rather than through the home ports of the
fishing nation.

40.   See, for example, E.D. Brown, The Legal Regime of
Hydrospace, 1971, at p. 83.

41.   Sedentary species are defined in Article 2, para. 4,

of the Continental Shelf Convention as "organisms which, at the harvestable stage, either are immobile on or under the sea-bed or are unable to move except in constant physical contact with the sea-bed or the subsoil."

42.   Article 2, para 4, of the Continental Shelf Convention lays down that "The natural resources referred to in these articles consist of the mineral and other non-living resources of the sea-bed and subsoil together with living organisms belonging to sedentary species..."

43.   Seabrook Hull writing in 1969 observed that this was possible then or in the following two years, without substantial development, E.W. Seabrook Hull, supra, at p.9.

44.   See, for example, Doc. E/5650.

45.   Shellfish have been farmed for some 2,000 years. Clustered in the shallows, more or less immobile, easy to study, convenient to handle, they presented no great difficulties, A.McKee, Farming the Sea, 1967, at p.100.

46.   J.H. Ryther and J.E. Bardarch, The Status and Potential of Aquaculture, (Washington, D.C., 1968) United States Department of Commerce Clearing House document BP-177767, cited in U.N. ECOSOC DOC. E/5120, 28 April 1972, at p.10.

47.   Doc. E/5650, at p.5; E/5648, at p.5; and E/5120, 28 April 1972, at pp.10-11.   It has been estimated that a 1000 square-mile area, if ecologically suitable, could produce annually an amount of mussel meat equal to almost three times the current world fish catch, ibid., at p.11, footnote 13. In Japan, the production from ocean aquaculture reached in 1972 650,000 tons, which was over 6 per cent of the total production figure for the nation, Sh. Oda Impact of the Fishery Technology on International Law, in Law of the Sea Institute, Ninth Annual Conference, January 6-9, 1975, Law of the Sea: Caracas and Beyond, 1975, p.251 at p.256 (hereafter cited as Law of the Sea Institute, Ninth Annual Conference).   However, the People's Republic of China is reported to have by far the largest yield from fish farming in the world.   Thus, in 1959, it produced 1.8 million metric tons of fish from fish farming, which represented 35.8 per cent of its total yield, and slightly more than half of this production was carried on in the sea, Peking Review, 12 Nov. 1965, at p.37.

48.   In Japan individual and enterprising fishermen have been constructing artificial reefs for centuries.   The first recorded example of a marine artificial reef in United States waters appears to be the so-called 'McAllister Grounds' laid down near Long Island in 1950.   The famous 'rubber reef' in 30 feet of water, some 15 miles north of Boston, started by using old tyres, A.McKee, supra, at pp.47-58 and 156 et seq.

49.   A major advantage of sea-farming, as opposed to agriculture, is that culture can also be three dimensional, and the principle of floating culture, i.e. culturing shellfish by suspending them in midwater has been known for hundreds of

years. Mussels are cultured in this way in quantity in the
province of Gallicia, at the north-west coast of Spain, which
is second only to Holland as the major producer in Europe, with
over 75,000 metric tons annually produced in Gallicia alone,
G.D. Waugh, A Crop from the Sea, The Geographical Magazine,
August 1966, No. 4, pp. 263-267; A. McKee, supra, at pp. 96-97.
    50.   Ibid.; It is difficult to state at present the
physical form of marine fish farms, as no system is yet fully
developed, apart from the fact that they will involve the use of
some kind or other of offshore structures.   See further L.K.
Newton and I.D. Richardson, Marine Fish Farming - Some Legal
Problems, in New Directions in the Law of the Sea, edited by
R. Churchill, K.R. Simmonds, J. Welch, 1973, Vol. III,   pp.61-70,
at p.66.
    51.   The creation of natural reserves, for example, which
have been proposed for the Swale in Kent, at the United Kingdom,
could effectively stop the extension of oyster-rearing grounds,
L.K. Newton and I.D. Richardson, supra, at p.67.
    52.   Report of the Committee on the Peaceful Uses of
the Sea-Bed and the Ocean Floor Beyond the Limits of National
Jurisdiction; General Assembly, Official Records: Twenty-
Fifth Session, Supplement No. 21 (A/8021), U.N. 1970, (hereafter cited as the 1970 Report of the Sea-Bed Committee),
Annex III, at p.96.
    53.   U.N. Third Conference on the Law of the Sea, Doc.
A/CONF. 62/WP.8/Rev. 1/Part I, 6 May 1976.
    54.   II ILC Yearbook, (1956), at p.298.
    55.   Doc. E/5650, at p.12.
    56.   THE GUARDIAN, 22 December 1975.
    57.   D.M. Johnston, Law, Technology and the Sea, 55
California Law Review (1967),   p.449 at p.457.   The Russian
experimental station is the forerunner of a 6,000 megawatt plant
designed for Mezen Bay, also on the Russian Arctic coast.
Estimates have further been made of the cost of tidal plants at
the Bay of Fundy and Passamaquoddy Bay on the U.S.-Canadian
border, at the Severn River in the United Kingdom and at San Jose
in Argentina, with generation costs varying by large amounts,
Doc. E/5650, at p.12.
    58.   Ibid.
    59.   THE TIMES, 30 April 1976 and 21 May 1976.
    60.   Doc. E/5650, at pp.13-14.
    61.   13 San Diego Law Review (1976), at p.657.
    62.   Doc. E/5650, at p.13.
    63.   Doc. E/5650, at p.14. On the tremendous potential of
solar energy in general see P.E. Glaser, The Case for Solar
Energy, Paper presented at the Annual Meeting of the Society
for Social Responsibility in Science, Conference on 'Energy
and Humanity', Queen Mary College, London, 3 September 1972.
    64.   NEWSWEEK, 24 November 1975, at p.9.
    65.   Doc. E/5650, at p.14.

66.   Third U.N. Conference on the Law of the Sea, Official
Records, Vol.II, 1975, at p.278.
67.   Doc. E/5650, at p.13.
68.   Ibid., at p.15.
69.   Doc. E/5650, at p.17.   Over 300 Very Large Crude
Carriers (VLCC's) of 250,000 d.w.t. or greater size are already
in service and another 400 are under construction, yet there
is no port in the U.S. at which such VLCC's can be unloaded.
Use of these supertankers can reduce transportation costs for
crude oil from distant places, such as the Middle East, by as
much as 68 per cent, American Bar Association, Resolution and
Report Re Deepwater Port Legislation adopted by the House of
Delegates, August 1974, in 7 Natural Resources Lawyer (1974),
p.693, at p.694.   See further H.G. Knight, International
Legal Aspects of Deep Draft Harbour Facilities, 4 (3) Journal
of Maritime Law and Commerce (1973), p.367 at p.369.
70.   H.G. Knight, supra, at p.370.   It has to be
emphasised, however, that not all of these alternatives will
always be feasible.   Andrew E. Gibson, for example, United
States Assistant Secretary of Commerce for Maritime Affairs, has
been quoted as saying that deepening and widening present harbours
is simply "prohibitive".   In addition to dredging costs there
are also the natural obstacles and man-made structures such as
pipelines, telephone cables and vehicular crossing installations,
which will have to be dealt with, in the course of such an
operation, Hellenic Shipping International, November/December
1972, at p.29.
71.   According to the U.S. National Academy of Engineering
1972, the technical feasibility of the development of new
deep water ports is well established (at p.48).
72.   The single buoy terminal consists of only one buoy and
is considered the least expensive method.   Costing from
$650,000 to $2m. it represents considerably less investment
than the construction of conventional harbour facilities, and it
can also become operational much more quickly than new shore
structures.
73.   The multiple buoy system consists of one buoy which
would serve solely as a discharge terminal, and a number of
other buoys which would serve as mooring points.
74.   Hellenic Shipping International, November/December
1972, at p.29.
75.   See in Noroil, Vol. 3, December 1975, at pp.76-7.
76.   H.G. Knight, supra, at p.371.
77.   J.J. Pot, Industrial Islands in the North Sea, at
p.19;   Ocean Science News, Vol. 12, No. 12, 20 March 1970, pp.3-4.
78.   W.H. Lawrence, Superports, Airports and Other Fixed
Installations on the High Seas, 6 Journal of Maritime Law and
Commerce 1975, p. 575 at p.577.
79.   C.W. Walker, Jurisdictional Problems created by
Artificial Islands, 10 San Diego Law Review (1973), p.638 et seq,

at p.639.
80.   See in 13 San Diego Law Review (1976), at p.659.
81.   A.H.A. Soons, Artificial Islands and Installations
in International Law, July 1974, Law of the Sea Institute,
University of Rhode Island, Occasional Paper No. 22, at p.1.
82.   S.K. Keaton and J. Judy, supra, note 12, at p.607.
83.   D.M. Johnston, supra, note 57, at p.454;
S.K. Keaton and J. Judy, supra, note 12, at pp.606-607.
84.   In the United Kingdom, for example, the Anglesey
Marine Terminal Bill has proved a very controversial Bill
indeed.   Shell Limited has proposed the construction of two
single buoy moorings about two miles off the west coast of
Anglesey in Wales, a proposal met with passionate and widespread
opposition.   Shell have already built 16 such single buoy mooring terminals all over the world, most of them in the Far East
or in Africa, used by 350 supertankers.   During the hearings
of the Select Committee which considered the Bill it was
revealed that there had been 150 spillages of oil at Shell's
single buoy mooring terminals, some of them disastrous.   During
the same hearings it was further established beyond doubt that
Shell's off-shore terminals throughout the world were constantly
liable to oil spillage and that spillages of similar size at
Anglesey would have a catastrophic effect on the island's beaches
and on the rich and rare marine and bird life in the area.
See the House of Lords Official Report, Vol.324, No. 153,
October 21, 1971, columns 483-494;   THE SUNDAY TIMES (London)
8 July 1973, 23 September 1973, and 30 September 1973.   For
the views of an oil company on the threat of oil pollution at
oil ports and terminals see further L.R. Beynon, Oil Pollution
of the Seas: Causes, Control and Clean-up, Paper presented
at the British Petroleum Ltd. Symposium, Leningrad, April 1973,
esp. at pp. 7-8.
85.   See in 11 San Diego Law Review (1974) at p.722 et
seq.;   see further A. Hirsch, Special Circumstances: Superports,
in J.K. Gamble and G. Pontecorvo (eds), Law of the Sea:
The Emerging Regime of the Oceans, Proceedings, Law of the Sea
Institute, Eighth Annual Conference, 1973, at p.217 et. seq.
86.   Act of 3 January 1975, Public Law 93-627, 93rd Congress, H.R. 10701;   for the text see in 14 I.L.M. 1975 at
pp.153-163.
87.   R.G. Hildreth, The Coast: Where Energy Meets the
Environment, 13 San Diego Law Review 1976, pp.253-305, at p.300.
88.   U.N. Doc. E/5120, 28 April 1972, at p.27.
89.   THE TIMES, 26 February 1973.
90.   Noroil, Vol. 3, December 1975, pp.41-47.
91.   THE TIMES, 19 January 1975, On nuclear explosion
techniques for the formation of oil storage cavities, see
further Petroleum Times, Vol. 79, 16 May 1975, at pp.21-23.
92.   D.M. Johnston, supra, note 57, at pp.456-457.   The
fact that containers are being developed for carriage of goods

by sea points to a likely similar development for the eventual
storage of goods in the sea.

93.   Lord Kennett, a leader of the fight against pollution
in the United Kingdom has called the storage tank at the
Ecofish field, "a bloody colossal risk to shipping: a solid
island of thousands of tons of oil to which tankers will come
like horses to a trough", THE SUNDAY TIMES, 7 May 1972.

94.   SHIPPING WORLD AND SHIPBUILDER, October 1972, at
p.1145; SHIP REPAIR AND MAINTENANCE INTERNATIONAL, January 1973.

95.   NEWSWEEK, 7 April 1975, at p.27.

96.   THE TIMES, 25 February 1970.

97.   Off-shore locations as well as coastal were among
the sites under consideration by the Roskill Commission for a
third London Airport, THE TIMES, 12 December 1968.

98.   San Diego Union, 18 April 1972, cited in C.W. Walker,
supra, at p.639.

99.   L. Lerner and M. Graham, New York Offshore Airport
Feasibility Study (executive brief, 1973), cited in W.H.Lawrence,
supra, at pp.577-8.

100.   A radar tower has been proposed recently to be built
in mid-Channel as an aid to safer navigation in the Strait of
Dover, with the purpose of giving surveillance and control in
a part of the busy shipping lanes not easily observable from
either the French or English mainland.   The tower is reported
to be one of a number of new proposals evolved by an Anglo-
French working party on safety of navigation, THE TIMES
(London), 15 January 1974.

101.   S.K. Keaton and J. Judy, supra, note 12, at p.609.

102.   D.M. Johnston, supra, note 57, at p.454.

103.   Oceanology International, October 1970, at p.14.

104.   SAN DIEGO MAGAZINE, July 1972, p.78, cited in
C.W. Walker, supra, at p.639.

105.   SCIENCE NEWS, 3 August 1969, p.235 and 3 October
1970, p.283; National Geographic, Vol. 140, August 1971,
pp.256-96.

106.   The Habitat was expected to be in operation by the
end of 1971 and it was hoped that it would "make the Virgin
Islands the Cape Kennedy of the underwater world programme,"
THE WASHINGTON POST, 14 February 1971.

107.   Oceanology International, October 1970, pp. 13-14.

108.   See below, Chapter 6.

109.   For measures now being taken worldwide toward
improvement in weather prediction and communications
instrumentation, see generally United States National Academy of
Engineering 1972, at p.226.

110.   D.M. Johnston, supra, note 57, at p.455.

111.   S.K. Keaton and J. Judy, supra, note 12, at p.609.

112.   Ibid., see also D.M. Johnston, supra, at p.456.

113.   In the United States, for example, about one half of
the population lives within 100 miles of the coast, and 29 per

cent within a 50-mile coastal belt representing 8 per cent of the country's total land area, U.N. ECOSOC DOC. E/5120, 28 April 1972, at p.29.

114. Ibid., at p.30; see also Doc. E/5650 at pp.23-4.

115. S.K. Keaton and J. Judy, supra, note 12, at p.610; D.M. Johnston, supra, note 57, at p.458.

116. THE TIMES, 21 May 1969.

117. U.N. ECOSOC. DOC. E/5120, 28 April 1972, at p.30.

118. SIPRI Research Report No. 7, Prospects for Arms Control in the Ocean, September 1972, at p.7.

119. M.S. McDougal and W.T. Burke, The Public Order of the Oceans, 1962, at p.716; P.C. Szasz, May the United States Build Radar Platforms on its Continental Shelf? 40 Cornell Law Quarterly, 1954-55, pp.110-125.

120. The 'Caesar' system is installed on the continental shelf at depths in the order of 200 metres off the coasts of the United States and it consists of a line of sonar installations linked to shore-based computer equipment; the 'Sea Sniper' system is installed along the Pacific and Hawaiian coasts. All these systems, together with a number of other related systems - 'Barrier' and 'Bronco' - are integral parts of the 'Sosus' overall comprehensive surveillance system and are based on the passive principle of hydro-acoustics. The active component of 'Sosus' is to be the 'Artemis' system, designed to detect submarines at long distance by means of ultra-powerful low-frequency active sonar stations. For a detailed description of ASW equipment, see the 1974 SIPRI monograph, Tactical and Strategic Anti-submarine Warfare.

121. Undersea Technology, December 1971, at p.9.

122. Undersea Technology, August 1971, at p.13.

123. On the increasing militarization of the seas and the attendant problems, see in general U.N. Doc. A/AC.135/28, 10 July 1968; E.D. Brown, Arms Control in Hydrospace: Legal Aspects, 1971; SIPRI Research Report No. 7, Prospects for Arms Control in the Ocean, Sept. 1972; E. Luard, The Control of the Sea-Bed, London 1974, ch.3; L.C. Petrowski, Military Use of the Ocean Space and the Continental Shelf, 7 Columbia Journal of Transnational Law 1968, pp.279-301; and The International Institute for Strategic Studies, Power at Sea, I. The New Environment, Adelphi Papers, No. 122, 1976.

124. SIPRI Research Report No. 7, supra, at p.15.

125. See H.F. Van Panhuys and Menno J. Van Emde Boas, Legal Aspects of Pirate Broadcasting, A Dutch Approach, 60 A.J.I.L. (1966), pp.303-341; J.C. Woodliffe, Some Legal Aspects of Pirate Broadcasting in the North Sea, 12 Netherlands International Law Review (1965), pp.365-384; E.D. Brown, Delimitation of Maritime Frontiers: Radio Stations in the Thames Estuary, 2 Australian Yearbook of International Law, (1966), pp.99-113; and M.M. Sibthorp (ed), The North Sea: Challenge and Opportunity, 1975, at pp.154-156.

126.   IMCO DOC. MSC XII/23/Add.2, 21 December 1965, pp.6-9; for a list of broadcasting stations outside territorial seas as of January 1966, see IMCO DOC. MSC/XII/23/add. 5, 18 January 1966.

127.   The European Agreement for the Prevention of Broadcasts Transmitted from Stations outside National Territories, opened for signature on 20 January 1965, in Strasbourg. Cmnd 2616;   634 U.N.T.S. 239;   reprinted also in 59 A.J.I.L., p.715;   14 I.C.L.Q., p.434;   and 4 I.L.M., p.115, (1965). The Agreement came into force on 19 October 1967.

128.   The R.E.M. station started its transmissions on 29 July, 1964 (radio), and 15 August 1964 (television).   It ceased operating on 17 December 1964, as a result of police action taken under the North Sea Installations Act (5 December 1964) specifically enacted for this purpose, see H.F. Van Panhuys etc. supra, at p.304;   for the text of the Act see ibid. at pp.340-341.

129.   The Fort is some 100 feet long and 30 feet wide on its main deck and it stands on two 75-feet high pillars.   The founder of 'Sealand' was offered money to convert it into a marina and casino and promoters were also promising money. His commercial agent in London said that "as in Liechtenstein, Sealand could be used by companies purely as a nameplate", THE SUNDAY TIMES,17 March 1968.

130.   Geo-Marine Technology, Vol. 3, No. 2, February 1967, pp.9-12;   Ocean Science News, 18 November 1966; and S. Eckhardt, Abalonia, 6 San Diego Law Review (1969), pp.498-501.   At about the same time a third company, operating independently of the Atlantis (U.S. v. Ray) and Abalonia promoters, attempted to obtain permission to construct Taluga, a new 'State' to consist of four islands on the Cortes Bank.   The company was, however, informed by the Corps of Engineers that the area was part of the continental shelf and that permission from the Secretary of the Army would be required, S. Eckhardt, supra, at p.498, footnote 64.

131.   14 Ocean Science News, 7 April 1972, at pp.2-3; F.M. Auburn, Some Legal Problems of the Commercial Exploitation of Manganese Nodules in the Pacific Ocean, Ocean Development and International Law Journal, Vol. 1, No. 2, 1973, pp.185-200, at pp.195-196.

132.   S.K. Keaton and J. Judy, supra, note 12, at pp.609-610. On the problem of free access to both sea and sea-resources by land-locked States see, generally, The Study of the Question of Free Access to the Sea of Land-Locked Countries and of the Special Problems of Land-Locked Countries Relating to the Exploration and Exploitation of the Resources of the Sea-Bed and the Ocean Floor Beyond the Limits of National Jurisdiction, Report of the U.N. Secretary-General, U.N. DOC.A/AC. 138/37 and Corr. 1, 1971;   see also The Interest of Land-Locked States in Law of the Sea, 9 San Diego Law Review (1972), at p.701.

133. Ocean Industry, December 1975, Vol. 10, at p.45.
On the technical problems see in general U.S. National Academy
of Engineering 1972, ch. IX, pp.134-172; "Experiments in
Excellence", pp.11-15; and North Sea Island Group, A Firm
Footing in the Sea, 1975.
    134. "Experiments in Excellence", at p.15.
    135. North Sea Island Group, supra, at p.7.   On the
overall economic implications see further "Experiments in
Excellence" at pp.15-19.
    136. "At the risk of losing credibility it should be
pointed out that serious suggestions have been made for
surgical experiments in adapting the human body for a normal
life under water so that communities can eventually be
established in the sea.   Such radical human resettlement may
be feasible, given the failure of all terrestrial solutions to
the population problem together with a preference for marine life
rather than resettlement on another planet.   The limited
alternatives available for human survival in the event of a
nuclear holocaust might also cause man to relocate his society
under water", D.M. Johnston, supra, note 57, at p.458
    137. "Environmental changes will be brought about through
the development of harbours and navigation channels, the
construction of breakwaters and jetties, off-shore oil field
platforms and collection systems, and the creation of new
land for residential or industrial use.   It is of paramount
importance that all construction and civil works operations
in the oceans be planned and carried forward with systematic
consideration of their favourable and unfavourable impacts on
the ocean environment", United States National Academy of
Engineering, 1972, at p.170.   Accordingly, more extensive use
should be made of physical and mathematical models to evaluate
the effect of any changes in the marine ecology through the
construction of artificial islands before they are authorized,
ibid. at p.163.
    138. On artificial islands constructed from the off-shore
disposal of dredged spoil and the possible effect on the
marine environment, see generally J.F. Hoffman, Industrial
Feasibility of Manmade Islands Constructed from the Offshore
Disposal of Dredged Spoil, United States, Naval Academy,
Annapolis-Maryland, Paper Th. I-G2-04.
    139. Ibid., Energy for the Sea-City designed by the
Pilkington Committee in the United Kingdom comes from an
undersea natural gas field nearby.
    140. Dr. J. Craven's address to the American Institute of
Architects, cited in the U.N. ECOSOC DOC. E/5120, 28 April 1972,
at p.31.

Chapter 2

THE RIGHT TO CONSTRUCT ARTIFICIAL ISLANDS

The seas can be divided into the following 5 (in certain cases overlapping) maritime zones, for the purpose of considering the jurisdiction exercised by States in them:
(1) Internal Waters; (2) Territorial Sea; (3) Contiguous Zone; (4) Continental Shelf; (5) High Seas.

In addition to these traditional zones, however, the concept of the Exclusive Economic Zone (EEZ) or Patrimonial Sea will also be considered as regards the right of States to construct artificial islands in such a zone (1). As has been said:

"At the present time, when State practice exhibits such a variety of claims and such a lack of stability, it is not practicable to examine claims in watertight compartments employing the traditional terminology. Some States are asserting traditional territorial sea claims, supplemented by claims to various functional zones, whereas others have dispensed with such refinements and are making comprehensive territorial sea claims of very considerable dimensions. Others again are experimenting de lege ferenda with new compromise formulae such as "the patrimonial sea" or the "exclusive economic zone" (2)."

I. INTERNAL WATERS

The whole maritime zone on the landward side of the baseline of the territorial sea is subject to the exclusive sovereignty of the coastal State (3). (Internal waters include also lakes, rivers, ports, harbours, inlets and bays). They are part of the territory of the State, thus subject to the control of the coastal State in a manner similar in degree to land territory (4).

Subject to one exception, arising from the provisions of the Geneva Convention on the Territorial Sea and the Contiguous Zone 1958, foreign shipping is not even entitled to the right of 'innocent passage' which is enjoyed in the territorial sea beyond internal waters. According to Article 4 of the Territorial Sea Convention, States may, in certain circumstances, adopt the 'straight baseline system' for the delimitation of the baseline from which the territorial sea is measured. Under Article 5 (2) of the same Convention, a right of innocent passage is preserved for foreign shipping in areas enclosed as internal waters by the establishment of this straight baseline system, if such waters were previously part of the territorial sea or of the high seas.

Thus, as regards construction of artificial islands, the coastal State may build and operate whatever installations it wishes in its own internal waters. In the absence of any treaty commitments to the contrary, a foreign State or national may not build nor operate any artificial structure within internal waters without the express permission of the coastal State.

II.   TERRITORIAL SEA

The entire maritime zone lying between the base-line and the outer limit of the territorial sea is under the exclusive sovereignty of the coastal State subject to a right of innocent passage for foreign shipping (5). Traditionally there has been a major uncertainty as regards the maximum permissible breadth of the territorial sea in international law, with claims running from three to 200 miles.

However, there seems now to be a general agreement on a 12 mile territorial sea in the Third United Nations Conference on the Law of the Sea. Thus, Art. 2, Part II of the Revised Single Negotiating Text, prepared during the fourth (New York) Session of the Conference in 1976, provides that "Every state has the right to establish the breadth of its territorial sea up to a limit not exceeding 12 nautical miles..." (6)

As regards the right to build artificial islands in the territorial sea, there is no doubt that the coastal State may in principle build whatever installations or other structures it wishes in its own territorial sea. Provision I of Informal Working Paper No. 12, prepared during the Second (Caracas) Session of the Third United Nations Conference on the Law of the Sea (UNCLOS III), provided that "The coastal State is entitled to construct artificial islands or immovable installations in its territorial sea" (7). It is also quite clear that in the absence of any treaty commitments to the contrary, a foreign State or national cannot construct or operate any artificial structures in the territorial sea of another State,

without the express permission of that State.   If, however,
the latter grants its permission for the construction of
artificial islands in that zone by a foreign State or national,
it will, ultimately, be responsible for the preservation of
the right of innocent passage through its territorial sea.

Indeed, when affirming the exclusive jurisdiction and control
of the coastal State over its territorial sea, it has to be
emphasized that the use of such waters must be consistent with
reasonable requirements of navigation, maritime safety, and the
right of innocent passage for foreign shipping.   The construction of artificial islands in the territorial sea must not
impede innocent passage through it, or hinder navigation in
general.   Article 5, para 6, of the 1958 Continental Shelf
Convention provides that :

> "Neither the installations or devices, nor the safety
> zones around them, may be established where inter-
> ference may be caused to the use of recognised sea
> lanes essential to international navigation."

Undoubtedly, the same principle applies as regards innocent
passage through the territorial sea, even though the said
Article applies to the waters superjacent to the continental
shelf, that is the high seas, and not to the territorial sea.
Article 15 of the Territorial Sea Convention 1958 lays down further
that:

> 1.   The coastal State must not hamper innocent passage
>   through the territorial sea.
> 2.   The coastal State is required to give appropriate
>   publicity to any dangers to navigation, of which
>   it has knowledge, within its territorial sea" (8).

It has further been suggested that, in the interests of
martitime safety and navigation, a coastal State should be
obliged to consult other States concerned when it undertakes
the construction of an artificial island in its territorial sea,

> "particularly as the territorial sea will very probably
> be extended and a structure in certain narrow waters might
> hinder access to the ports of a neighbouring State.   It
> would be desirable to impose on a coastal State the
> obligation to publish the plans of any structure which
> it proposed to erect and to take into consideration any
> observations addressed to it by other States;   it would
> doubtless be advisable to provide for the right of appeal
> to an impartial organisation such as IMCO" (9).

Belgium has accordingly proposed the following texts as
working bases for the preparation of sets of draft articles :

> "Article (a):   The coastal State is entitled to construct
> artificial islands or immovable installation in its
> territorial sea;   it must not, through such structures,
> impede access to the ports of a neighbouring State or
> cause damage to the marine environment of the territorial

seas of neighbouring States.

Article (b): Before commencing the construction of artifcial
islands or installations as mentioned in the preceding
Article, the coastal State shall publish the plans thereof
and take into consideration any observations submitted to
it by other States. In the event of disagreement, an
interested State which deems itself injured may appeal to
IMCO, which though not empowered to prohibit the construction, may prescribe such changes or adjustments as it considers essential to safeguard the lawful interests of other
States" (10).

III. CONTIGUOUS ZONE

Article 24 of the Geneva Convention on the Territorial Sea
and the Contiguous Zone (1958), lays down that in a zone of the
high seas contiguous to its territorial sea, which may not extend
beyond twelve miles from the baseline from which the breadth
of the territorial sea is measured, the coastal State may
exercise the control necessary to:

"(a) Prevent infringement of its customs, fiscal, immigration or sanitary regulations within its territory or
territorial sea;
(b) Punish infringement of the above regulations committed
within its territory or territorial sea" (11).

The sole purpose, therefore, of the establishment of the
contiguous zone is the prevention or punishment of infringements
of regulations concerning customs, fiscal, immigration or sanitary matters. It is thus clear from these provisions that the
coastal State does not possess any right to control or prohibit
the construction of artificial islands in the contiguous zone
by virtue of its status as such. The contiguous zone is a
zone of the high seas and as such it falls under the regime of
the high seas. The coastal State will, however, have certain
rights as regards such construction in cases where the waters
of the contiguous zone are superjacent to the continental shelf.

IV. HIGH SEAS

Article 3 of the Geneva Convention on the Continental Shelf
1958, lays down that, "The rights of the coastal State over
the continental shelf do not affect the legal status of the
superjacent waters as high seas...." It may, therefore, be
advisable before discussing the right to construct artificial
islands in thè area of the continental shelf, to clarify the
legal status of the high seas in relation to such construction
therein.

The doctrine of the freedom of the high seas in present

international law is authoritatively stated in Article 2 of the
Geneva Convention on the High Seas, 1958. There is no doubt
that Article 2 is simply a restatement of the generally
accepted principle of the freedom of the high seas under international customary law. That Article reads as follows :
"The high seas being open to all nations, no State may
validly purport to subject any part of them to its
sovereignty. Freedom of the high seas is exercised
under the conditions laid down by these articles and
by the other rules of international law. It comprises,
inter alia, both for coastal and non-coastal States :
1. Freedom of navigation;
2. Freedom of fishing;
3. Freedom to lay submarine cables and pipelines;
4. Freedom to fly over the high seas.
These freedoms, and others which are recognised by the
general principles of international law, shall be
exercised by all States with reasonable regard to the
interests of other States in their exercise of the freedom
of the high seas."
Article 2, thus, makes clear that the four named freedoms do
not exhaust the uses of the sea covered by the principle of the
freedom of the high seas. In para. 2 of the Commentary to draft
Article 27 (now Article 2) the ILC said that,
"The Commission has merely specified four of the main
freedoms, but it is aware that there are other freedoms,
such as freedom to undertake scientific research on the
high seas - a freedom limited only by the general principle
stated in the third sentence of paragraph 1 of the
Commentary to the present Article," that is that
"States are bound to refrain from any acts which might
adversely affect the use of the high seas by nationals
of other States " (12).
As regards the sea-bed, this has traditionally been considered as res nullius or res communis. Subscription to
first theory implies that rights acquired are exclusive in
nature, whereas adherence to the latter implies recognition of
rights non-exclusive in nature (13). Relevant state practice
has, of course, been limited in the past by the virtual impossibility (technologically and economically) of establishing control
over the deep sea floor. Exclusive State rights in sedentary
fisheries have been generally recognised. Another use of the
sea-bed has been the laying of submarine cables and pipelines
which is now expressly mentioned in Article 2 of the High Seas
Convention as one of the rights comprised in the freedom of the
high seas.
The legal status of seamounts should also be mentioned in
the present context. Here again, relevant State practice has
been limited in the past by the virtual impossibility of product-
ive exploration and exploitation and there have been no specific

references or concern, for seamounts in the international conventions on the law of the sea so far.   As has been said,
"the significance of seamounts has remained unacknowledged by
most commentators, and the existing legal status of these
structures must be presumed to be the same as that of the sea-
bed itself" (14).

In relation to the subsoil of the high seas, the ILC commented in 1956 that:
"The Commission has not made specific mention of the
freedom to explore or exploit the subsoil of the high
seas.   It considered that apart from the case of the
exploitation or exploration of the soil or subsoil of a
continental shelf..... such exploitation had not yet
assumed sufficient practical importance to justify
special regulation" (15).

However, now that the exploration and exploitation of
the mineral resources of the sea-bed and subsoil beyond the
limits of national jurisdiction has already started, such
exploration and exploitation has, indeed, "assumed sufficient
practical importance to justify special regulation"(16).

Accordingly, the fact that the law is changing as regards
the ocean floor and subsoil, "if it has not already changed"
(17), is echoed in the U.N. General Assembly Moratorium
Resolution of 1969 (18) and the Declaration of Principles
Governing the Sea-Bed and the Ocean Floor and the Subsoil
Thereof, Beyond the Limits of National Jurisdiction (19).
The first three operative paragraphs of the Declaration provide
that :
"1.   The sea-bed and ocean floor and the subsoil
thereof, beyond the limits of national jurisdiction
(hereinafter referred to as the area), as well as the
resources of the area, are the common heritage of mankind.
2.   The area shall not be subject to appropriation by
any means by states or persons, natural or juridical, and
no State shall claim or exercise sovereignty or sovereign
rights over any part thereof.
3.   No state or person, natural or juridical, shall claim,
exercise or acquire rights with respect to the area or
its resources incompatible with the international regime
to be established and the Principles of this Declaration."

While a detailed examination of the legal significance
of U.N. General Assembly resolutions is beyond the scope of
the present study, it can, however, be said that the Declaration
of Principles is reflecting the general opinion of the international community of states (20).   Indeed, in view of the fact
that the Declaration was adopted unanimously (except for 14
abstentions), the least which can be said is that its principles
formulate emerging rules of international law, while at the
same time, they impose a political and moral commitment on
states to prevent their nationals from carrying out activities

in the area contrary to the Declaration of Principles. Profes-
for Cheng has suggested that while a General Assembly resolution
is without binding force, strictly speaking, it can nevertheless
provide strong evidence that the law stated therein, is a rule
of customary international law among the states voting for it (21).
Another jurist from the Soviet Union has further stated that:
"Although General Assembly resolutions enunciating
general principles for state activities have a recommend-
atory character and cannot be seen as compulsory juridical acts
they, nevertheless, have great political and moral significance. This is especially true for resolutions adopted
unanimously or by an overwhelming majority of votes of all
three basic state groupings – the socialist, western and
neutral countries, including the major powers....
They may also be the first formulation of provisions that
in the future can turn into compulsory juridical rules of
common or treaty character" (22).
It should finally be added that even if the Declaration of
Principles fails to materialize in the form of a binding conventional regime "its adoption underlines the difficulties inherent
in reliance on the rules of international customary law to
provide a framework for submarine exploitation"(23).
As regards Article 2 of the High Seas Convention and
the content of the freedom of the high seas, two opposite views
have been historically developed. According to the first view
all peaceful uses of the seas are covered, whereas the second
only admits a limited number of long established uses.
Thus, the advocates of the first view have supported that
Article 2 of the High Seas Convention does not imply that the
freedom of the seas comprises only a limited number of well-
established categories of freedoms. Accordingly, it would
appear that the freedom of the high seas comprises, apart from
the four named freedoms, and any other uses of the high seas
which are recognised as flowing from the principle that the
latter are open to all nations for any peaceful purposes (24).
These freedoms must, of course, be exercised with reasonable
regard to the interests of other States in their exercise of
the freedom of the high seas. It has further been submitted
that State practice supports such a view. McDougal and Burke,
for instance, have supported the view that any use of the seas
for peaceful purposes is permissible under international law:
"Both the practice of States and the explicit agreements
they have formulated concerning free access to the sea
seem in accord with common interest..... There would
appear, in short, a very widespread consensus, clearly in
accord with the common interest, that access to the oceans
is permissible for any peaceful purpose" (25).
According to this view, therefore, the construction,
maintenance and operation of an artificial island or structure
on the high seas is a right which falls within the principle of

the freedom of the high seas.   As a freedom of the high seas
it has, of course, to be exercised with reasonable regard to
the interests of the other States.

Sir Humphrey Waldock has, also forcefully argued in the
R.E.M. station case, that Article 2 of the High Seas Convention
comprises, apart from the four named freedoms, and any other use
of ±he high seas for peaceful purposes (26).   He has, thus,
argued"....   the right of a State to make whatever use it thinks
fit of the high seas has never really been challenged, except
on the basis that the particular use in question constituted an
unreasonable interference with the rights of other States upon
the high seas" (27).   With regard to artificial islands he
concluded that :

"Both the Geneva Convention of 1958 and State practice
thus support the view that the erection of an artificial
structure on the sea-bed of the high seas is an act which
in itself falls within and is sanctioned by the principle
of the freedom of the high seas" (28).

The Dutch maritime expert, M.W. Mouton, had earlier adopted
a similar view :

"We maintain that building constructions in the high seas
is using the freedom of the seas just as much as navigating
on these seas, or fishing in these seas or laying telegraph cables on the bottom of these seas.   If Grotius
had known about telegraph cables and oil derricks, he would
have included them in the kind of use one can make of
the high seas" (29).

With regard to certain types of artificial islands it may
be argued further that their construction on the high seas is
permitted under existing international law, in so far as they
are incidental to the exercise of one of the freedoms already
recognised by the general principles of international law.
Thus, it could be argued, for example, that, given the present
technological developments, off-shore harbour facilities fall
within presently permitted uses of the high seas because they
are incidental to navigation, fishing installations are incidental
to fishing, ODAS are incidental to scientific research, and so
forth (30).   A similar argument has been advanced by Professor
Riphagen who has proposed "the adoption of a clear priority-
rule in favour of such activities as are necessarily sea-based"
(31).   Thus, according to this view artificial islands constructed on the high seas to serve traditionally land-based and
land-orientated activities, such as sea-cities, must not necessarily be prohibited, but simply they must have a lower priority
than recognised sea-based activities.   In his words: "...the
construction of an artificial island for the sole purpose of
transferring to such island traditionally land-based and land-
orientated activities of necessity must have a lower priority
than any recognised sea-based activity" (32) .

According to the second theory now, this view of the law

is diamterically opposed. The advocates of this strict view consider that only a limited number of well-established freedoms are allowed under international law. As was stated by C.J. Colombos in the R.E.M. station case :

"That the fact that a given act is not prohibited by international law does not imply that it is allowable. Any interference with the freedom of the seas must be clearly expressed and cannot be presumed" (33).

The permissibility of new uses of the high seas is, thus viewed with great suspicion by many scholars advocating this strict view. Professor Tammes, for example, considered that "any new activity on the high seas which does not belong to the freedoms recognised by the general principles of international law, such as installations facilitating the use of the sea, or intended for scientific research or use as fisheries equipment... need not be respected by other uses of the high seas" (34). It would appear, therefore, that "under this strict view, a State's declaration of jurisdiction to construct or control activities on an artificial island would be contrary to the freedom of the high seas, destroying as it would, the principle of res communis" (35).

Already in 1954, certain delegates raised, during the ILC's discussions on the subject of islands, doubts regarding the right of States to erect artificial islands beyond their own territorial sea "as that would allow them to appropriate large stretches of the high seas." It was then said that such an act would be contrary to international law, but nevertheless, it was conceded that ultimately it was a matter of recognition by other States (36). Some thirty years earlier Gidel also made the establishment of artificial islands on the high seas dependent on acceptance by other States (37).

The doubts voiced are based on the premise that recognition of such a right would be tantamount to recognising the exclusive occupation of portions of the high seas "which would be an evident violation of the principle of the freedom of the seas and would invite the most varied claims" (38). In his report to the Council of Europe on the legal status of artificial islands built on the high seas, the Rapporteur, Mr. Margue, noted that, "The creation of an artificial island amounts to exclusive occupancy of a maritime area" and that "The exclusive occupation of a portion of maritime area constitutes an a priori encroachment on the general interests of the international community" (39). However, Mr. Margue supported further the view that :

"As a corollary of the freedom of the high seas the creation of an artificial island on the high seas shall be free on condition that it does not encroach upon the rights of other States, that is, that it does not interfere with the free use of the seas. No special authority is required to create an artificial island situated outside the territorial waters of any State" (40).

After the preceding analysis of the position under international customary law, it is the writer's view that the erection of artificial islands on the high seas is a desirable and necessary development, if not inevitable, potentially serving the general interests of mankind. As such, the construction of artificial islands can be legally justified either under the theory that "although constituting a new use of the high seas, and one not contemplated in any existing international agreement or customary international law norms, nonetheless such a use is not inconsistent with other uses of the high seas, and the unilateral action initiating such a use would not likely meet with protest" (41), or under the doctrine that it is "an act which in itself falls within and is sanctioned by the principle of the freedom of the high seas" (42). It is of little practical value to engage in sterile doctrinal disputes and narrow legalistic interpretations when State practice indicates that we are on the way to recognising the necessity of this new 'freedom'. Whenever in the past the necessity for a new use of the seas has arisen, such as laying submarine cables and pipelines, flying over the seas, etc., States have had recourse to such uses without seeking the consent of other States and without protestation from the States concerned. This has also been the case with the construction of light-houses (43) and navigational aids, buoys and various other structures used for scientific purposes, weather predictions and so forth, and installations constructed on the sea-bed of the high seas for the exploitation of natural resources (44). This is the case today with the deployment of Ocean Data Acquisition Systems (ODAS) on the high seas and the construction of off-shore harbours beyond the limits of the territorial sea. The underlying common interest of all States in such activities makes it unlikely that they will protest at the engagement in such activities by other States and their nationals. Indeed, so far as we know, no such protests have been recorded. In case of doubt, acquiescence and express or implied recognition legitimise these acts in international law.

Furthermore, the "freedom to construct artificial islands and other installations" in the high seas is now expressly recognised by the Draft Convention prepared by UNCLOS III (45). Art.76 provides that the freedom of the high seas "comprises, inter alia, both for coastal and land-locked States:
(a) Freedom of navigation; (b) Freedom of overflight;
(c) Freedom to lay submarine cables and pipelines... ;
(d) Freedom to construct artificial islands and other installations permitted under international law... ;
(e) Freedom of fishing...; (f) Freedom of scientific research.."
"2. These freedoms shall be exercised by all
States, with due consideration for the interests of other
States in their exercise of the freedom of the high seas,

and also with due consideration for the rights under the
present Convention with respect to activities in the
International Area."

Thus, the problem is not really whether the right to
erect artificial islands is a 'freedom' of the high seas or not.
The real problem is how best to (a) safeguard this activity
vis-a-vis other legitimate uses of the seas, and (b) ensure that
the construction of artificial islands on the high seas will not
facilitate the exploitation of the wealth of the oceans only
for the benefit of the few powerful, economically and technologically, States.

With regard to (a) above, artificial islands, as has
already been indicated, can be a serious danger to shipping and
fishing, and a significant source of pollution and nuisance.
It becomes increasingly clear that, as the use of the oceans is
intensified, both in variety and in volume, the various freedoms
of the seas can only survive as regulated freedoms. This is
already the case with the freedom of navigation (46). The
construction of artificial islands should, thus, take place in
an orderly and well thought out way so as to avoid any unjustifiable interference with the other legitimate uses of the high
seas and the sea-bed such as, apart from navigation, the laying
of submarine cables and pipelines, fishing, conservation of the
living resources of the sea, scientific research and so forth
(47). For example, artificial islands should not be constructed
in, or near, straits used for international navigation, in or
near, approaches to ports and harbours, and in general in places
where there is congestion of shipping.

Thus, Art. 16 of the Draft Convention on the International
Sea-Bed Area provides in para 2 (ii) that "stationary and
mobile installations relating to the conduct of activities in the
Area.... shall not be located in the Area where they may obstruct
passage through sea lanes of vital importance for international
shipping or in areas of intense fishing activity" (48).

To sum up then, it would appear that the best way to tackle
the problem of artificial islands would be a multilateral
approach resulting in a conventional regime, where the ambiguities
and general guidelines of international customary law could be
transformed into more precise and definite rules concerning the
legal regime of artificial islands and the accommodation of the
conflicting uses of the sea.

The Council of Europe, as has already been indicated, is
aware of the problem and has made an attempt to tackle it
from a European angle, urging its member States to a multilateral
approach. A Recommendation presented by the Legal Affairs Committee of the Council of Europe states that :

"The Assembly,
....
3. Noting that an increasing number of artificial islands
    are being built on the high seas by natural persons

and bodies corporate under private law, for the
most varied purposes (oil prospecting, scientific
exploration, pirate radio stations, tourist
development);

4. Considering the obstacles to freedom of
navigation and fishing, the dangers of fraud and of
infringement of the laws of coastal States and the
risks of pollution and nuisances inherent in the
phenomenon of artificial islands;

5. Considering that these islands do not come under
the legal order of any particular State and that the
absence of authoritative international regulations
in the matter constitutes a source of conflicts and
problems;

6. Considering that the creation of an artificial
island on the high seas amounts to the exclusive occupation of a portion of international public property;

7. Considering that it would be advisable to try and
regulate this situation on a multilateral basis;
.......10. Considering that it is necessary to subject
the creation of artificial islands on the high seas
to control, possibly under the aegis of an international organisation, in order to reconcile the
general interests of the international community,
the national interests of States, especially of
coastal States, and the lawful claims of those who
build, own and develop these islands;
Recommends that the Committee of Ministers ask
member States to define a common attitude to the
problem of the legal status of artificial islands
on the high seas, taking into account the interests
of coastal States, and to make joint proposals on
this subject at the International Conference on the
Law of the Sea in 1973" (49).

It would appear further that this proposed multilateral
approach should ideally culminate into the establishment of
international control and supervision over all types of
artificial islands erected on the high seas for the benefit of
the international community as a whole. Moreover, it would
seem that in the present state of affairs this could be best
achieved within the context of the International Regime to be
established for the exploitation of the ocean resources, by
placing the artificial islands under the effective control and
authority of the International Machinery for the sea-bed.

Indeed, to recognise in the present climate of international
relations the construction of artificial islands on the high
seas as a 'freedom of the seas' within the traditional sense of
unrestricted and unregulated access to the oceans, is tantamount to accepting the full domination of the few States with
the resources and the most advanced technology upon the riches

of the seas, and even further their conceivable claims of sovereignty over large areas of the high seas, with very little
of the ocean wealth left for the less developed and land-locked
States.   There is no doubt that the few privileged States
would take as quickly as possible all attractive locations in
the high seas, such as sites rich in mineral resources and
hydrocarbons, and notably the seamounts which at present appear
to be the most promising sites, for the construction of any
artificial islands they see fit.   It is exactly the fear of
such a dangerous development that has led many commentators to
subscribe to the theory of the strict interpretation of the
freedom of the high seas.   As has been put by one such
commentator :

> ".....Also to be considered is the strong possibility
> of conflict as States compete for the wealth of the
> high seas.   Add to this the spectre of unfriendly
> nations building artificial islands off each other's
> coasts, and the probability of conflict approaches
> certainty.   The strict interpretation of the freedom
> of the high seas would avoid these anomalous results.
> At the same time it does not prohibit the international
> community from creating a regime prescribing jurisdiction
> over artificial islands of all uses" (50).

The construction of artificial islands on the high seas,
then is indeed a freedom of the high seas, but nevertheless it
must be understood and accepted not as an unrestricted and
unregulated freedom, which could easily be transformed into a
"first come first served" principle, but as a regulated and
rationally exercised 'freedom' for the benefit of all nations.
The principle of the freedom of the high seas cannot be viewed
as a rigid, unchanging principle, but as one capable of adapt-
ation to changing circumstances.   Professor Lauterpacht, for
instance, has this to say with regard to the said principle:

> "The principle of the freedom of the seas cannot be
> treated as a rigid dogma incapable of adaptation to
> situations which were outside the realm of practical
> possibilities in the period when that principle
> first became part of international law" (51) .

Accordingly, the traditional res communis concept, underlying for centuries the customary law of the sea, may suitably
be adapted to contemporary conditions by a shift of emphasis
from "freedom" (i.e. unrestricted access) towards "international
management and regulation" (i.e. restricted access and rational
use) (52).   It naturally follows that the establishment of

> "..... an international regime encompassing artificial
> islands for all uses is necessary and proper."   And
> whereas, "such a regime should recognise that the coastal
> State has inherent economic and security interests in the
> seas appurtenant to its coast and is best able to promote
> and protect these interests and should thus have primary

jurisdiction to construct and control activities on
artificial islands within an area encompassing some distance seaward, which would be set by agreement between
nations..... Beyond the area of primary coastal State
jurisdiction the construction and use of artificial
islands should be under the exclusive .control of the
international community for the benefit of all States,
especially the landlocked, the shelf-locked and the
under-developed." To be sure "the creation of this
regime will take a great deal of planning, negotiation and
goodwill, especially on the part of the developed countries
who, in essence, will be giving up the opportunity to
exercise their greater ability to reap the wealth of the
oceans on a first-come, first-served basis. But they
should realise that they will gain insured freedom of
the seas, insured peaceful use of the seas, and control
of pollution: in general, an orderly development of the
oceans which is beneficial to all nations and which
surpasses any limited benefits which might accrue to a
few nations from a laissez-faire attitude toward artificial islands " (53).

It is, therefore, to be seen as a hopeful sign the fact
that States themselves have started realising the necessity for
an international regime as regards artificial islands. Thus,
the Belgian Government has, for example, submitted to the
United Nations Sea-Bed Committee the following text to serve
as a working base for the preparation of sets of draft articles
on the construction of artificial islands "on the high seas
beyond the limits of the continental shelf":

"Any construction of an artificial island or immovable
installation on the high seas beyond the limits of the
continental shelf shall be subject to the authority and
jurisdiction of the international machinery for the sea-
bed. The international authority may authorize a State
to erect such islands or installations and delegate
jurisdiction over such structures to that State " (54).

Ecuador, Panama and Peru expressly recognise further
in their working paper, submitted to the Sea-Bed Committee in
1973, the freedom to emplace artificial islands on the "international seas" as a freedom of the high seas, subject, however,
to international regulations (55). Thus, Articles 19 and 24
of the draft read as follows :

"Article 19
The following freedoms shall be exercised on the inter-
national seas ....
(4) freedom to emplace artificial islands and other
    installations permitted under international law,
    without prejudice to the provisions of article 24;
Article 24
The emplacement of artificial islands or any other type

of installations apart from submarine cables or pipelines shall be subject to international regulations."

Moreover, it is further submitted that the difficult problem of the conflicting uses of the seas could be best faced within the context of such an international regime and machinery. Plans of any projected structure on the sea would have to be published before any such construction is undertaken, and any observations submitted by other States, and particularly by the immediately affected ones, such as neighbouring States, as well as any other interested parties, would have to be taken into consideration. As Dr. Mouton already noted in 1952: "In order to achieve a reasonable application of different ways of using the high seas, it would be recommendable to create an international body, judging plans submitted to it and giving binding decisions" (56).

However, provisions to that effect are unfortunately missing from the existing Draft Convention on the International Sea-Bed Area which is concerned exclusively with installations used for the exploration and exploitation of the resources of the Area. One relevant provision contained in the Informal Working Paper No.12, of 20 August 1974, has now been omitted from the said Draft Convention. That Provision reads as follows :

"Any construction of an artificial island or immovable installation on the high seas beyond the limits of the continental shelf shall be subject to the authority and jurisdiction of the international machinery for the sea-bed. The international authority may authorise a state to erect such islands or installations and delegate jurisdiction over such structures to that State" (57).

The legal regime of the seamounts calls, finally,for a brief comment in the present context since the utilisation of these valuable structures is envisaged to be closely connected with the construction of artificial islands in the deep oceans. Here again respective recommendations call for the establishment of an all-embracing international regime so as to avoid further conflicts created by the possible occupation of the seamounts by a few developed countries:

"What is desired, in view of the rapid advances of technology, is a regime for seamounts and guyots which will prevent their unilateral claim and exploitation by nations to the exclusion of other nations, and avoid those problems inherent in claiming and occupying unowned territory. A regime for the entire sea-bed has long been sought, but the urgency which often fosters such agreements is lacking because most of the sea-bed is still economically out of reach for all practical purposes. Such is not the case with seamounts and guyots. As previously indicated, they are within reach, and are currently prospects for massive exploitation, and possibly occupation, by a few developed countries. Accordingly, a regime governing the status

of seamounts is essential now, and must be adopted without
undue delay..... The regime established for seamounts
must of necessity, therefore, be part of an all-inclusive
programme covering every aspect of the ocean as an area for
exploitation and development...... The initial step in the
creation of a regime of this nature would be the claim
by an internationally created organisation of a vested
right to all territory outside the exclusive jurisdiction
of the coastal States, and all non-living resources of the
high sea-bed for the benefit of mankind. The title
claimed would not encompass the area of the "legal"
continental shelf.... the living resources of the oceans,
nor the water of the high seas" (58).

V.   CONTINENTAL SHELF

The legal regime of the continental shelf is governed by
the international customary law doctrine of the continental
shelf and, for State Parties thereto, by the Geneva Convention
on the Continental Shelf 1958.   Both international customary
law and the 1958 Continental Shelf Convention confer upon
the coastal State sovereign and exclusive rights for purposes
of exploration and exploitation of the natural resources of the
continental shelf.   Thus Article 2 of the Continental Shelf
Convention provides that :
"1.   The coastal State exercises over the continental
      shelf sovereign rights for the purpose of exploring
      it and exploiting its natural resources.
 2.   The rights referred to in paragraph 1 of this article
      are exclusive in the sense that if the coastal State
      does not explore the continental shelf or exploit
      its natural resources, no one may undertake these
      activities, or make a claim to the continental shelf,
      without the express consent of the coastal State.
 3.   The rights of the coastal State over the continental
      shelf sovereign rights for the purpose of exploring
      notional, or on any express proclamation."
The formula 'sovereign rights' rather than 'sovereignty'
was chosen because the ILC wanted to make clear the decisive
importance of safeguarding the full freedom of the superjacent
sea, and the air space above it.   In commenting upon draft
Article 68 (now Article 2) the ILC said :
"The Commission desired to avoid language lending itself
to interpretations alien to an object which the Commission
considers to be of decisive importance, namely, the safeguarding of the principle of the full freedom of the
superjacent sea and the air space above it.   Hence, it
was unwilling to accept the sovereignty of the coastal
State over the sea-bed and subsoil of the continental
shelf.   On the other hand, the text as now adopted

leaves no doubt that the rights conferred upon the coastal State cover all rights necessary for and connected with the exploration and exploitation of the natural resources of the continental shelf. Such rights include jurisdiction in connection with the prevention and punishment of violation of the law. The rights of the coastal State are exclusive in the sense that, if it does not exploit the continental shelf, it is only with its consent that anyone else may do so" (59).

Accordingly, Article 3 of the Convention makes it explicit that the coastal State's sovereign rights over the continental shelf do not affect the legal status of the superjacent waters as high seas, or that of the airspace above those waters.

Article 5 (2) of the Continental Shelf Convention provides further that "... the coastal State is entitled to construct and maintain or operate on the continental shelf installations and other devices necessary for its exploration and the exploitation of its natural resources....." It is beyond any doubt that the said paragraph 2 covers only installations connected with the exploration and exploitation of the natural resources of the continental shelf. The coastal State, therefore, is not entitled to construct or operate artificial islands and installations for any other uses, by virtue of the said Article 5.

In view of these provisions it is thus clear that both the ILC and the 1958 Conference were completely opposed to "according any rights to the coastal State over the continental shelf other than those strictly connected with the exploration and exploitation of the natural resources" (60). The restricted character of the coastal State's jurisdiction is further illustrated by the following observation of the ILC in its final report to the General Assembly:

"It is clearly understood that the rights in question do not cover objects such as wrecked ships and their cargoes (including bullion) lying on the sea-bed or covered by the sand of the subsoil" (61).

In short, the 1958 Continental Shelf Convention grants the coastal States the exclusive authority required for exploration and exploitation of the shelf resources, including of course, the right to erect in the shelf area any artificial islands and installations necessary for that purpose (62). Artificial islands for any other purposes cannot thus be (a) constructed by virtue of the Continental Shelf Convention and (b) covered by the provisions of that Convention.

It naturally follows that the problem of the authority to use the continental shelf for purposes other than for exploration and exploitation of resources still persists despite the Convention. Moreover, in the present context, the most important question appears to be whether any State, or only the coastal State, can construct artificial islands on the continental shelf for purposes other than those contemplated in the 1958 Convention, independently of the Convention.

Prima facie it would appear that any State and not only the coastal State may construct artificial islands on the latter's continental shelf for peaceful purposes other than for exploration and exploitation of the shelf resources. This view could well be based on the doctrine of the freedom of the high seas. Since both the Geneva Convention on the Continental Shelf 1958, and customary international law, recognise the coastal State's exclusive rights on the continental shelf only for specific limited purposes, namely exploration and exploitation of natural resources, it follows that they do not limit this freedom with regard to any other uses permissible under international law. The continental shelf area, therefore, is subject to the regime of the high seas as regards these other uses. Indeed, Article 3 of the Continental Shelf Convention does preserve the legal status of the superjacent waters as high seas. It follows that any State may construct and/or operate any floating or fixed installations for peaceful purposes on the continental shelf of another country, excluding, of course, those associated with exploration and exploitation of natural resources. This right, if accepted, would naturally have to be exercised with reasonable regard to the interests of other States in their exercise of the freedom of the high seas. In particular, the artificial islands and installations under consideration should not be sited in such a way as to constitute any unreasonable interference with the coastal State's right to explore and exploit the shelf resources. Sir Humphrey Waldock, for example, would appear to have accepted the freedom of the high seas argument in his 'Opinion' on the R.E.M. station case, subject, of course, to the rule of unreasonable interference:

"No doubt, the coastal State would have a right to complain if the siting of the installation was such as to constitute an unreasonable interference with the exploitation of the natural resources. But it would not seem entitled to assume jurisdiction over an installation not open to that complaint" (63).

By covering both structures deployed in the superjacent waters and structures built on the sea-bed of the continental shelf this argument would certainly be adopted by those who consider that the legal status of the sea-bed is the same as that of the superjacent high seas: "A clear distinction must be drawn between the bed of the sea and its subsoil. As regards the former, the better opinion appears to be that it is incapable of occupation by any State and that its legal status is the same as that of the waters of the open sea above it" (64).

For those who do not subscribe to the theory that the doctrine of the freedom of the high seas comprises and the sea-bed, the sea-bed title argument may be employed alternatively.

Thus, "if the view is accepted that title to specific areas of
the sea-bed underlying the high seas may be initiated by
effective control and consolidated by recognition and acquiescence,"
then it follows that a State may establish the exclusive control
necessary for such construction activities, both on the bed
of the high seas and on the continental shelf. "In both cases,
such control would, of course, have to be exercised with reasonable regard to the interests of other States in their use of
the high seas" (65).   Moreover, with regard to the bed of the
continental shelf such control should not interfere unreason-
ably with the exploration and exploitation activities of the
coastal State.

However, the "free for all" approach would appear to suffer
from two fundamental drawbacks: (a) it dangerously ignores
the security interests of the coastal State; and (b) it
rather lightly by-passes the obvious danger of interference with
the coastal State's exploration and exploitation of the natural
resources.

With regard to the security interests of the coastal State,
structures originally constructed for mineral extraction and
other peaceful purposes may at a later stage be used for
military purposes.   Indeed, "The United States has employed
the shelf for military purposes by using the structures originally designed to extract oil and other minerals" (66).   It
is only too clear that no State would welcome such a development
so near its territorial sea.   No State would like to see
foreign installations, let alone artificial islands, built so
near its coast.

The Dutch specialist on the continental shelf, Dr. Mouton,
in commenting upon the first national instruments, such as the
Truman Proclamation, which extended the coastal sovereign rights
over the continental shelf, expressed the view that those
instruments did not rely on the theory of contiguity, but were
moved by reasons of security:
> "We believe that in spite of the wording the authors of
> the instruments do not rely on the theory of contiguity,
> but were moved by reasons of security.   No State would
> like to see valuable resources so near its coasts to be
> exploited by another State.   No State would like to see
> foreign installations being built so near its territorial
> waters.   Let us admit immediately that the fear is more
> of a theoretical than of a practical nature, because the
> building of installations in front of a foreign coast does
> not seem practicable in most cases" (67).

As Dr. Mouton has pointed out further these security considerations may be compared with the considerations of Judge
Sir William Scott in the case of the Anna (1805) (68), where he
held a number of off-shore little mud islands to be "the natural
appendages of the coast on which they border and from which
indeed they are formed," forming thus part of the territory of

the United States from which the protection of the territory
was to be reckoned.   Sir William Scott then continues :
> "Consider what the consequence would be if lands of
> this description were not considered as appendant to the
> mainland, and as comprised within the bounds of territory.
>
> If they do not belong to the United States of America,
> any other power might occupy them; they might be embanked
> and fortified.   What a thorn would this be in the side of
> America."

As regards further the threat of interference with the
coastal State's rights in the exploration and exploitation of
the shelf resources, posed by the erection of foreign installations, the possibilities of conflict are only too obvious
to be emphasized once more.

In the writer's view a fundamental distinction has to be
made, de lege lata, between installations and structures
deployed and operated in the superjacent waters and installations
fixed on, or otherwise supported by, the bed of the continental
shelf.   In view of Article 3 of the 1958 Continental Shelf
Convention which preserves the legal status of the superjacent
waters as high seas, and also in view of the minimum security
risks and the rather negligible interference with the exploration
and exploitation activities which is likely to occur by the
deployment of the former installations, it is submitted that
these are subject to the principle of the freedom of the high
seas.   Thus, any State could deploy and/or operate these on the
superjacent waters of the continental shelf of another country,
subject, of course, to the rule of the reasonable regard to the
interests of other States in their exercise of the freedom of
the high seas.   Moreover, such installations should not be
deployed in such a way as to constitute an unreasonable interference with the coastal State's right to explore and exploit
the shelf resources, when such exploration and exploitation is
conducted from the superjacent waters.   Prior notification and
consultation between the coastal State and the owners or
operators of the installations is, normally, to be expected.
Conflicts would, thus, by and large be avoided and a reasonable
accommodation of the competing users achieved.

With regard to fixed installations it is submitted that
considerations of coastal security as well as the paramount
importance of the continental shelf for exploitation purposes,
make it necessary to recognise exclusive coastal authority and
control over any use of the shelf which would require the
construction of fixed installations.   McDougal and Burke have
also supported a similar view :
> ".....considerations of coastal security and of honouring
> the now-recognised authority over the continental shelf,
> for exploitative purposes make it imperative to recognise
> exclusive coastal control over any use of the continental
> shelf which requires emplacing relatively fixed installations.

It would be most inadvisable, for example, to permit an uncontrolled competence in non-coastal States to erect structures on the continental shelf, while at the same time authorising the coastal State to exploit the natural resources of the continental shelf. The possibilities of conflict are too obvious" (69).

It is also interesting to note that under Provision VI of the Informal Working Paper No. 12, of 20 August 1974, no State or foreign nationals may establish "on or over the continental shelf of another State any military installations or devices or any other installations for whatever purposes without the consent of the coastal State". Of considerable significance is further Article 68 of the draft Convention prepared by the Second Committee of UNCLOS III (70). That Article, which must be read in conjunction with Articles 48 and 44 in Chapter III dealing with the Exclusive Economic Zone, provides in effect that: On the continental shelf, the coastal State shall have the exclusive right to construct, authorize and regulate the construction, operation and use of :

(a) Artificial islands;
(b) Installations and structures for
1. the exploration and exploitation of the natural resources of the shelf;
2. economic purposes in general, and
3. scientific research;
(c) Installations and structures which may interfere with the exercise of the rights of the coastal State on the shelf.

It is thus clear that under the Revised Single Negotiating Text, the coastal State has the exclusive authority to construct artificial islands and economic installations on its shelf area. Furthermore, in view of (c) above, it would appear that non-economic installations are also in effect subject to authorization and regulation by the coastal State. In short, coastal States will most probably claim in practice exclusive authority to construct artificial islands and installations on the continental shelf, whether economic or non-economic, floating or fixed.

It is further submitted that, embryonic State practice, as emerges from recent municipal legislation, national courts' decisions and proposals for international action, would seem to confirm the views supported here with regard to construction activities on the continental shelf. Indeed, a brief examination of the existing material will illuminate further the above supported views.

ARGENTINA. Articles 23 and 24 of the Draft Articles on the Territorial Sea, "Epicontinental Sea" and Continental Shelf, submitted to the Sea-Bed Committee in 1973, read as follows :
"23. A coastal State shall authorize the laying of submarine cables and pipelines on the continental shelf,

without restrictions other than those which may result
from its rights over the same.
24. The establishment of any other type of installation
by third States or their nationals is subject to the
permission of the coastal State" (71).

It will be noted that both floating and fixed installations
would appear to be covered by the formulation of Article 24 under
which the coastal State is granted exclusive authority for construction activities on its continental shelf.

BELGIUM. With regard to the erection of fixed installations or
artificial islands on the continental shelf it would seem fair,
in the Belgian Government's view, to provide for the authorisa-
tion of the coastal State, since an artificial island which
does not serve exploitation purposes may directly interfere
with that exploitation. It would further be necessary to follow
the restrictive provisions of the 1958 Continental Shelf Convention and also provide for a right of appeal against any
project which a State considered detrimental to its interests.
Such an appeal could not be lodged with the international
authority proposed for the sea-bed unless the latter's authority
extended to the territorial sea. "It might thus be necessary
to provide for a right of appeal to IMCO if the objection related
to interference with navigation; to the regional fisheries organisation, if it related to interference with fishing; or to an
international organisation for the marine environment, if one
is established, in the case of objections concerning the environment or pollution."

As regards floating artificial islands or installations
Belgium considers that "in view of the notional mobility, could
be treated as vessels," subject thus to the principle of the
freedom of the high seas (72).

SOVIET UNION. Article 5 of the Russian Decree of 6 February
1968, relating to the Continental Shelf, provides that (73):

"Foreign physical and juridical persons shall be
prohibited from surveying, exploring or exploiting the
natural resources or carrying on any other activity on
the continental shelf of the USSR unless such activity
is specifically provided for by an agreement between the
USSR and the foreign State concerned or by special permission granted by the competent authorities of the USSR."

Undoubtedly, the formulation "any other activity on
the continental shelf" would also include the construction of
artificial islands or installations on the bed or subsoil of
the continental shelf for non-extractive uses. Article 5 would
appear to grant exclusive authority and control to the Soviet
Government with regard to any uses and activities on the continental shelf area. However, this should be interpreted so as to
exclude the superjacent waters which under the 1958 Continental
Shelf Convention remain high seas. An extensive interpretation
would certainly run contrary to both letter and spirit of the latter.

Article 6 prescribes rather severe penalties for violations of the Decree (74), including of course the violation of Article 5, while Article 7 lays down further that:

"If Article 5 of this Decree is violated, the vessel and all the instruments and tools used by the person committing the violation and anything which has been obtained illegally shall be liable to confiscation."

Finally, Articles 2 and 3 of the Decision of the Presidium of the Supreme Soviet of the USSR Concerning the Application of the Decree of the Presidium of the Supreme Soviet of the USSR Concerning the Continental Shelf of the USSR, 13 August 1969 (75) read as follows :

"2. Special authorizations for the conduct of research the exploration and exploitation of natural resources, and the execution of other works on the continental shelf of the USSR by foreign individuals and bodies corporate, as provided by article 5 of the Decree of the Presidium of the Supreme Soviet of the USSR of 6 February 1968, shall, where the execution of such works is not expressly provided for in an agreement between the USSR and the foreign State concerned, be issued in a manner and under conditions to be determined by the Council of Ministers of the USSR.

3. The following violations shall make the offender liable to the penalties prescribed in article 6 of the Decree of the Presidium of the Supreme Soviet of the USSR of 6 February 1968 Concerning the Continental Shelf of the USSR:

The erection of installations and other works on the continental shelf of the USSR and the creation around them of safety zones without the appropriate authorization;

Failure to provide protection for installations and other works on the continental shelf of the USSR, to maintain permanent devices for warning of their presence, to remove installations and works which have been permanently taken out of operation, or to take steps within the safety zone to protect the living resources of the sea from harmful waste-products;

The conduct of the exploration and exploitation of natural resources, and the execution of other works on the continental shelf of the USSR by foreign individuals and bodies corporate in contravention of the requirements of article 5 of the above-mentioned Decree."

UNITED STATES. In the United States the legal regime of the continental shelf is regulated by the Outer Continental Shelf Lands Act, 7 August 1953 (76). Under the Act "...the subsoil and sea-bed of the outer Continental Shelf appertain to the United States and are subject to its jurisdiction, control, and power of disposition...." (77). Section 4 extends the "Constitution and laws and civil and political jurisdiction of the United States... to the subsoil and sea-bed of the outer

Continental Shelf and to all artificial islands and fixed
structures which may be erected thereon for the purpose of
exploring for, developing, removing and transporting resources
therefrom, to the same extent as if the outer Continental Shelf
were an area of exclusive Federal jurisdiction located within a
State" (78). Finally, the Act extends the "authority of the
Secretary of the Army to prevent obstruction to navigation in
the navigable waters of the United States... to artificial
islands and fixed structures located on the outer Continental
Shelf" (79), and states explicitly that it is to be "construed
in such manner that the character as high seas of the waters above
the outer Continental Shelf and the right to navigation and
fishing therein shall not be affected" (80).

The 1953 Act thus authorizes leasing only for the purpose
of mineral development. However, the United States authorities
have in several instances prohibited or stopped construction of
artificial islands for non-extractive uses on the continental
shelf, by invoking the power of the Secretary of the Army to
prevent obstructions to navigation and also the "vital interests"
of the United States in the shelf. Thus, in United States v.
Ray (81) two rival companies, a Bahamian corporation called
Atlantis Development Corporation, Ltd. and a Florida corporation
called Acme General Contractors, had hoped to establish artificial islands, and ultimately sovereign States, on reefs four and
a half miles east of Elliot Key, off the south east coast of
Florida, and outside its territorial sea, to be named respectively, "Atlantis, City of Gold" (82) and "Grand Capri Republic."
The United States Government brought an action against the two
corporations on two counts: the first alleged trespass on
government land, and the second alleged construction of artificial
islands without the permission of the Army Secretary. The
Florida District Court dismissed the trespass claim, but it sus-
tained the United States position that a government permit was
necessary for construction on the reefs. The court held further
that no private proprietary claims could be asserted to the
reefs over the interest of the United States:

"The government has not consented to private construction
on these reefs..... Whatever proprietary interest exists
with respect to these reefs belongs to the United States
under both national (Shelf Act) and international (Shelf
Convention) law. Although this interest may be limited
it is nevertheless the only interest recognised by law,
and such interest in the United States precludes the
claims of the defendants and intervenor" (83).

As one commentator has noted further "it may be fair to
say that the holding of the Ray case is based more upon a concern
for national security than national resources" (84). Indeed,
the district court was obviously concerned with the implications
for national security, if the authority of the United States
did not apply to the continental shelf :

"If these reefs were available for private construction
totally outside the control of the United States Government,
they could conceivably support not only artificial islands
and unpoliced gambling casinos, but even an alien missile
base, all within a short distance of the Florida Coast" (85).

On appeal by all parties involved, the United States Court
of Appeals affirmed the lower court's findings of fact and grant
of injunctive relief to the Government (86). The Court made
reference to ..... "restraint from interference with rights to
an area which appertains to the United States and which under
national and international law is subject not only to its jurisdiction but its control as well." By combining these "rights"
and the "vital interests" of the United States, the Court found
the result sufficient to warrant injunctive relief:

"Neither ownership nor possession is, however, a necessary
requisite for the granting of injunctive relief......
The evidence overwhelmingly shows that the Government has
a vital interest, from a practical as well as an
aesthetic viewpoint, in preserving the reefs for public
use and enjoyment...... Obviously the United States has
an important interest to protect in preventing the establishment of a new sovereign nation within four and one-half
miles of the Florida Coast, whether it be Grand Capri
Republic or Atlantis, Isle of Gold.
The rights of the United States in and to the reefs and
the vital interest which the Government has in preserving
the area require full and permanent injunctive relief
against any interference with these rights by defendants
and intervenor" (87).

Similarly, and at approximately the same time, another
private company attempted to establish an independent 'State'
on the Cortes Bank seamount, which is rich in abalone and
lobster, about 110 miles off the coast of San Diego, California.
However, the Corps of Engineers quickly declared this to be a
hazard to navigation and the Government declared the area to
be part of the Outer Continental Shelf (88).

Conclusion: The preceding, albeit brief, analysis of existing
embryonic State practice would appear to confirm the view
supported here as regards the construction of artificial
islands on the continental shelf. Indeed, a careful examination of the existing material leads to the inescapable conclusion that coastal States are very suspicious of any foreign
activities taking place on their continental shelves and they
thus tend to subject them to their control on an ever increasing
scale. Finally, and as the United States practice indicates
further, States are not prepared to tolerate even the construction of artificial islands undertaken by their own nationals
without their permission and outside their control.

VI.   EXCLUSIVE ECONOMIC ZONE (EEZ)

Of the functional zones claimed by a number of States
in recent years, the most important and well known is that of
the Exclusive Economic Zone (EEZ), or Patrimonial Sea (89).
Indeed, the EEZ is a new concept of critical importance since
its adoption would include within national jurisdiction almost
40 per cent of the total area of the sea – an area in which most
of the known hydrocarbons and commercial fisheries of the sea
are found.

There seems to be little doubt that "the progressive
development of international law entails the recognition of the
concept of the Patrimonial Sea" as Judge Luis Padilla Nervo
has put it (90).   There is now a wide agreement among nations
on the establishment of a 200-mile EEZ and the international
community is steadily moving to that position.   It is known,
for example, that over 100 countries have spoken at UNCLOS III
in support of the EEZ concept as part of an overall treaty
settlement.

As regards further recent State practice, the trend is
only too clear.   Iceland has already adopted a 200-mile
fishery resource zone, within which all foreign fishing is
prohibited (91).   A decree establishing a 200-mile EEZ off
Mexico's coast was enacted on January 22, 1976 (the implementing
legislation came into force on June 6, 1976).   Under the
decree, Mexico assumes full control over all natural resources
and artificial islands within that zone (92).   In the United
States, President Ford has already signed a Bill extending
the country's fishing limits to 200 miles.   The Bill will
come into force on March 1, 1977.   Canada is also committed to
declaring a similar zone by mid-1977 (93).   In Europe, the
EEC Commission released in early 1976, a policy document concerning the EEC's fisheries policy, which envisages exclusive
national coastal zones of up to 12 miles and a community-wide
zone beyond this up to 200 miles (94).   The Norwegian Government has said that it may be forced to extend its fishery
limits to 200 miles before the end of 1976 without waiting for
a joint EEC fishery policy to be decided, and Denmark has
announced that it intends to declare a 200-mile zone off
Greenland unless agreement is reached at UNCLOS III (95).
Finally, the U.K. Government has confirmed the preparation of
enabling legislation for a 200-mile fishing zone to be enacted
should the EEC fail to adopt a community-wide EEZ (96).

The EEZ concept is rather comprehensively dealt with by
Chapter III, Part II, of the Revised Single Negotiating Text (97).
Under Article 45, the EEZ shall not extend beyond 200 nautical
miles from the baselines from which the breadth of the territorial
sea is measured.   The rights of the coastal State in the EEZ
are elaborated in the previous Article 44, under which the
coastal State has :

"(a)   Sovereign rights for the purpose of exploring and
exploiting, conserving and managing the natural resources,
whether living or non-living, of the bed and subsoil and
the superjacent waters;
(b)   Exclusive rights and jurisdiction with regard to the
establishment and use of artificial islands, installations
and structures;
(c)   Exclusive jurisdiction with regard to :
     (i)   Other activities for the economic exploitation
        and exploration of the zone, such as the
        production of energy from the water, currents
        and winds; and
     (ii)   Scientific research.
(d)   Jurisdiction with regard to the preservation of the
marine environment, including pollution control and
abatement;....."

Provision is further made in Article 46 for the preservation
of the freedoms of navigation, overflight, submarine cable and
pipe-laying, "and other internationally lawful uses of the sea
related to navigation and communication," in the EEZ.

With respect to artificial islands, installations and
structures, Article 48 (1) provides that :
"In the exclusive economic zone, the coastal State shall
have the exclusive right to construct and to authorize and
regulate the construction, operation and use of :
    (a)   Artificial islands;
    (b)   Installations and structures for the purposes
        provided for in Article 44 and other economic
        purposes;
    (c)   Installations and structures which may interfere
        with the exercise of the rights of the coastal
        State in the zone."

It is thus clear that the coastal State has the exclusive
authority to construct and operate artificial islands and
economic installations within its EEZ.   Moreover, in view of
paragraph 1 (c) above, it would appear that non-economic
installations are also in effect subject to authorization and
regulation by the coastal State.   As has been noted by two
leading members of the U.S. delegation to UNCLOS III :
"This issue has undergone a very long period of difficult
discussion in the Evensen Group and elsewhere.   The text
is an attempt to bridge the gap between those that wished
to maintain the strict economic-non-economic distinction
inherent in the zone and those that did not by resolving
the accommodation of conflicting uses problem in favour of
the coastal State.   It is clear that all artificial
islands and all resource and other economic off-shore
installations (e.g. artificial deep water ports) are ipso
facto, subject to coastal State exclusive rights;   however
it is equally clear that the "may interfere" test in

sub-paragraph (c) "tilts" heavily towards the coastal
State even with respect to non-economic installations in
the economic zone. It should also be noted that Article
67 (Art 69 of RSNT) gives the coastal State "the exclusive
right to authorize and regulate drilling on the continental
shelf for all purposes" ; the Article 62 (Article 64 of
RSNT) definition of the continental shelf includes the
full 200-mile zone...." (98).

CONCLUSIONS

1. Both the internal waters and the territorial sea are
   subject to the exclusive sovereignty of the coastal
   State. The latter, therefore, may construct therein
   whatever artificial islands and installations it wishes.
   However, such construction activities must be consistent
   with reasonable requirements of navigation, maritime
   safety and the preservation of the right of innocent
   passage for foreign shipping through the territorial sea.
   In the absence of any treaty commitments to the contrary,
   foreign States and nationals may not build and/or operate
   any artificial structures in those zones without the
   express permission of the coastal State.

2. The coastal State does not possess any rights of jurisdiction and control over the construction of artificial
   islands in the contiguous zone by virtue of its status.
   The contiguous zone is a zone of the high seas and as such
   it falls under the regime of the high seas.

3. In the writer's view, the construction of artificial
   islands on the high seas is a desirable and necessary
   development, potentially serving the general interests of
   mankind. As such it can be legally justified either under
   the theory that although it constitutes a new use of the
   high seas, nonetheless it is not inconsistent with other
   uses of the high seas, or under the doctrine that it is
   an act which in itself falls within and is sanctioned by
   the existing principle of the freedom of the high seas.
   However, a multilateral approach to the problem of
   artificial islands is hereby advocated, which could ideally
   culminate in the establishment of international management
   and control over all types of artificial islands erected
   on the high seas.

4. In theory a fundamental distinction has to be made,
   de lege lata, between non-economic installations deployed
   in the superjacent waters and artificial islands, including
   fixed installations, constructed on the continental shelf.
   The deployment of the former should in principle be subject
   to the doctrine of the freedom of the high seas, while the
   construction of the latter should be subject to exclusive
   coastal authority and control. In practice, however,

coastal States will most probably claim exclusive authority to construct artificial islands and installations in the shelf area, whether economic or non-economic, floating or fixed. The relevant provisions of the Revised Single Negotiating Text constitute a clear indication of this trend.

5. The coastal State has exclusive authority and control over the construction, operation and use of all artificial islands and all economic installations within the EEZ. Non-economic installations and structures would also appear to be subject to coastal authorization and control.

NOTES

1. This expression is meant to cover the building, construction, erection, placement, anchoring, deployment, etc. of any artificial island, fixed on the sea-bed or floating, any fixed or floating installation, object, etc. not being a ship.

2. E.D. Brown, Maritime Zones - A Survey of Claims, in new Directions in the Law of the Sea, Collected Papers, Vol. III, published by the British Institute of International and Comparative Law, 1973, pp.157-192, at p.160.

3. Geneva Convention on the Territorial Sea and the Contiguous Zone, 1958, Articles 1 and 5.

4. M.S. McDougal and W.T. Burke, The Public Order of the Oceans, 1962, at p.64.

5. See Articles 1, 2 and 14-17 of the Geneva Convention on the Territorial Sea and the Contiguous Zone, 1958. Article 1 (1) provides that "The sovereignty of a State extends, beyond its land territory and its internal waters, to a belt of sea adjacent to its coast, described as the territorial sea;" Article 2 provides further that "The sovereignty of a coastal State extends to the air space over the territorial sea as well as to its bed and subsoil;" and Articles 14-17 regulate the right of innocent passage through the territorial sea.

6. U.N. DOC. A/CONF. 62/WP.8/Rev.1/Part II, 6 May 1976.

7. UNCLOS III, Committee II, Informal Working Paper No.12, 20 August 1974.

8. See also draft Art. 23 of the Revised Single Negotiating Text, Part II, DOC.A/CONF. 62/WP.8/Rev. 1/Part II, 6 May 1976 (hereafter cited as R.S.N.T. Part II) and The Corfu Channel Case (Merits), I.C.J. Rep., 1949, p.4. However, it is equally clear that the right of innocent passage would be subject to any mandatory shipping lanes and traffic separation schemes established in the territorial sea in the interests of maritime safety and navigation. See for example, the relevant draft

Arts.21 and 39 of R.S.N.T., Part II.

9. "Working Paper Concerning Artificial Islands and Installations", submitted to the U.N. Sea-Bed Committee by Belgium, DOC.A/AC.138/91, 11 July 1973.

10. Ibid., p.11. For an interesting comment on this Belgian proposal, see A.H.A. Soons, Artificial Islands and Installations in International Law, July 1974, Law of the Sea Institute, University of Rhode Island, Occasional Paper No.22, at pp.5-7.

11. In view of Art.2 of R.S.N.T., Part II, which provides for a 12-mile territorial sea, Art.32, para 2, lays down that "the contiguous zone may not extend beyond 24 nautical miles from the baselines from which the breadth of the territorial sea is measured."

12. II ILC Yearbook (1956) at p.278. The ILC made no express pronouncement on the "freedom" to undertake nuclear weapon tests on the high seas. It merely stated that this "freedom" was subject to the same principle stated above, i.e. that States are bound to refrain from any acts which might adversely affect the use of the high seas by nationals of other States (ibid).

13. See, for instance, E.D. Brown, The Legal Regime of Hydrospace, 1971, at pp.82-85; J.A.C. Gutteridge, The 1958 Geneva Convention on the Continental Shelf, 35, B.Y.I.L. (1959), pp.102-123, at p.102; H.W. Briggs, Jurisdiction over the Sea-Bed and Subsoil beyond Territorial Waters, 45, A.J.I.L. (1951), pp.338-342, at pp.338-339; and W. Friedman, The Future of the Oceans, 1971, pp.46-48.

14. S.K. Keaton and J. Judy, Seamounts and Guyots: A Unique Resource, 10 San Diego Law Review (1973), pp.599-637, at p.611; for an extended discussion on the legal status of seamounts see ibid. at p.610 et seq.

15. II ILC Yearbook (1956), p.278, para 2 of Commentary on Article 27.

16. The Hughes Tool Co. has started mining manganese nodules in the Pacific, THE OBSERVER, 28 October 1973. Deep-sea Ventures, Inc., a subsidiary of Tenneco, Inc, on 15 November 1974, filed with the U.S. Secretary of State a "Notice of Discovery and Claim of Exclusive Mining Rights and Request for Diplomatic Protection and Protection of Investment," over an area of 60,000 sq. km. in the Pacific Ocean. For the text of the 'Notice' see in 14 I.L.M. 1975, at pp.51-65.

17. E.D. Brown, supra, at p.84.

18. U.N. Gen. Ass. Res. 2574 D, 24 UN GAOR supp.30, at p.11, U.N. DOC. A/7630 (1969). This Resolution was adopted by 62 in favour, 28 against with 28 abstentions.

19. U.N. Gen. Ass. Res. 2749 (XXV), Dec. 17, 1970, 25 UN, GAOR Supp. 28, at p.24, U.N. DOC. A/8097 (1970) (hereafter cited as Declaration of Principles). The Declaration was adopted by 108 in favour, none against, with 14 abstentions.

20. On the legal significance of U.N. General Assembly
resolutions, see in general Bin Cheng, United Nations
Resolutions on Outer Space: Instant International Customary
Law?, 5 Indian J.I.L. (1965) at p.23; E.D. Brown, The
Consequences of Non-agreement, in The Law of the Sea: A
New Geneva Conference, Proceedings of the Sixth Annual
Conference of the Law of the Sea Institute, 1971. For the
scholarly opinion of a jurist from the Soviet Union see G.F.
Kalinkin, Problems of Legal Regulation of Sea-bed Uses Beyond
the Limits of the Continental Shelf, 3 Ocean Development and
International Law, 1975, p.127 at pp.145-151.
21. Bin Cheng, supra, at p.37.
22. G.F. Kalinkin, supra, at p.146. However, it must
also be noted that a number of States have repeatedly
attempted to limit the significance of the Declaration while
many others have made statements on its non-binding effect.
Thus, the U.S. Department of State, for example, replied as
follows to the Deepsea's 'Notice of Discovery': ".... The
position of the United States Government on deep ocean
mining pending the outcome of the Law of the Sea Conference
is that the mining of the seabed beyond the limits of national
jurisdiction may proceed .as a freedom of the high seas under
existing international law," 14 I.L.M. 1975, at p.66. For
a similar view see further L.F.E. Goldie, A General International
Law Doctrine for Sea-bed Regimes, 7 International Lawyer, 1973,
at p.796. On the Declaration of Principles and the controversy
surrounding its effects, see in general E.D. Brown, supra,
note 20; R.S. Gibson, An Illusion of Camelot, the Validity
of a Claim, and the consequences of the negotiations: The
Great Nodule Spectacle, 13 San Diego Law Review 1976, pp.667-706.
23. E.D. Brown, supra, note 13, at p.84. A draft
Convention on the ocean floor, beyond the limits of national
jurisdiction, has now been prepared by UNCLOS III, see Revised
Single Negotiating Text, U.N. DOC A/CONF. 62/WP.8/Rev.1)
Part I, 6 May 1976 (hereafter cited as R.S.N.T., Part I).
24.   There are, of course, uses of the high seas which
are prohibited under international customary law, as is the
case with slave trade and piracy; See the relevant Articles
13 (slave trade) and 14-22 (piracy), of the High Seas
Convention, 1958.
25. M.S. McDougal and W.T. Burke, The Public Order of
the Oceans, 1962, at p.763. In an earlier section upon the
ILC's Commentary on Article 2 of the High Seas Convention they
concluded that "in sum, the Commission seems to have affirmed,
implicitly and awkwardly, that the sea is open to use for
every purpose, subject to the limitations of the requirement
of reasonableness in relation to other users," ibid, at p.761.
Van Panhuys and Van E. Boas have also supported the view that
'freedom of the high seas' comprises all peaceful uses of the
seas, H.F. Panhuys and M.J. Van E. Boas, Legal Aspects of

Pirate Broadcasting: A Dutch Approach, 60, A.J.I.L. (1966), pp.303-341, at pp.312-313 and 338-339.

26. "..... Accordingly, I doubt very much whether it would be correct to interpret the language of Article 2 as implying that the freedom of the high seas comprises only a limited number of well-settled categories of freedoms. It seems rather to contemplate that the freedom of the high seas comprises the four named freedoms and any other use of the high seas which are recognised as flowing from the general principle that the high seas are "open to all nations", Professor Sir Humphrey Waldock, The R.E.M. Broadcasting Station and the Equipments North Sea Act, in RECHTSGELEERDE ADVIEZEN, 1964, pp.22-39, at pp.23-24. During its conflict with the Dutch Government the R.E.M. invited and obtained "Opinions" on the international legal aspects of the R.E.M. station from six international law scholars; Dr. C. John Colombos, Prof. D.H.N. Johnson, Prof. Charles Rousseau, Prof. Sir Humphrey Waldock, Prof. Henri Rolin and Prof. Frans de Pauw. These "Opinions"have been collected in RECHTSGELEERDE ADVIEZEN (Legal Opinions), published in 1964 by the R.E.M.

27. Ibid., at p.24.

28. Ibid., at p.25.

29. M.W. Mouton, The Continental Shelf, 1952, at p.229.

30. For a further discussion on this, see H.G. Knight, International Legal Aspects of Deep Draft Harbour Facilities, 4 (3) Journal of Maritime Law and Commerce, (1973), pp.367-395, at p.377, et seq.

31. W. Riphagen, International Legal Aspects of Artificial Islands, IV (4) International Relations, (1973), pp.327-347, at p.333.

32. Ibid., at p.342.

33. C.J. Colombos, In the Matter of the so-called Anti-R.E.M.-Law, in RECHTSGELEERDE ADVIEZEN, supra, pp.2-4 at p.4.

34. Cited in Van Panhuys and Van Boas, supra, note 25, at p.315.

35. C.W. Walker, Jurisdictional Problems Created by Artificial Islands, 10 San Diego Law Review (1973), pp.638-663, at p.650.

36. I ILC Yearbook (1954), pp.91-92. The problem was tackled by the Rapporteur Mr. Francois, Mr. Spiropoulos and Mr. Zourek.

37. Gidel, Le Droit International Public de la Mer, 1932, Vol. I, p.503.

38. Mr. Zourek, I ILC Yearbook (1954), at p.92, para 26.

39. Report on the Legal Status of Artificial Islands Built on the High Seas, by Mr. Margue, Council of Europe, Consultative Assembly, DOC.3054, 9 December 1971, at pp.7, para.18, and 8, para.23 (hereafter cited as the Margue Report).

40. Ibid., p.10, para 31.

41. H.G. Knight, supra, note 30, at p.377. As regards off-shore harbours in particular the same author has concluded that "a deep draft port may or may not be an existing permitted use of the high seas', but even if it is not permitted the process of emerging norms of customary international law provides a mechanism for undertaking the construction of such facilities pending international agreement on the subject," ibid., at p.380.

42. Sir Humphrey Waldock, supra, note 26, at p.25.

43. In the instance of light-houses farther than six miles from the mainland or islands, see Colombos, The International Law of the Sea, 6th ed., 1967, pp.127-129, esp. footnote 5 at p.128.

44. Presently, of course, the matter is covered by the provisions of Article 5 of the Continental Shelf Convention, 1958. However, Sir Humphrey Waldock has supported the view that even before the 1958 Convention, when the doctrine of the coastal State's right to the natural resources of the continental shelf received general recognition, it could not appear that doubts existed about the legitimacy of erecting a drilling installation for the purpose of exploiting the natural resources of the sea-bed and subsoil if this did not interfere with other legitimate uses of the high seas, such as navigation and fishing. The only controversy concerned the coastal State's claim to exclusive jurisdiction over the natural resources of its continental shelf, Sir Humphrey Waldock, supra, note 26 at p.25.

45. See R.S.N.T. Part II, Chapter V: High Seas. Draft Art. 75 defines the "high seas" as "...all parts of the sea that are not included in the exclusive economic zone, in the territorial sea or in the internal waters of a State, or in the archipelagic waters of an archipelagic State".

46. It is necessary to provide sea-traffic separation lanes in busy shipping areas and in the Gulf of Mexico, where there are approximately 6,000 oil and other platforms "Shipping Safety Fairways" have been marked on Nautical Charts, E.D. Brown, supra, note 13, at pp.88-89. On the contemporary problems of the freedom of navigation see further C. Warbrick, The Regulation of Navigation, in New Directions in the Law of the Sea, (edited by R. Churchill, K.R. Simmonds, J. Welch), 1973, Vol. III, pp.137-154. The Sub-Committee on Safety of Navigation of the IMCO Maritime Safety Committee has been very much concerned in the last few years with matters relating to Traffic Separation Schemes and a great number of these have already been recommended to its member States on a world-wide scale. See, for example, the recent IMCO DOCS. MSC XXVIII/22 26 September 1973, Annex IV; NAV XVI/2(a)/1-4, January-March 1974; NAV XVI/WP.7, 2 April 1974; and IX/Res.340, 18 December 1975.

47. "Today this freedom (of the seas) is not yet directly challenged, but as the ocean beds are increasingly opened up at ever-greater depth to exploration and exploitation by various national and corporate interests, the limitations of the traditional freedoms of the sea become both more numerous and more disturbing.....And as drilling rigs, floating islands, stationary platforms, submersibles and artificial structures above and below the surface of the sea multiply, the traditional freedoms of fishing and shipping, however strongly they may be affirmed theoretically, must be qualified, restricted, and ultimately excluded," W. Friedman, The Future of the Oceans, 1971, at p.3.   For a detailed study on the conflict of the numerous old and new uses of the sea, see U.N. ECOSOC DOC. E/5120, 28 April 1972 (Study prepared by the Secretary-General).

48. R.S.N.T. Part I, "Accommodation of Activities in the Area and in the Marine Environment", at p.16.   See also the relevant provision VIII of the Informal Working Paper No. 12, 20 August 1974, (Committee II).

49. See the Margue Report, supra, note 39.

50. C.W. Walker, supra, note 35, at pp.651-652.

51. Lauterpacht, Sovereignty over Submarine Areas, 27 B.Y.I.L. (1950), p.376 at p.399.

52. See also W. Riphagen, supra, note 31, at p.334.

53. C.W. Walker, supra, note 35, at p.663.

54. Working Paper Concerning Artificial Islands and Installations, submitted by Belgium, DOC. A/AC.138/91, 11 July 1973.

55. U.N. DOC. A/AC.138/SC.II/L.27, 13 July 1973.

56. M.W. Mouton, The Continental Shelf, 1952, at p.229.

57. For a similar proposal see also A.H.A. Soons, supra, note 10, at p.24.

58. S.K. Keaton and J. Judy, supra, note 14, at pp.628-630.

59. II ILC Yearbook (1956), p.297.   In an earlier section the Commission had emphasized that it "accepted the idea that the coastal State may exercise control and jurisdiction over the continental shelf, with the proviso that such control and jurisdiction shall be exercised solely for the purpose of exploiting its resources," ibid, pp.295-6.

60. Sir Humphrey Waldock, supra, note 26, at p.32.   In an earlier section he commented that "in short, the 1958 Conference deliberately refrained from conferring a general jurisdiction on coastal States with respect to the sea-bed and subsoil," ibid., at p.25.

61. II ILC Yearbook (1956), at p.298.   See further M.S. McDougal and W.T. Burke, supra, note 25, at p.718, and Van Panhuy's and Van E. Boas, supra, note 25, at p.321.

62. In the case of Ministre d'Etat charge de la Defense Nationale et Ministre de l'Equipment et du Logement v. Starr et British Commonwealth Insurance Co., 1970 Revue Generale

de Droit International Public 1114 (Conseil D'Etat, 4 December 1970), the Conseil D'Etat fully accepted the following conclusions of the Commissaire du Gouvernement: "....Does the riparian State exercise over the shelf a sovereignty analogous to that which covers the territorial waters? The Commissaire du Gouvernement stated unambiguously that "one must not confuse sovereign rights and sovereignty. The littoral State enjoys rights over the continental shelf which are exclusive and independent of any occupation but these rights are limited to the aims fixed by the (Continental Shelf) Convention and defined in France by the Law of December 30 1968. The continental shelf thus does not form part of the national territory. This ends at the limit of the territorial waters." This case is reported and analysed by P.M. Eisemann, in 3 Journal of Maritime Law and Commerce (1971-72), at pp.189-192.

63. Prof. Sir Humphrey Waldock, supra, note 26, at p.33.

64. C.J. Colombos, International Law of the Sea, 6th ed., 1967, p.67.

65. E.D. Brown, Arms Control in Hydrospace: Legal Aspects, 1971, at p.23. Prof. Brown was concerned in that study with the problem of military installations, and with regard to the right of establishment he considered three arguments - the sea-bed title argument; the freedom of the high seas argument; and the self-defence argument. Clearly, however, the first two arguments may be also considered as regards construction of installations for peaceful purposes.

66. M.S. McDougal and W.T. Burke, The Public Order of the Oceans, 1962, at p.718.

67. M.W. Mouton, The Continental Shelf, 1952, p.293.

68. 5 C. Rob. 373; 165 English Reports 815.

69. M.S. McDougal and W.T. Burke, The Public Order of the Oceans, 1962, at p.719.

70. R.S.N.T. Part II, Ch. IV: Continental Shelf.

71. U.N. DOC. A/AC.138/SC.II/L.37, 16 July 1973. It is also interesting to note that in describing the coastal authority over the continental shelf the Draft uses the term "sovereignty" instead of "sovereign rights": "The sovereignty of a coastal State extends to its continental shelf......", (Article 15), Ibid.

72. Working Paper Concerning Artificial Islands and Installations, DOC. A/AC.138/91, 11 July 1973, esp. at pp.9 and 11.

73. Decree of the Presidium of the Supreme Soviet of the USSR, dated 6 February 1968, entitled "On the Continental Shelf of the USSR", see in U.N. Leg. Ser. DOC. ST/LEG/SER.B/15, 1970, pp.441-443; and also in 7 I.L.M. (1968), pp.392-394.

74. Fines up to 10,000 roubles or imprisonment up to one year, or both, are prescribed by this Article.

75. See in U.N. Leg. Ser. DOC.ST/LEG/SER.B/16, Vol.II,

8 May 1972, at p.159.

76. Public Law 212 - 7 August 1953: "U.S. Code" (1964 ed.),
Title 43. For an extensive analysis of this Act see R.B. Krueger,
The Background of the Doctrine of the Continental Shelf and the
Outer Continental Shelf Lands Act, 10 Natural Resources Journal
(1970), pp.442-514 and 763-810. The text of the Act may also
be found in U.N. Leg.Ser. ST/LEG/SER.B/15, 1970, p.462.

77. 43 U.S.C.S.1332 (a) (1953).

78. 43 U.S.C. S. 1333 (a) (1) (1953).

79. 43 U.S.C. S. 1333 (f) (1964).

80. 43 U.S.C. S. 1332 (b) (1964).

81   294 F. Supp. 532 (S.D. Fla. 1969);   423 F.2d 16
(5 Cir. 1970), reported in 63 A.J.I.L. (1969), pp.642-644 and
64 A.J.I.L. (1970), pp.954-955.   For an extensive discussion
and analysis of this case see further Geo-Marine Technology,
Vol. 3, No. 2, February 1967, pp.12-13; S. Eckhardt, Atlantis,
"Isle of Gold", 6 San Diego Law Review (1969), pp.487-498;
55 Virginia Law Review (1969), pp.1005-1011.

82. The Atlantis plan, the more ambitious of the two,
included construction of 2,600 acres on which there would be
a casino, bank with numbered accounts, post office, foreign
offices, government palace and congress; the value of the
waterfront property to be constructed was estimated to approach
the billion dollar figure.   The Atlantis Corporation managed
to construct four buildings, three of which were later
destroyed by a hurricane.

83. 294 F. Supp. 532 (S.D. Fla 1969), at 542, cited in
63 A.J.I.L. (1969) at p.644.

84. S. Eckhardt, supra, at p.497.

85. 294 F. Supp. 532 (S.D. Fla 1969) at 542, cited in
55 Virginia Law Review (1969), at p.1008, footnote 12.

86. 423 F. 2d 16 (5 Cir. 1970).

87. Ibid, at pp. 22-23; cited in 64 A.J.I.L. (1970) at
p.955.

88. S. Eckhardt, Abalonia, 6 San Diego Law Review
(1969), at pp. 498-501.

89. In order to clarify the problem of terminology, it
should be noted that the Patrimonial Sea concept, originally
propagated by the Carribean countries is, in fact, a variant
of the EEZ concept.   On this concept see in general E.D. Brown,
Maritime Zones - A Survey of Claims, in New Directions in the
Law of the Sea, Collected Papers, Vol. III, published by the
British Institute of International and Comparative Law, 1973,
pp.157-192; and L.D.M. Nelson, The Patrimonial Sea, 22 I.C.L.Q.
(1973), pp.668-686.

90. See the Dissenting Opinion of Judge Luis Padilla
Nervo in the Fisheries Jurisdiction case (United Kingdom of
Great Britain and Northern Ireland v Iceland), Interim
Protection Order of 17 August 1972, I.C.J. Reports (1972), p.12,
at pp. 20-28.

91. For the relevant regulations issued by Iceland's Ministry of Fisheries on 15 July 1975 see in 14 I.L.M. (1975), at p.1282.   See further in 25 I.C.L.Q. (1976),at p.687.

92.   Ibid., at p.685.

93.   THE TIMES, 1 March 1976

94.   THE TIMES, 19 February 1976.

95.   THE TIMES, 4 June 1976.

96.   THE TIMES, 30 June 1976.   For similar plans by the Governments of Colombia, India and Sri Lanka, see in 25 I.C.L.Q. (1976), at p.688.

97.   See further, the relevant main Drafts that have been submitted to U.N. Sea-Bed Committee and Conference in the last few years: The General Report of the African States Regional Seminar on the Law of the Sea, held in Yaounde 20-30 June 1972, U.N. DOC. A/AC/138/79; The Declaration of Santo Domingo, 7 June 1972, U.N. DOC A/AC.138/80; The Maltese Draft, U.N. DOC. A/AC.138/SC.II/L.28; The Fourteen Power Draft Articles on the EEZ, DOC. A/AC.138/SC.II/L.40; OAU Declarations on the Issues of the Law of the Sea, DOCS. A/AC 138/89 and A/CONF. 62/33.

98.   J.R. Stevenson and B.H. Oxman, The Third United Nations Conference on the Law of the Sea: The 1975 Geneva Session,69 A.J.I.L. (1975), p.763 at p.777.

Chapter 3

JURIDICAL STATUS OF ARTIFICIAL ISLANDS

INTRODUCTION

The problem of the juridical status of artificial islands
is one of primary importance.   In the past, they have often
been assimilated to islands or have been regarded as ships (1).
The significance of assimilating artificial islands to
natural islands will be appreciated, if it is remembered that
every island has its own territorial sea and continental shelf.
Undoubtedly, the assimilation of artificial islands to natural
islands poses difficult questions such as territorial sovereignty, jurisdictional zones and exploitation of the resources
lying around the artificial structure.   States might be
encouraged to erect artificial islands so that they could
claim jurisdiction over large stretches of the seas.   This
problem has attracted some attention in the past, particularly
in the delimitation of the territorial sea.   Lighthouses, of
course, are a notorious example.   In the Behring Sea
Arbitration (1893), Sir Charles Russell, the Attorney-General,
supported the view that lighthouses are entitled to a belt of
territorial sea.   He argued that :

> "..... if a lighthouse is built upon a rock or upon piles
> driven into the bed of the sea, it becomes, as far as that
> lighthouse is concerned, part of the territory of the
> nation which has created it, and as part of the
> territory of the nation which has created it, it has,
> incident to it, all the rights that belong to the
> protection of the territory - no more and no less.....
> That point has never been doubted and if it were, there
> is ample authority to support it.   The right to acquire

by the construction of a lighthouse on a rock in the
ocean a territorial right in respect of the space
so occupied is undoubted" (2).

The arguments advanced by Sir Charles Russell aroused
much controversy amongst publicists.   Westlake, for instance,
rejected Russel's view: "It would be difficult to admit
that a mere rock and building, incapable of being so armed as
really to control the neighbouring sea, could be made the source
of a presumed occupation of it, converting a large tract into
territorial water" (3).

The question of lighthouses was also discussed by
Oppenheim in his report to the Institute of International Law
in 1913.   He denied that such a structure was entitled to
a territorial sea belt, any more than a lightship (4).
Jessup, commenting upon Oppenheim's view, found it valid: "It
would be dangerous doctrine in many parts of the world to allow
States to appropriate new areas of water by means of structures
on hidden shoals.   On the other hand, it should be conceded that
where dredging operations or the like result in the formation
of permanent "made land" the coast of the State and its
territorial waters are extended accordingly. This would also
be true of a stone jetty or breakwater connected with the shore.
On these points, however, it is impossible to dogmatize" (5).

Gidel also considered the question of lighthouses.   He
concluded that the determining factor is the type of elevation
on which it is erected and not the nature of the lighthouse
itself (6).   This principle, propounded by Gidel some 40 years
ago, appears to be an adequate approach to the problem and is
actually sanctioned by the Territorial Sea Convention, 1958.
The right to a territorial sea belt is not derived from the
status of the lighthouse as such but from the status of the
natural formation on which it is built (7).

It would appear, therefore, that the authorities have
been rather uncertain and divided on this matter.   Consequently,
no general principle of international law could be established
from which an appropriate rule regarding artificial islands could
be deduced (8).

Apart from lighthouses, however, attempts have also been
made to assimilate artificial islands in general to natural
islands, under various conditions and circumstances.   Gidel,
for instance, in his definition of an island, has assimilated
artificial islands to natural islands, provided that the
former conform to the same conditions as the latter.   The
conditions laid down by Gidel were: (a)   a formation
surrounded by water;   (b)   permanently above water at high tide;
and (c) the natural conditions of the formation being such as
to permit the stable residence of human communities.   In
addition, the artificial island must have been a natural formation transformed into an "island" by human help, that is, an
artificial "alluvion" (9).

Attempts have further been made to assimilate certain
artificial islands to ships. Thus, in a Report to the
Council of the League of Nations, 1927, the following passage
appears : "Islands" which are "artificially created by
anchorage to the bed of the sea, and which have no solid
connection with the bed of the sea, but which are employed
for the establishment of a firm foundation, e.g. for enterprises designed to facilitate aerial navigation...... Such fictit-
ious islands must be assimilated to vessels voyaging on the
high seas" (10). The same view was taken by Mouton in 1952.
He believed that "such contraptions should not be called artificial islands, because they float and in fog they should sound
the bell like a ship." He argued further that "Even if
they are anchored by two anchors so that they cannot sway
on the tide or current or wind, they have all the characteristics of a ship and nothing in common with an island" (11).

On the other hand, the view has been supported, regarding
floating 'islands', (floating platforms for drilling etc), that
"It is no use trying to assimilate them with ships. Neither
their construction nor their mode of operation or the risk to
which they are subjected turn them into ships" (12).

It follows from the above that neither of these solutions
(assimilation to islands or ships) appears satisfactory. It
is true, that certain artificial islands could be assimilated
either to islands or ships, and certain legal characteristics
pertaining to islands and ships could be attributed to some
artificial islands. However, in the writer's view the best
procedure would be to consider the individual categories of
artificial islands. It is believed that the consideration of
artificial islands according to their function and purpose is
the most useful approach to determining their juridical status.
At the same time it is thought necessary to consider briefly
the notions of an island and ship in international law. Such
an examination will clarify what structures and formations
qualify for the juridical status of an island or ship in
international law.

I. NATURAL ISLANDS

1. The Notion of an Island under International
Customary Law prior to the Geneva
Convention, 1958

There has been some controversy in the past, prior to
the 1958 Geneva Conference on the Law of the Sea, concerning
the legal requirements for the existence of an island in
international law. At the Hague Codification Conference
in 1930, for instance, many Governments, including the
United Kingdom, advocated the view that in order to have
territorial sea, an island must be a piece of territory capable

of occupation and use (13).   Against such a definition, the
German Delegation suggested that an artificial island (artificial construction) should possess territorial sea provided
that (a) it rests on the sea-bottom;   and (b) it has human
inhabitants (14).   According to another opinion, an island
was any naturally formed area of land showing above the sea.
Some were supporting the view that this would cover both low-
tide and high-tide elevations (15), whereas others maintained
that only high-tide elevations should qualify for the juridical status of an island.

However, the criteria of occupation and use were not
accepted by the 1930 Conference in its formulation of the
definition of an island.   Sub-Committee II of the Second
Committee rejected such a formulation and adopted instead
the following rules :

"(i)   Every island has its own territorial sea.
        An island is an area of land, surrounded by
        water, which is permanently above high-water mark.
(ii)   Elevations of the sea-bed situated within the
        territorial sea, though only above water at low
        tide, are taken into consideration for the
        determination of the base line of the territorial
        sea" (16).

According to the Harvard Research, on the other hand,
low-tide elevations are entitled to a territorial sea belt.
The relevant draft Article 7 reads as follows :   "The marginal
sea around an island, or around land exposed only at some stage
of the tide, is measured outward three miles therefrom in
the same manner as from the mainland" (17).   Under this
definition "any rock, coral, mud, sand or other natural solid
formation which is exposed above the surface of the water
at any stage of the tide even though at other stages it be
totally submerged" has its own territorial sea (18).

2.   The Geneva Convention on the Territorial
        Sea and the Contiguous Zone, 1958

The traditional dispute as to the legal requirements
for the existence of an island in international law has been
resolved in favour of the view that islands are only high-tide
elevations.   Article 10 of the Geneva Convention on the
Territorial Sea and the Contiguous Zone, 1958, provides as
follows :

"(i)   An island is a naturally-formed area of land
        surrounded by water, which is above water at high
        tide.
(ii)   The territorial sea of an island is measured in

accordance with the provisions of these articles."

It is clear from this formulation that artificial islands, however composed, showing above water at high tide, do not qualify for the juridical status of an island, as this is understood in Article 10. The expression 'natural island' or 'naturally' may refer either (a) to the material composing the island under consideration, or (b) to the way the island is formed. Or, to put it another way, the 'artificiality' of an island may depend either on the nature of the material composing it - as in the case of an island constructed by concrete - or on the way it is formed, as for instance where land is artificially placed on the sea-bed. Paragraph 1 of Article 10 covers both cases: (a) 'naturally formed', that is by natural process, without human intervention, as in the case with dumping of sand and stones in shallow waters, and (b) 'area of land', exluding, that is, any human construction like building up with concrete, installations etc.

This formulation will certainly exclude low-tide elevations where concrete, or other material, has been used to build them up, so that they can show above water at high tide. The King of Tonga, for example, used concrete to build up two uninhabited low-tide elevations of his scattered South Pacific Kingdom, so that he could claim them as being islands under international law. By doing so, he claims to have extended the area of his Kingdom, consisting of 150 islands, by a hundred miles, (presumably by using the method of 'the group basis' employed for measuring the territorial sea of an archipelago) (19).

It is another matter whether these 'islands' can be taken into account for the delimitation of the territorial sea in an archipelagic straight baseline system, but certainly they do not qualify for the juridical status of an island under the Geneva Convention, 1958.

On the other hand it has to be admitted that it is sometimes extremely difficult to decide whether an island is natural or artificial. If, for instance, a natural island is in process of gradually disappearing beneath the waves and it is decided to erect earthworks so as to keep the island above sea level, is that island natural or artificial? Or, again, if a State builds up a construction in the seas, which indirectly results in the changing of the currents with the consequence of accelerating the natural process of accumulation of sand and stones, so that gradually an island showing above sea level will be formed, is that island natural or artificial? Is an island formed as a result of an artificially induced explosion causing a volcanic eruption on the sea-bed natural or artificial?

Do the areas of land in all these cases qualify for the juridical status of an island and can they be taken into account for purposes of delimitation of the territorial sea, or not?

Perhaps the answer lies in the criteria of reasonableness
and "construction for practical use" which have been
suggested by Professors McDougal and Burke: "The chief
criterion for appraising the reasonableness of a claim to
delimit the territorial sea, or an area of internal waters,
from an artificially formed area of land surrounded by water,
is whether it is constructed for practical use or rather only as
a disguised attempt to extend the territorial sea or internal
waters without other relation to local interest.   When the
construction of an area of land serves a consequential coastal
purpose, it would seem to be in the common interest to permit
the object to be used for delimitation purposes.... Nor would
it appear desirable from community perspectives to permit
delimitation from an artificial island after it has ceased to
serve useful purposes, at least if destruction is an economical
procedure" (20).

The reasonableness of this proposition is obvious, since
otherwise a State could extend its territorial sea, or create
new internal waters, merely by placing rocks or sand and stones
in the water to such a height as to ensure their continued
emergence above the sea-surface

It would appear, therefore, that the criterion of the
"reasonable and useful purpose" might be the decisive factor in
determining which of the "areas of land" or constructions in
these marginal cases should be entitled to the juridical status
of an island or should be taken into consideration for
delimitation purposes.

The importance of the second paragraph of Article 10 lies
in what it conceals rather than in what it displays; it does
not deal with the important question of groups of islands or
archipelagos.   Thus indirectly, by not providing any special
rules for the delimitation of the territorial sea of such
groups on any "group basis", this provision lays down that
each island-unit of the group has its own territorial sea,
measured in accordance with the ordinary provisions of the
Geneva Convention (21).   The discussion of this topic is not,
however, of direct concern in the present context (22).

3.   The Third United Nations Conference on the
      Law of the Sea

The preparatory work for UNCLOS III was carried out
by the Committee on the Peaceful Uses of the Sea-Bed and the
Ocean Floor Beyond the Limits of National Jurisdiction (Sea-
Bed Committee), which was established by Resolution 2467 A
(XXIII), 21 December 1968, of the U.N. General Assembly.   In
order to facilitate the work of the Committee, three sub-
committees were set up in March 1971 and the regime of islands
was allocated to Sub-Committee II.   To the limited extent
that the discussion on Islands took place in Sub-Committee II,

the regime of islands was examined :
    (a) in connection with islands under colonial dependence
       or foreign domination or control or under the
       sovereignty of a State and located in the continental
       shelf of another State in a different continent; and
    (b) in a specific context, such as the territorial sea,
       continental shelf, exclusive economic zone and
       international ocean space (23).

As regards in particular the regime of islands in the
context of the vital issue of jurisdiction over ocean space and
resources, two opposing view, motivated by different national
interests, clearly emerged from the discussions of the
Sea-Bed Committee.

According to the first view "the maritime spaces of certain
types of islands, other than those island States and
archipelagic States, should be determined by equitable principles
taking into account special factors and circumstances such
as their size, population and contiguity to the principal
territory, whether or not they were situated on the continental
shelf of another State, the physical, geological and geomorph-
ological structure of the marine area involved, the general
configuration of the respective coasts and the existence of
islands or islets of another State" (24).

According to the second view, "the principle for determining the territorial sea of islands and their continental shelf
and zones of national jurisdiction should be the same as the
principle for determining the territorial sea, continental
shelf and zones of national jurisdiction of the continental or
other part of the State of which the islands formed an integral
part. In that connection reference was made to the applicability of the principles of median line of equidistance as well
as to the principle of sovereign equality of States, of the
indivisibility of sovereign integrity and its implications under
international law and the Charter of the United Nations" (25).
Furthermore, "no distinction whatsoever should be made between
islands, irrespective of their size and population, and the
continental land masses; and that the criteria relating to the
delimitation of the territorial sea, the continental shelf, the
exclusive economic zone or patrimonial sea... must apply to
islands in the same way as they applied to continental land
masses" (26).

The Caracas session of UNCLOS III produced an Informal
Working Paper on the regime of islands, the sole purpose
of which "is to reflect in generally acceptable formulations
the main trends which have emerged from the proposals submitted
either to the United Nations Sea-Bed Committee or to the Conference itself" (27). Indeed, this working paper contains six
Provisions, each with a number of alternative formulations,
which reflect mainly the two opposing views as elaborated above.

However, the regime of islands is now dealt with by

Article 128 of the Revised Single Negotiating Text (Part II).
Paragraph 1 of that Article repeats verbatim the definition of
an island as provided for by Article 10 (1) of the·1958
Territorial Sea Convention: "An island is a naturally formed
area of land, surrounded by water, which is above water at
high tide." Paragraph 2 provides further that :

"Except as provided for in paragraph 3, the territorial
sea, the contiguous zone, the exclusive economic zone and
the continental shelf of an island are determined in
accordance with the provisions of the present Convention
applicable to other land territory."

Paragraph 3 introduces the following exception to the
said rule:

"Rocks which cannot sustain human habitation or economic
life of their own shall have no exclusive economic zone
or continental shelf " (28).

4. Low-Tide Elevations

The term 'low-tide elevations' refers collectively to
drying rocks, reefs and shoals, which are off-shore structures
exposed at low tide but submerged at high tide. As has been
indicated above, there has been some discussion in the past
as to whether such structures generate any territorial waters,
or as to whether they possess territorial sea of their own.
However, in present day international law, low-tide elevations
are not entitled to a territorial sea belt of their own.
Article 11 of the 1958 Territorial Sea Convention, after
defining a low-tide elevation as "a naturally formed area of land
which is surrounded by and above water at low tide but submerged
at high tide", lays down in paragraph 2 that a low-tide
elevation wholly situated at a distance exceeding the breadth
of the territorial sea from the mainland or an island has
no territorial sea of its own. On the other hand, paragraph 1
provides for an exception: "where a low-tide elevation is
situated wholly or partly at a distance not exceeding the
breadth of the territorial sea from the mainland or an
island, the low water line on that elevation may be used as
the baseline for measuring the breadth of the territorial sea"
(29).

Conclusions

The above analysis of the definition of an island
in international law shows that the following structures cannot
constitute islands de lege lata :

1. Natural materials artificially placed on the seas, as, for instance, sand, stones, clay or rocks dumped on the seas in the shallow waters, even though they show permanently above water at high tide.

2. Natural formations which show above water only at low tide, known as low-tide elevations or drying rocks and shoals.

3. Permanently submerged natural formations, such as permanently submerged reefs, banks, etc.

4. Navigational aids, such as lighthouses, light-ships, beacons and buoys.

5. Artificial structures, for example, installations erected on the sea-bed, drilling platforms and floating objects.

6. Artificial structures erected on a pre-existing natural formation, for example, on shallow sand-banks or drying rocks, even though they are visible at high tide.

7. The projected Sea-Cities.

8. The Ocean Data Acquisition Systems, Aids and Devices (ODAS).

None of the said natural or artificial formations generate any territorial sea, unless they fall within the terms of :

(a) Article 4 (3) of the 1958 Convention on the Territorial Sea and the Contiguous Zone, concerning lighthouses and similar installations built on low-tide elevations: or

(b) Article 11 (1) of the same Convention, concerning low-tide elevations situated within the territorial sea.

II.   SHIPS AND ARTIFICIAL ISLANDS

Lord Finlay asserted in the Lotus case that a ship is "a movable chattel of a very special nature" (30).   Indeed, a ship is considered in the great majority of legal systems to be a movable chattel, a thing, but it is treated as a chattel with certain personality (31).   However, the plurality of definitions of the word 'ship', which are to be found in the various municipal systems of law and international conventions, indicate that these define the ship only for the purposes of the relevant statute or convention.   No definition can be large enough to contain all the virtually infinite variety of maritime craft and at the same time precise enough to satisfy the

lawyer.   Yet, in international law the problem appears to be
somewhat simpler if one bears in mind that "International maritime law governs primarily maritime navigation" and that "the
expression 'ships' in international customary law relates, it
would seem, essentially to sea-going ships or vessels, terms which
it uses, moreover, synonymously" (32).

It is impossible to draw a universally applicable principle
as to what 'chattel' qualifies for the juridical status of
'ship' since even within each municipal system different
definitions are employed for different purposes.   In the
United Kingdom, for instance, a simple boat propelled by oars
is not a 'ship' within the definitions of the Merchant Shipping
Act 1894, but it appears to be a 'vessel' within the same act
(S.742).

The same boat is equally not a 'ship' within the definition
of the Port of London (Consolidation) Act 1920, but it is a
'ship' within the definition of the Administration of Justice
Act 1956 (S.8 (1)), as it is, also under the Shipbuilding
Industry Act, 1967.

It is considered further a 'vessel' within the meaning of
the Harbours, Docks and Piers Clauses Act 1847, but it is
not a 'vessel' in the meaning of the Isle of Man Harbours Act
1874 (33).   Certain national laws, on the other hand, provide
specially for certain types of vessels or other maritime craft,
such as barges, tugs, boats, lighters, floating docks, dredgers,
pontoons, etc.

Coming to the realm of international law, it will again
be seen that different definitions of ships are given according
to the specific purposes of the particular conventions, treaties,
international regulations, etc.   However, it has to be emphasised that "there is nothing to indicate that the definition of
the words 'ship' or 'vessel' is wider or narrower in international law than in national (municipal) laws" (34).

The International Law Commission has attempted in the
past to formulate a definition but without success.   Draft
Article 6 on ships, drawn up by the special Rapporteur,
Mr. Francois, reads as follows :

"A ship is a device capable of traversing the sea, but
not the airspace, with the equipment and crew appropriate
to the purpose for which it is used" (35).

In his report in 1950, Mr. Francois had commented that :
"..... The floating docks, the seaplanes, and in general the
floating islands are not assimilated to vessels.... Dredgers
must be assimilated to vessels as being capable of navigation.
There are, possibly, doubts as to the floating cranes and
the wrecks......." (36).

The International Law Commission, however, unanimously
agreed in 1955, after a short discussion, to delete Draft
Article 6.   The Rapporteur himself stated that he doubted
the appropriateness of his own definition and that he was not

"wedded to it". The view has been supported that, as the Geneva Convention now stands, the word 'ship' must be taken as including all types of ships whatever their size or purpose (37).

Bearing in mind, therefore, the diversity in State practice, lack of uniform rules or adoption of common standards as to what 'objects' qualify for the juridical status of a ship, it is advisable in maritime matters that any new related conventions should define the term 'ship' clearly so as to avoid further confusion and complexity.

Turning now to artificial islands, could a fixed or floating platform, etc., be proclaimed a ship and granted the nationality of the State whose flag it flies? After all, no common definition is attainable for municipal law purposes and this is very clear if one looks at the various statutes and practice of States. On the other hand, treaty law and State practice on maritime subjects "do not prove conclusively, that international customary law has created a definition of its own" (38). Meyers has supported the view that only "Objects which cannot float and which are not capable of traversing the sea cannot in reason be considered as ships under the rules obtaining at sea. But the conclusion that there exist further reaching characteristics, internationally, which are of a universal applicability is not permissible" (39).

It would thus appear that there are at least a few characteristics pertaining only to 'ships' as a legal category. Meyers has proclaimed two of these: In order for an object to qualify as a 'ship' it must be (a) capable of floating, and (b) capable of traversing the sea. A careful analysis of the definition of ship as given by both municipal laws and international conventions might not permit the inference of universally applicable conclusions, but it nevertheless reveals that a few elements of the definition are common to all, or at least, to a great majority of definitions. What are these common elements? It would appear that the following main elements appear more or less frequently in the various definitions given by both national and international law (40).

    1. Means of Propulsion;   2. Tonnage;
    3. Profit; 4. Transport of Passengers and/or Goods;
    5. Ownership;   6. Parts of ship included in definition;
    7. Navigability and Navigation.

These are the main elements to be found in the various definitions of the word 'ship' or 'vessel'. Some are to be found more frequently than others. For present purposes, however, the elements of tonnage, profit, transportation, ownership and the parts of a ship included in the definition can be immediately disregarded. Definitions including these elements are not commonly met with, particularly in international legal definitions of the word 'ship'.

These elements do not, in any case, indicate much about the nature of a 'movable chattel' qualifying as a 'ship'.

They are employed for the specific purposes of the various
statutes, without, thus, constituting a basis for the concept
of 'ship'. They are not, in other words, of a fundamental
nature, as is the case with the ability to navigate.   Indeed,
the ability to navigate appears to be the paramount test (41).
"Except with ships on the stocks, there is but one test to go
upon in all international legal definitions of 'sea-going vessel'
for all subject-matters: its being capable of maritime navigation" (42).   The means of propulsion, on the other hand, is
an element of relative importance compared with those mentioned
above.   It can, thus, be used as a supplementary criterion as
to what object qualifies for the legal status of a 'ship', without, of course, being of primary importance.   There is no
evidence that this element is an attribute of a 'ship' internationally required and of universal application.

Regarding the ability to navigate it has to be emphasised
that what is normally required is that the ship.must be
capable of being used for navigation, not that the ship is
actually being used.   Thus a ship capable of navigation but
in general permanently moored does not cease to be a ship on
account of the fact that it is not actually in use.   The
existence on the other hand of the frequently encountered
sutomary restriction that the ship must actually be used for
navigation, not merely that it must be capable of being so used,
is recognised.   Definitions including this requirement would
certainly exclude "objects which are usually employed as floating
islets" (43).   This, for instance, appears to be the purpose
of the above mentioned English Statutes M.S.A. 1894, S.742,
M.S.A. 1921, S.1, Administration of Justice Act 1956, S.8 (1),
etc., which contain the phrase "used in navigation" (44).

The foregoing analysis makes it clear that it is impossible
to give a general definition of what constitutes a ship or
vessel.   The question whether a particular object is a ship
or vessel must be a question of fact in each case.   The
following points should be kept in mind when deciding whether
a floating craft is a ship or vessel (45). It is generally
accepted, in the first place, that a ship or vessel is :
(a)   a movable chattel;   (b)   floating on the seas; and
(c)   capable of navigation, that is, capable of traversing the
sea either in tow or by using its own power.   Starting from
that premise, the following considerations will, also, be taken
into account:

The design of the object;

The purposes for which it has been built, its function
and its actual use (this will prove material when considering whether the ship is used in navigation)(46);

The means of propulsion (it is not necessary, however,
for the attribution of the legal status of ship
that she should be able to navigate under her own power)
(47);

The existence of a rudder and the manning of the vessel.
This may indicate that a floating object is a ship;
however, the absence of either does not mean that a
floating object is not a ship (48);

The degree of stationariness and mobility (49);

Finally, the risk under which a floating object operates.
The Judge will ask whether this is an ordinary maritime
risk normally encountered by a ship sailing the seas.

Turning now to artificial islands it can be safely
assumed that structures fixed on the sea-bed cannot in reason
be considered ships.   They are not of the nature of a movable
chattel and they can neither float on the seas nor are they
capable of navigation.   The Netherlands Government, for example,
regarded the R.E.M. broadcasting station, a platform which
rested on columns of concrete secured in the sea-bed, as an
'artificial island', and the radio-ship Veronica as a 'ship'
(50).   During the discussions in the Dutch Parliament, for the
adoption of the North Sea Installations Act, whose purpose was
to make illegal the R.E.M. station, the difference between a
ship and a platform was discussed in view of the fact that the
Dutch Government intended to take action only against the
R.E.M. station.   The Government justified its not taking
action against Veronica by pointing out that she was a ship,
and as such she had a different international legal status
compared to the R.E.M. station.   The Minister of Justice
observed that "a ship, in view of its mobility, is essentially
different from fixed installations....." (51).   The
opinion was also expressed that "it can hardly be maintained
that the radio-ship Veronica is not a ship (any longer) in the
sense of international law" and, thus, the "difference between
the artificial island, fixed at one point and secured in the
sea-bed, and the ship which is pre-eminently intended for
displacement" (52) was further affirmed (53).
    The case of floating platforms, and floating objects in
general, presents a somewhat more difficult problem.   Prima
facie, many of these floating structures, if not all of them,
would appear to qualify for the juridical status of a ship in
international law.   They are of the nature of a 'movable
chattel,' they float on the seas and they are capable of
traversing the sea, either in tow or by using their own power,
even though the first mode of movement would appear to be used
by the great majority of the floating structures under consider-

ation.   However, this similarity with ships is rather deceptive
and, in any case, ends there.   The design of these platforms
and structures, their size and the purposes for which they
are built, make them somewhat different from ships.   They
are not intended to be used in navigation and they are not, in
fact, being so used, even though they are capable of traversing
the sea either in tow or by using their own power.   Certain
of these floating structures are self-propelled and navigable
to a certain degree.   Yet they are not primarily designed for
navigation but for other purposes.   The purpose of an off-shore
terminal system, for instance, is to provide harbour facilities
far from the shore.   Again, the purpose of a floating dock
is not to navigate but to provide repair facilities.   It is
not actually used in navigation and its main characteristic is
its lifting capacity and its accommodation of ships.   Similar
remarks may be made about floating airports.   Their purpose
is to provide airport facilities on the seas.   They will be
fairly stationary, as it would take considerable time to
mobilise such massive structures, let alone to navigate.   The
same or similar principles, then, apply to any other floating
platforms on the seas not being built for the purpose of, or
intedned for, navigation in the proper sense of the term, and
which in fact are used for other purposes.   They are neither
ships stricto sensu, as a rule, nor islands.   It would, therefore, be inappropriate to treat these platforms as, or assimilate them to, ships.   As has already been seen the Rapporteur
of the International Law Commission, Mr. Francois, was of the
same opinion when he commented that, "The floating docks,
the seaplanes and in general the floating islands are not
assimilated to vessels......"

It should, however, be remembered that "there is, of
course, nothing in international law .to prevent States, in
treaty arrangements governing either maritime or inland
navigation, to attach any special meaning to these words,
('ship' or 'vessel)" (54).   Indeed, a number of recent international conventions, and in particular those concerned with
pollution control, appear to attach an intentionally wide
meaning to these terms.   Thus, according to Article II, para.2,
of the International Convention Relating to Intervention on
the High Seas in Cases of Oil Pollution Casualties, Brussels,
29 November 1969 to 31 December 1970, (55), the term 'ship'
means:

"(a)   any sea-going vessel of any type whatsoever, and
 (b)   any floating craft, with the exception of an
        installation or device engaged in the exploration
        and exploitation of the resources of the sea-bed
        and the ocean floor and the subsoil thereof."

This definition is clearly broader than that in the
Convention for the Prevention of Pollution of the Sea by Oil

(1954-1969), but, in any case, it does not cover drilling
platforms, rigs and devices engaged in the exploration and
exploitation of the sea-bed resources.

Article 19, para 2, of the Convention for the Prevention
of Marine Pollution by Dumping from Ships and Aircraft, Oslo,
February 15, 1972 (56), lays down that :

> "For the purpose of this Convention :
> (1) ....
> (2) "Ships and aircraft" means sea-going vessels and
> airborne craft of any type whatsoever. This
> expression includes air-cushion craft, floating
> craft whether self-propelled or not, and fixed on
> floating platforms."

On the other hand, Article III of the IMCO Convention on
the Prevention of Marine Pollution by Dumping of Wastes and
other Matter, London, November 13, 1972, (57), clearly excludes
from its definition of 'vessel' fixed platforms:

> "2. 'Vessels and aircraft' means waterborne or airborne
> craft of any type whatsoever. This expression
> includes air cushioned craft and floating craft,
> whether self-propelled or not."

In conclusion, it would appear that whereas there are a
few characteristics pertaining only to 'ships' as a legal
category, restricting thus the scope of that term, nevertheless
States may in treaty arrangements attach any special meaning
to the terms 'vessel' or 'ship' for the particular purposes
of those treaty arrangements.

III.   A PROPOSAL FOR THE LEGAL STATUS OF
            ARTIFICIAL ISLANDS

The best solution to the problem of the legal status
of artificial islands, de lege ferenda, appears to be the
creation of a new legal category comprising all artificial
structures which can be assimilated to neither ships nor
islands. The most suitable means for the achievement of this
goal would probably be an international convention with the
maximum participation possible. Specific rules would be
laid down for the different categories of artificial islands,
according to their structure and purposes. Undoubtedly, many
of the rules pertaining, and presently applying, to the legal
category 'ships', would either apply or could be modified so
as to apply to the legal category 'floating structures'. Such
rules would appear to refer to deployment, registration, marking
and signals, safety regulations, collision, salvage and so on.

There are already two precedents in international practice

which show the way to the development of new notions and
new rules appropriate to regulate continuing technological
innovations. They relate to installations for the exploration
and exploitation of the natural resources of the continental
shelf, and the Ocean Data Acquisition Systems (ODAS).
The Continental Shelf Convention 1958, has attempted to
define certain guidelines for the legal regime of such installations. These installations are treated neither as ships
nor islands. Rules have been laid down for the safety of
these installations, the rights and obligations of the coastal
State, jurisdiction over them, the protection of navigation
and other uses of the seas. General principles have also
been provided for the accommodation of the conflicting uses of
the seas, such as those referring to navigation, preservation
of the marine environment and scientific research. Admittedly,
these constitute general guidelines and principles rather than
specific and unequivocal rules of international law and they
are far from being complete or precise, but, nevertheless, they
may be taken as a starting point. Moreover, subsequent
national legislation is modelled on the Convention principles.

The second precedent is furnished by the Ocean Data
Acquisition Systems (ODAS). Article 1 of the Preliminary
Draft Convention on ODAS defines an ODAS as follows :

"..... 2. ODAS means a structure, platform, installation
buoy or other device, not being a ship, together with
its appurtenant equipment, deployed at sea....essentially
for the purpose of collecting, storing or transmitting
samples or data relating to the marine environment or
the atmosphere or the uses thereof" (58).

Article 1 (2) clearly excludes both ships and installations
for the exploration and exploitation of the sea-bed resources,
from the definition of ODAS. Any other platforms, such as
floating docks, floating airports, power stations, etc.,
are also excluded. Generally speaking, it only covers devices
used for the collection of scientific data.

In the writer's view a fundamental distinction has to be
drawn de lege ferenda, betweeen artificial islands erected and
used for urban purposes - Sea-Cities - and any other artificial
structures, platforms, and floating or fixed installations in
general. Further distinctions among the latter category may
be made and separate consideration be given to the main types,
such as installations for the exploration and exploitation of
the sea-bed and ODAS.

1. Sea-Cities

In terms of legal status, the paramount feature of a Sea-
City is that it must have a territorial sea in the same way that

a natural island has one. It is true that this is not a
principle of lex lata. The problem of the Sea-City has not
been faced yet in a practical way and probably it will not
have to be faced for quite a number of years to come.
        It is further submitted that the following considerations
have to be taken into account in attributing the legal status
of a Sea-City to an artificial island. First, the artificial
island in question must essentially be an island in the same
sense that a natural island is an island; that means that it
must (a) be 'surrounded by water', and (b) show permanently
above water at high tide. Secondly, in so far as it is an
artificial island, as opposed to a natural island, it must,
nevertheless, be 'of the nature of territory'. This last
qualification is not intended to mean that the artificial
island must literally be a 'portion of territory' or a 'true
tract of land', as a natural island is, but that it must have
the essential characteristics of a portion of territory.
Its capability of being subjected to the sovereignty of a State
as 'territory', and a degree of permanence similar to that
possessed by a natural island appear to be the essential
characteristics required. As far as the latter test of permanence is concerned, there is no indication that a greater
degree of permanence is required of an artificial island
than a natural island. After all, even a natural island is
permanent only in a relative sense. Islands have been known
to appear and disappear as a result of volcanic eruptions.
This is, for example, the case with Surtsey Island, the first
new permanent island to be formed in the North Atlantic in
several hundred years. Surtsey, a now-dormant shield volcano,
erupted from the sea-floor in about 120 metres of water, south
of Iceland's Westman Islands, only 500 miles north-west of
Scotland, in 1965, (59). Even in the absence of such major
events, however, their shores are subject to erosion and
accretion or alluvion, with the result that the extent of their
maritime belts varies from time to time
        Finally, the foremost criterion is that the artificial
island in question must be inhabited and, for all practical
purposes, form a self-sufficient community (60). Such an
island only differs from a natural island housing a similar
community, in its formation and name. It has to be emphasized
further that the notion of self-sufficiency is understood
within the context of an artificial island housing a community
as a natural island does. It would thus appear that this
criterion is satisfied only by an artificial island erected,
and in fact used, for urban purposes, that is a Sea-City (61).
On the other hand, this criterion is not satisfied by such
structures as an industrial artificial island, an oil production
platform or a power station, let alone by an unmanned device
on the seas. The same, of course, holds true for any other
artificial island whose primary purpose is not the accommodation

of a large, self-sufficient community. A mere safety zone
would appear to be a satisfactory solution to the problem of
the protection of these structures.

The rationale behind this proposal becomes clear if it
is considered why a coastal State extends its sovereignty outside the limits of its land territory over a sea-belt around
its coast. The reasons for the establishment of a territorial
sea zone have been stated aptly as follows :

> "The reasons which justify the extension of the
> sovereignty of a State outside the limits of its
> land territory are always the same. They may be
> summarized under the following heads :
>> (i)   the security of the State demands that it should
>>   have exclusive possession of its shores and
>>   that it should be able to protect its approaches;
>> (ii) for the purpose of furthering its commercial,
>>   fiscal and political interests, a State
>>   must be able to supervise all ships enter-
>>   ing, leaving or anchoring in its territorial
>>   waters;
>> (iii) the exclusive exploitation and enjoyment of
>>   the products of the sea within a State's
>>   territorial waters is necessary for the existence
>>   and welfare of the people on its coasts. Hall
>>   upholds the necessity of the maritime belt on
>>   the ground that unless the right to exercise
>>   control were admitted, no sufficient security
>>   would exist for the lives and property of
>>   the subjects of the State upon land" (62).

It is only too clear that these reasons hold true for the
projected Sea-Cities. The security, economic, fiscal, political
and other interests of the population of the Sea-City have
to be protected in the same way that the interests of any
other populations living on naturally formed land are protected
according to principles sanctioned by international law. It
should make no difference in law the formation of 'land' upon
which a population is living. The paramount feature is the
protection of the interests and welfare of the people, and
the establishment of a mere safety zone around a Sea-City,
however extensive, is not sufficient to safeguard the interests
of the local population.

The question may then arise whether a Sea-City could and/or
should have a 'continental shelf'. The answer to that is
negative for two major reasons. First, the continental shelf,
geologically, is the natural prolongation of a State's land
territory into and under the sea. The International Court
of Justice has upheld the principle of natural prolongation as
being the most fundamental of all the rules relating to the

continental shelf (63). It can hardly be argued that the
sea-bed and subsoil lying near and around an artificial
island forms a natural prolongation of its 'land territory'
into and under the sea, or that it may be regarded as an
extension of its 'land mass', and thus naturally appurtenant
to it. Second, from a functional viewpoint, an artificial
island should not again be attributed a 'continental shelf'.
The importance of the latter for a coastal State lies mainly
in the natural resources to be found therein. Ratione loci,
an artificial island may be situated, generally speaking,
either in national ocean space, that is, in a zone upon which
a certain coastal State exercises jurisdiction and control and
enjoys more or less exclusive jurisdiction regarding the
exploitation of natural resources- or it may be placed in the
international ocean space, beyond the limits of national
jurisdiction. In the first case the coastal State shall
already enjoy exclusive rights of exploration and exploitation
on its own continental shelf or in the EEZ, so that in this
respect there will be no change. With regard to Sea-Cities
constructed in the international ocean space, it is submitted
that their regime should be accommodated in the context of
the International Regime to be established. Erection of
artificial islands on the high seas should be no excuse for
the appropriation of large parts of the seas, particularly
by the economically and technologically advanced States.

Article 4 (1) of the draft convention on the international
sea-bed area (Revised Single Negotiating Text, Part I),
provides that: "No State shall claim or exercise sovereignty
or sovereign rights over any part of the Area or its resources,
nor shall any State or person, natural or juridical, appropriate any part thereof. No such claim or exercise of sovereignty
or sovereign rights, nor such appropriation shall be
recognized" (64).

So far, the discussion concerns only Sea-Cities fixed on
the sea-bed. The territorial sea concept fits in well with
the novel idea of an artificial island Sea-City fixed on the
sea-bed with definite boundaries and certain limits. Yet the
same cannot be said for the extraordinary concept of the
floating Sea-City. For one thing, there are no definite
boundaries and fixed limits. Certainty, therefore, as to
the extent of the 'territorial sea' cannot exist. The
boundaries will change as soon as the floating platform-city
moves to another place, if it does. A constantly changing
jurisdictional zone can already be seen. It all depends on
how stationary or mobile the platform will be. In the first
case, the floating city will be assimilated to a fixed one.
In the second case, however, a certain zone of transient
jurisdiction will have to be created so that the various
interests of the inhabitants of such a floating island will
be adequately protected.

2.   Artificial Islands Other than Sea-Cities

As regards the legal regime of artificial islands other than Sea-Cities, it is submitted that the principles and rules presently applying to the installations erected on the continental shelf for the exploration and exploitation of its natural resources, under the Geneva Convention 1958, should be used as guidelines for such a regime.   This is, for instance, the line taken by the major Draft Treaties on the International Sea-Bed Regime and the Revised Single Negotiating Text (Parts I-II), regarding the installations for the exploration and exploitation of the resources of the international sea-bed area and the exclusive economic zone (65).

There is no inherent reason why artificial islands, other than Sea-Cities, should be entitled to a territorial sea belt, or to a similar jurisdictional zone with obvious sovereign implications.   The primary purpose of any legal regime covering artificial islands is to ensure the safety and normal functioning of these structures without illegal interference from, and with, any other uses of the seas.   It would appear that the establishment of safety zones around artificial islands is adequate to satisfy that need.   It should further be made clear that States may not claim jurisdiction over ocean space by virtue of their control over artificial islands, and that the latter may not be used for delimitation purposes. Once again, it has to be emphasized that the construction of artificial islands should not be used as a pretext for the assumption of jurisdiction over large stretches of the seas (66). Article 16, para 2 (V) of the RSNT, Part I, provides that, stationary and mobile installations relating to the conduct of activities in the Area "shall not possess the status of islands.   They shall have no territorial sea, nor shall their presence affect the determination of territorial or jurisdictional limits of any kind."

However, of much broader scope is Article 48 of the RSNT, (Part II), since it covers in effect all artificial islands, installations and structures constructed in the exclusive economic zone.   Paragraph 8 of that Article reads as follows :

"Artificial islands, installations and structures have no territorial sea of their own and their presence does not affect the delimitation of the territorial sea or of other zones of coastal State jurisdiction or of the continental shelf."

Rather detailed rules concerning deployment, notice of construction, accommodation of conflicting uses of the seas, establishment of safety zones and jurisdiction therein, protection of the marine environment and scientific research,

and so on, have to be laid down.   Certain changes and
modifications will, of course, have to take place according to
the different characteristics, mode of operation and safety
requirements of the new structures.

It would appear, for example, that the 500-metre safety
zones provided for by the 1958 Continental Shelf Convention,
are not adequate for many artificial islands and/or installations.

Safety zones could certainly vary in breadth, and possibly
in the kind of activities allowed therein, according to the
requirements of the use of the particular artificial island or
installation.   For instance, off-shore airports would require
safety zones both in the air and on the sea.

As regards off-shore harbour and terminal facilities, one
writer has proposed "a safety zone around any such facility
with a radius not less than 3 nautical miles nor more than 10
nautical miles in which no other installations, structures, or
uses will be permitted.   A provision of this type is felt
necessary because of the tremendous amount of manoeuvring room
which supertankers require and the total incompatibility of
offshore structures for the exploration of oil and gas with
the proximate navigation of such vessels" (67).

It is interesting to note that the United States Deepwater
Port Act of 1974 does not provide for safety zones of a fixed
distance (68).   Section 10 (d) of the Act simply refers to
"a zone of appropriate size:"

"Subject to recognized principles of international law
and after consultation with the Secretary of the Interior,
the Secretary of Commerce, the Secretary of State, and
the Secretary of Defence, the Secretary (of Transportation)
shall designate a zone of appropriate size around and
including any deepwater port for the purpose of navigational
safety.   In such zone, no installations, structures, or
uses will be permitted that are incompatible with the
operation of the deepwater port.   The Secretary shall by
regulation define permitted activities within such zone....
    In addition to any other regulations, the Secretary
is authorized... to establish a safety zone to be effective during the period of construction of a deepwater port
and to issue rules and regulations relating thereto."

A 10-mile safety zone may be somewhat excessive and
probably unnecessary, but, on the other hand, it is to be
regretted that the Revised Single Negotiating Text provides for
an inflexible 500-meter distance for safety zones around
artificial islands, installations and structures erected in the
EEZ.   The relevant provisions of Article 48 of the RSNT
(Part II), read as follows :

"....

4. The coastal State may, where necessary, establish
reasonable safety zones around... artificial
islands, installations and structures in which it
may take appropriate measures to ensure the safety
both of navigation and of the artificial islands,
installations and structures.

5. The breadth of the safety zones shall be determined
by the coastal State, taking into account applicable
international standards. Such zones shall be
designed to ensure that they are reasonably related
to the nature and function of the artificial islands,
installations or structures, and shall not exceed
a distance of 500 metres around them....

6. All ships must respect these safety zones and shall
comply with generally accepted international
standards regarding navigation in the vicinity of
artificial islands, installations, structures and
safety zones. Due notice shall be given of the
extent of safety zones."

Part I of the RSNT does not provide for safety zones of
a certain distance around stationary and mobile installations
relating to the exploration and exploitation of the
resources of the international sea-bed area. Paragraph 2 (iii)
of Article 16 lays down simply that, "Safety zones shall be
established around such installations with appropriate markings
to ensure the safety both of the installations themselves and
of shipping..."

Clearly, due notice must be given of the construction of
any artificial islands, and permanent means for giving
warning of their presence must be maintained. Any installations which are abandoned or disused must be entirely removed (69).

Thus, according to Article 48 (3) of the RSNT, Part II,
which covers artificial islands, installations and structures
in the exclusive economic zone,

"Due notice must be given of the construction of
such artificial islands, installations or structures,
and permanent means for giving warning of their presence
must be maintained. Any installations or structures
which are abandoned or disused must be entirely removed."

The construction of artificial islands on the seas must
not, further, result in any unjustifiable interference with
other legitimate uses of the seas, such as navigation, fishing,
conservation of the living resources of the sea, and scientific
research. As regards the protection of the freedom of
navigation, in particular, it is clear that artificial islands
may not be established where interference may be caused to the

use of recognized sea lanes essential to international navigation (70). Thus, artificial islands may not be constructed
in, or near, straits used for international navigation, in, or
near, approaches to ports and harbours, and, generally, in places
where there is congestion of shipping. Under Article 48 (7)
of the RSNT, Part II, artificial islands, installations and
structures in the exclusive economic zone "and the safety
zones around them may not be established where interference
may be caused to the use of recognized sea lanes essential to
international navigation."

Certain principles and rules, on the other hand, need
further elaboration. It is submitted, for example, that
the general principle laid down by the 1958 Continental Shelf
Convention concerning the "protection of the living resources
of the sea from harmful agents," (71), is not deemed to be
adequate for the protection of the marine environment from major
(potentially catastrophic) polluting incidents emanating from,
or directly connected with, the exploitation of the sea-bed
and the installations involved. More precise rules are
needed for the protection of the marine environment from the
potentially highly polluting artificial islands and the
associated hazards.

Indeed, as one writer has observed :

"In the long run, environmental concern may be the
biggest legal obstacle to artificial islands. For
example, Delaware has passed a law specifically prohibiting superports. Responding to proposals to build a
nuclear power plant off their coast, the New Jersey
Legislature immediately passed a resolution calling
for legislation that would bar off-shore nuclear power
plants. In Zabel v. Tabb, (430 F.2d 199 (5th. Cir.1970,
cert. denied, 401 U.S. 910), it was held that the Secretary
of the Army can refuse to issue a permit for a structure
on ecological grounds, even if it is not a hazard to
navigation. A superport would be particularly subject
to opposition from environmentalists fearing the
prospect of oil or other mineral spills from a huge
tanker unloading a few miles off the coast" (72).

Under the Revised Single Negotiating Text, Part III,
Chapter I of which attempts to deal with the protection and
preservation of the marine environment, States shall take all
necessary measures to prevent, reduce and control pollution
of the marine environment from any source whatsoever. According to Article 4 (3) of the RSNT, Part III, "These measures
shall include, inter alia, those designed to minimize to the
fullest possible extent :
....
(c) Pollution from installations and devices used in
the exploration and exploitation of the natural

resources of the sea-bed and subsoil, in particular
for preventing accidents and dealing with emergencies,
ensuring the safety of operations at sea, and regulating the design, construction, equipment, operation
and manning of such installations or devices.

(d) Pollution from all other installations and devices
operating in the marine environment, in particular
for preventing accidents and dealing with
emergencies, ensuring the safety of operations at
sea, and regulating the design, construction,
equipment, operation and manning of such installations or devices."

Another problem which requires clarification, concerns the
jurisdiction exercised upon artificial islands and installations and in the safety zones surrounding these structures.
Does the coastal or flag state enjoy the same degree of
jurisdiction over both, or should a distinction be made between
them? Delicate problems of interpretation in this respect have
already arisen in connection with the installations used for
the exploration and exploitation of the shelf resources under
the 1958 Continental Shelf Convention (73).

Finally, the question whether new sovereign States can be
established through the construction of artifial islands will
be considered in the present context of the juridical status.
As has already been seen, attempts have been made by a number
of individuals and corporate bodies under municipal law to
create new 'sovereign States' by erecting artificial islands
on the high seas.

It is clear in the first place that artificial islands
constructed by, or under the auspices of, a State, and
occupied by it, shall be subject to its sovereignty and control
as any other part of its territory (74). Practically speaking, States will be able to extend their sovereignty beyond
their traditional 'natural' boundaries. Thus, the inhabitants of an artificial island shall be subject to the legal
order of the coastal or national State as any of its citizens
or inhabitants on the mainland. As Mr. Margue has noted
in his Report to the Council of Europe (75) :

"A coastal State that extends its jurisdiction beyond
the boundaries of its territorial sovereignty must
first justify its action under international law. This
guarantee seems, admittedly, rather theoretical unless
the occupiers of the artificial island are nationals of
another State which is sufficiently powerful and interested
for a problem of diplomatic protection to arise.
If a coastal State extends its legal order beyond
the boundaries of its territorial sovereignty, it also

extends the effects of the guarantees provided for
under its municipal legal order.   This creates a
case of forum prorogatum.   Police action on an artificial island must be carried out in as regular way as
police action on national territory. - The occupiers of
an artificial island should have vis-a-vis the administration of the coastal State the legal and judicial guarantees
provided for under its municipal order.   They should be
able to have recourse to the courts of the coastal State.
It follows also that they should be able to invoke
Conventions ratified by the coastal State.   Thus, if
the coastal State has ratified the European Convention
on Human Rights, occupiers of an artificial island
against whom this State has instituted proceedings
should be able to invoke its guarantees" (76).

However, the problem becomes more complex when considering
the case of artificial islands erected by private individuals
or bodies corporate under municipal law, and it is not claimed
that such construction takes place under the auspices, or on
behalf, of a State.   Could such individuals and/or corporations
establish new 'sovereign States' on the high seas?
Under international customary law it is settled that
unoccupied dry land is res nullius, and sovereignty over it
may be acquired by a State which establishes an effective
occupation (77).   There has, of course, been some debate as
to what acts are necessary to constitute occupation, and
"the United States in the 19th century successfully maintained,
in a series of disputes concerning Guano islands off the
American continent, that only exercise of sovereignty and
actual possession of islands situated outside territorial waters
can give title" (78).   The United States Secretary Hughes also
stated in 1924 that "actual settlement" was required for a
valid claim of sovereignty over a discovered country (79).
However, regardless of what acts are necessary to constitute
occupation, it would appear to be an established rule that such
acts may be performed only by States.   In other words, only
States may claim an unoccupied territory by discovery and subsequent use or occupation:

"In order that occupation shall be legally effected it
is necessary, either that the person or persons appropriat-
ing territory shall be furnished with a general or specific
authority to take possession of unappropriated lands on
behalf of the State, or else that the occupation shall
be subsequently ratified by the State" (80).

The King of Italy has also stated in his decision of
6 June 1904, as arbitrator between Great Britain and Brazil
under the treaty concluded in London on 6 November 1901, that :

"To acquire the sovereignty of regions which are not
in the dominion of any State, it is indispensable
that occupation be effected in the name of the
State which intends to acquire the sovereignty of
those regions" (81).

It has finally been pronounced more recently that ,

"Claims of dominion by right of discovery are reserved
to nations and sovereigns alone. It is a principle
which cannot be asserted by an individual" (82).

It would appear, therefore, that individuals and/or
bodies corporate under municipal law, which have no legal
existence independent of their respective sovereign states,
cannot establish new sovereign States under existing international law, through the construction of artificial islands
on the high seas, i.e. through the construction of artificial
territory, subsequently claimed as unoccupied territory.
Furthermore, it would appear that individuals are still no
more than objects in existing international law. According
to Professor Schwarzenberger, for example,

"The rules governing recognition are so elastic that
there is no limit to the objects which, by recognition,
may be transformed into subjects of international law.
Thus, the international personality of the individual
is not a question of principle, but simply one of fact:
Is there enough evidence to substantiate the claim that
the individual, the basis of national and international
life, is more than an object in existing international law?"
(83).

After asserting that this is "as yet unproven on the
level of international customary law", Professor Schwarzenberger
concludes that,

"On the level of organised international society,
that is the United Nations, the protection of
fundamental human rights and freedoms is still
so embryonic as not to alter the picture" (84).

Ultimately, of course, the establishment of new sovereign
States by private individuals and/or corporations may be
legitimized through general recognition by the existing subjects
of international law (85).
Moreover, even if one accepts further, either de lege lata
or de lege ferenda, that individuals and/or corporations may
establish new sovereign States on the high seas, such States
must be capable of acquiring the generally accepted criteria

of independent statehood, that is :
    (a)   a permanent population;   (b)   a defined territory;
    (c)   government;   and (d) capacity to enter into relations
    with other States (86).

With regard to the known cases involving attempts to
establish independent 'sovereign States' on the high seas,
such as the 'Grand Capri Republic', the 'Atlantis, Isle of
Gold', or the 'Minerva Republic', none of these would seem
to be anywhere near possessing, or being capable of acquiring,
the generally accepted indicia of statehood, as described above
(87).In short, two points must be emphasized following the
above brief analysis concerning the establishment of new
sovereign States :

    (a)   Private individuals and/or corporations cannot
          establish new independent States, under existing
          international law, through the construction of
          artificial islands.   Ultimately, of course, such
          establishment may be legitimized through general
          recognition by the existing States;   and

    (b)   States must be capable of acquiring the generally
          accepted criteria of independent statehood as
          described above.   None of the attempted
          new 'sovereign States' so far would appear to
          possess the said criteria of statehood, and they
          cannot, therefore, claim an independent existence
          as States in present international law.

NOTES

1.   See, for instance, the Margue Report.
2.   Moore, International Arbitrations, Vol. I, pp.900-1.
3.   Westlake, International Law, Vol. I (1904 ed), at
p.186.
4.   26 Annuaire 409, cited in Jessup, The Law of
Territorial Waters and Maritime Jurisdiction, 1927, p.69.   The
same view is supported by the present editor of Oppenheim,
International Law, Vol. I, 8th. ed., (Lauterpacht), p.501,
para 190a.
5.   Jessup, supra, pp.69-70.
6.   Gidel, Le Droit International Public de la Mer, 1934,
Vol. III, p.677.
7.   The relevant Articles of the Territorial Sea Convention are mainly Articles 3, 4, 10 and 11.
8.   D.H.N. Johnson, Artificial Islands, 4 I.L.Q. (1951),

pp.203-215, at p.211.

9.   Gidel, supra, p.684.

10.   League of Nations, Committee of Experts for the Progressive Codification of International Law, Report to the Council of the League of Nations on the Questions Which Appear Ripe for International Regulation.   (Questionnaires 1-7) adopted by the Committee at its third session held in March-April 1927, C 196 M 70, 1927 V, C.P.D.I.95 (2), Geneva 1927. (Public. of League of Nations V Legal 1927, V 1), cited in M.W. Mouton, The Continental Shelf, 1952, p.235.

11.   Ibid.

12.   G. Lasaratos, The Definition of Ship in National and International Law, Revue Hellenique de Droit International, Juillet-Decembre 1969, pp.57-99, at p.74.

13.   Bases of Discussion, Vol. II, at p.53.

14.   Ibid., at p.52.

15.   This view was taken, for instance by the U.S. Government, ibid., at pp.52-53.

16.   Acts of Hague Conference, 1930, Vol. III, at pp.217 and 219.

17.   Harvard Research, 23 A.J.I.L 1929, Special Supp, at p.275.

18.   Ibid., at p.276.

19.   THE TIMES, 22 August 1972.

20.   M.S. McDougal and W.T. Burke, The Public Order of the Oceans, 1962, at pp. 387-388.

21.   See G. Fitzmaurice, The Law of the Sea, 8 I.C.L.Q. (1959) at p.88.

22.   For a further discussion on the problem of archipelagos, see Fitzmaurice, ibid., at pp. 88-90;   McDougal and Burke, supra, at p.315;   and E.D. Brown, Passage Through the Territorial Sea, Straits Used for International Navigation and Archipelagos, 1974 (Published by the David Davies Memorial Institute of International Studies).

23.   See the 1972 Report of the Sea-Bed Committee at p.46, and the 1973 Report of the Sea-Bed Committee, Vol. I, at pp.56-57.

24.   1973 Report of the Sea-Bed Committee, Vol. I, item 87, at p.57.

25.   Ibid., item 85, at p.56.

26.   Ibid., item 86, at p.57.

27.   Informal Working Paper No. 13, 20 August 1974, Second Committee.   For the relevant discussions on the regime of islands held at the Caracas Session, see Third United Nations Conference on the Law of the Sea, Official Records, Vol. II, 1975, at pp.278-289.

28.   For the problems raised by this formulation see R.D. Hodgson and R.W. Smith, The Informal Single Negotiating Text (Committee II):   A Geographical Perspective, 3 Ocean Development and International Law 1976, p.225 et seq., at

pp.230-234; see also J.R. Stevenson and B.H. Oxman, The Third United Nations Conference on the Law of the Sea: The 1975 Geneva Session, 69, A.J.I.L. 1975, p.763, at p.786.

29. See also draft Article 12 of the R.S.N.T. Part II, entitled "Low-tide elevations", which is of identical formuation to Article 11 of the 1958 Territorial Sea Convention.

30. Dissenting Opinion, P.C.I.J. Reports 1927, Series A, No. 10, at p.53.

31. H. Meyers, The Nationality of Ships, 1967, pp8-23, esp. at p.14, et seq; G. Lazaratos, The Definition of Ship in National and International Law, Revue Hellenique de Droit International, Juillet-Decembre 1969, pp.57-99, at p.61.

32. Bin Cheng, State Ships and State Aircraft, 11 C.L.P. 1958, pp.225-257, at p.226. The terms 'vessel' and 'ship' are interchangeably used in the various statutes. In French-speaking countries, we find the terms 'navire', corresponding more or less with 'ship' and 'batiment de mer', corresponding with 'vessel'.

33. Lazaratos, supra, at p.64.

34. Lazaratos, supra, at p.79. See, for example, the definition of 'vessel' or 'ship' in the following conventions: International Regulations for Preventing Collision at Sea, 1960; International Convention for the Prevention of Pollution of the Sea by Oil 1954, as amended in 1962 and 1969, U.K.T.S. No. 59 (1967), Cmnd. 3354, and Cmnd. 4347 (1970); International Convention on Civil Liability for Oil Pollution Damage, Brussels, 29 November 1969 to 31 December 1970, Cmnd. 4403 (1970).

35. The English translation of the Draft Article is to be found in I ILC Yearbook (1955) at p.10.

36. U.N. Doc.A/CN 4/17, at p.4.

37. Lazaratos, supra, at p.84.

38. Ibid., at p.92.

39. H. Meyers, supra, at p.23.

40. See, for instance, Lazaratos, supra, at p.61 et seq.

41. Merchants Marine Insurance Co. v. North of England, Protection and Indemnity Association 1926, 42, T.L.R. 724; 32 Comm. Cas. 165. This case is normally taken as laying down the broad test of navigability, although it was there held to be a question of fact in each case and impossible to frame an exhaustive definition, or to lay down an exhaustive test.

42. H. Meyers, supra, at p.18.

43. H. Meyers, supra, at p.22.

44. A craft which is very rarely "used in navigation" will probably not be held by a judge to be a ship under these definitions.

45. Halsbury's Laws of England, 3rd edition, Vol.35, pp.73-74; Merchants Marine Insurance Company Ltd. v. North of England P. and I. Association, 1926, 32 Comm. Cas. 165.

46. Merchants Marine etc. v. North of England, per L.J.

Bankes, (ibid.), at p.169; The Mac, (1882), 7 P.D. 126, C.A.;
Wells v. Gas Float Whitton (No.2) (Owners), 1897, A.C. 337, H.L.
   47.   The Mac (1882), 7 P.D. 126, C.A.; The Harlow (1922),
P.175
   48.   The St. Machar (1939), 65 LI.L. Rep. 119; The Mac
(1882), 7 P.D. 126, C.A.
   49.   Merchants Marine v. North of England (1926), 32 Comm.
Cas.165, per L.J. Scrutton, at p.173.
   50.   The Veronica was a former German light-ship, lying
just outside the Dutch territorial sea.   She was heavily anchored
and did not have her own means of propulsion.   Advertising
announcements and popular music had been transmitted from
Veronica to Netherlands since 16 February 1961, IMCO DOCS.
MSC XII/23, 30 November 1965; MSC XII/23/Add. 2, 21 December
1965; and MSC XV/9/Add. 1, 6 February 1967.
   51.   Handelingen 2 ek, Session 1964-1965, third meeting,
17 September 1964, at p.83, cited in H. Meyers, supra, at pp.23-24,
footnote 2.
   52.   Memorandum of Reply, Handelingen, 2 ek, Session 1963-
64, 7643, No. 7, pp.15, 18, cited in H. Meyers, supra, at pp.23
-24, footnote 2.
   53.   It is submitted that the words used and the distinction made by the Dutch Government, were at least unfortunate
and should not be taken as a basis for discrimination in
the treatment of Veronica and the R.E.M. station.   It can,
indeed, very well be maintained that Veronica was not a ship
any longer and that she was as much intended for displacement
as the R.E.M. station was.   Both were there to stay and both
could be removed by tugs - the Veronica by raising its heavy
anchors and the R.E.M. by raising its concrete columns.
Neither of the two was intended for navigation, and neither
in fact was being used for navigation.   A judge would have
probably decided that Veronica had ceased to be a ship, and
the coastal State was certainly entitled to regard it no
longer as a ship.   The question of the nationality of a ship
would then be dismissed, and structures such as the R.E.M.
station and Radio Veronica might receive equal treatment.
See also H. Meyers, supra, at pp.23-24, footnote 2.
   54.   Bin Cheng, supra, at p.226.
   55.   Cmnd. 4403 (1970).
   56.   11 I.L.M. (1972), pp.262-266.
   57.   67 A.J.I.L. (1973), pp.626-636.
   58.   DOC. SC-72/CONF. 85/8, Paris, 30 March 1972.
   59.   Other examples known are the Fuglasker Rocks, also
in Icelandic waters, which are volcanic islands about eighty
miles to the west, where the volcano Myoe appeared above
sea-level 30 miles south-west of Reykjanes in May 1783.   Similar
volcanoes have been noticed in other seas as well, see
Dr. A.T.J. Dollar, Under-Sea Volcanoes, The Geographical
Magazine, No. 4 August 1966, pp.245-252, and G.P. Tamrazyan,

Volcano in the Caspian Sea, The Geographical Magazine, January 1968, No. 9, pp. 774-775.

60. It will be remembered that at the Hague Codification Conference 1930, certain Governments advocated the view that artificial islands resting on the sea-bed and having human inhabitants should be assimilated to natural islands.

61. The Sea-City, designed as a glass-and-concrete off-shore island by the Pilkington Committee, is to house a self-sufficient community of 30,000, with its own sources of energy, its own industries and its own means of transportation.

62. Colombos, International Law of the Sea, 6th edition, 1967, at p.87.

63. North Sea Continental Shelf Case, Judgment, I.C.J. Reports 1969, p.3, at p.22.

64. See also the relevant Article 9 of the Maltese Draft on State jurisdiction in ocean space, DOC.A/AC.138/SC.II/L.28, 16 July 1973.

65. See, for example, the Soviet Union Draft, in the 1971 Report of the Sea-Bed Committee, at pp.67-75; the Maltese Draft, ibid., at pp.105-193, orig. issued as DOC.A/AC.138/53; and the United States Draft, in the 1970 Report of the Sea-Bed Committee, at pp.130-176, orig. issued as DOC.A/AC.138/25.

66. See Article 5 (4) of the 1958 Continental Shelf Convention.

67. H.G. Knight, International Legal Aspects of Deep Draft Harbour Facilities, 4 (3) Journal of Maritime Law and Commerce (1973), pp.367-395, at p.395.

68. U.S. Public Law 93-627, 93rd Congress, H.R. 10701, 3 January 1975. For the text of the Act see in 14 I.L.M. 1975, at pp.153-163.

69. See Article 5 (5) of the 1958 Continental Shelf Convention.

70. See Article 5 (6) of the 1958 Continental Shelf Convention.

71. See Article 5 (7) of the 1958 Continental Shelf Convention.

72. C.W. Walker, Jurisdictional Problems Created by Artificial Islands, 10 San Diego Law Review (1973), pp. 638-663, at p.645.

73. This question is fully explored in Chapter 5 dealing with the Geneva Convention on the Continental Shelf 1958.

74. There is, of course, a difference between the new and the old territory, in that whereas the latter is natural the former is artificially created 'territory'. The concept of territory has, of course, always been understood in the sense of naturally created land. However, the law has now to reckon with artificially created territory, which shall be subject to the same rules and principles of inter-

national law.

75. Margue Report at pp.14-15.

76. As will be seen later in Chapter 5, installations and devices constructed and operated on the continental shelf for exploration and exploitation purposes "are under the jurisdiction of the coastal State for the purpose of maintaining order and of the civil and criminal competence of its courts", II ILC Yearbook (1956), para. 6, at pp.299-300.

77. ".....No real controversy existed as to the status of unoccupied dry land. It is res nullius in the true sense and sovereignty over it can be acquired by the first State which establishes an effective occupation." Waldock, The Legal Basis of Claims to the Continental Shelf, 36 Grotius Society Transactions (1951), pp.115-148, at p.115. See further Hall's International Law, 8th. edition, 1924, at p.125; Hackworth, Digest of International Law, Vol. I, p.401 et seq; and Moore, International Law Digest, Vol. I, 1906, p.258 et seq.

78. Waldock, supra, at pp.120-121.

79. Hackworth, supra, at pp.400, 402. See further Moore, supra, at p.258: "Title by occupation is gained by the discovery, use and settlement of territory not occupied by a civilized power. Discovery gives only an inchoate title, which must be confirmed by use or settlement." For a different view, see Lindley, Acquisition and Government of Backward Territory in International Law, 1926, at pp.6-7, where the author maintains that certain uninhabited islands are under the undoubted sovereignty of a number of States. See also Smedal, Acquisition of Sovereignty over Polar Areas (Oslo, 1931; translation by Chr. Meyer), pp.38-39, and Von der Heydte,"Discovery, Symbolic Annexation and Virtual Effectiveness in International Law", in 29 A.J.I.L. (1935), pp.462-465, where the author supports the view that, "Without prejudice to the general principle which requires effective occupation, sovereignty over a region completely uninhabited and seldom frequented is acquired merely by symbolic annexation", cited in Hackworth, supra, at p.402.

80. Hall's International Law, 8th edition, 1924, at p.128.

81. Award of His Majesty the King of Italy with Regard to the Boundary Between the Colony of British Guyana and the United States of Brazil Cd. 2166 (1904) 4; 99 Br. and For. St. Paps (1905-6) 930, cited in Hackworth, Digest of International Law, Vol. I, at p.401.

82. Bernfeld, Developing the Resources of the Sea - Security of Investment, 2 INTERNATIONAL LAW, p.67, at p.75 (1967) cited in 55 Virginia Law Review (1969), at p.1009, footnote 15.

83. G. Schwarzenberger, A Manual of International Law, 5th edition, 1967, at p.80.

84. Ibid., at p. 81.

85. "Unless limited by prohibitory rules of international

customary law, the subjects of international law are entitled
to use their discretion in granting and refusing recognition
of any kind", G. Schwarzenberger, supra, at p.69.

86.   See Article I of the Montevideo Convention on
Rights and Duties of States, signed 26 December 1933;   see
in Hudson, Int. Leg., Vol. VI, p.620.   See further
G. Schwarzenberger, supra, at p.55;   D.P. O'Connell,
International Law, Vol.I, 2nd edition, 1970, at pp.284-285;
and I. Brownlie, Principles of Public International Law, 2nd
edition, 1973, at p.74, et seq.

87.   See also in 55 Virginia Law Review, 1969, p.1005
et seq., esp. at pp.1008-1009.

Chapter 4

JURISDICTION OVER ARTIFICIAL ISLANDS

States have essentially territorial sovereignty over
their internal waters and territorial sea, and hence within
these zones there are no problems as to the jurisdictional
status of artificial islands.   Internal waters are part of
the territory of the coastal State, thus subject to its control in a manner similar in degree to land territory.   It
follows that the coastal State has jurisdiction and control
over activities on any artificial islands built within its
internal waters.   The same holds true further for the
territorial sea which is under the exclusive sovereignty of
the coastal State subject to a right of innocent passage for
foreign shipping.   Thus, artificial islands constructed within the territorial sea are subject to exclusive coastal
jurisdiction and control (1).

However, once beyond the coastal State's territorial sea,
we come into the domain of the high seas, "and here the
jurisdictional problems are tremendous and there are no formulated answers" (2).   Thus, the question of the legal system
applicable to the life and activities of the persons on, or
the inhabitants of, the artificial island arises.   "Will the
criminal law of the coastal State be applicable to the artificial island or will it be the national criminal law of the
owners?   But in this case, who will be competent to prosecute
should offences be committed on the artificial island?   All
of these questions are difficult to answer" (3).

It is deemed advisable to consider the problem of jurisdiction under the headings of (a) High Seas; (b) Continental
Shelf; and (c) Exclusive Economic Zone.   It is unnecessary
for our purposes to consider the Contiguous Zone separately.
According to Article 24 of the Geneva Convention on the

Territorial Sea and the Contiguous Zone, 1958, this Zone is part
of the high seas and will, therefore, be considered under that
heading. First, however, the principle of State jurisdiction
under international customary law will be briefly considered.

I. STATE JURISDICTION UNDER INTERNATIONAL CUSTOMARY LAW (4)

It is undisputed that a State has jurisdiction to deal
with any offence committed within its territory, regardless of
the nationality of the offender - territorial jurisdiction (5).
It is generally agreed further that a State may assume jurisdiction over offences committed by its own nationals abroad,
wherever they may be - personal jurisdiction (6). However,
there is no general agreement as to when and under what
circumstances a State may assume jurisdiction over offences
committed by foreigners outside its territory. Indeed, "the
practice of States in applying their criminal laws to foreigners
for acts committed outside their territory is notoriously
inconsistent" (7). Thus, one group of States (e.g. the United
States and United Kingdom) adopt the theory of the territoriality of criminal jurisdiction and, in principle, do not admit
that a State is competent to prosecute aliens for acts committed
outside its territory. Even this group, however, admit that
jurisdiction may, under certain conditions, be exercised
legitimately where an act initiated outside the territory of the
State takes effect within it - objective territorial jurisdiction (8). A second group (e.g. France and Germany, and,
according to J.L. Brierly, perhaps the majority of States),
while accepting the territoriality principle as the general rule,
admit certain exceptions, for example when acts committed outside the territory are directed against the security of the
State or its financial credit, its territorial integrity and
political independence (9). Indeed, this 'protective' principle would appear to be a major exception to the principle of
territoriality. The third group (e.g. Turkey and Italy)
reject the territoriality principle and instead adopt the
universal theory of crime under which a crime, wherever committed, is justiciable by any State interested in suppressing it;
in practice, however, these States restrict the application of
their jurisdiction to acts prejudicial to the State or one
of their nationals, avoiding thus the anarchy of jurisdictions
to which the universal theory of crime might lead (10).

II. JURISDICTION OVER ARTIFICIAL ISLANDS CONSTRUCTED ON THE HIGH SEAS

1. Ships

The fundamental principle is that international law

prohibits appropriation of the high seas by individual States. Consequently, no State may claim territorial jurisdiction over the high seas and this dominant principle is today codified in Article 2 of the 1958 High Seas Convention: "The high seas being open to all nations, no State may validly purport to subject any part of them to its sovereignty....." Thus,

"States are limited to exercising their jurisdiction over ships and aircraft of their own nationality while sailing on, or flying over, the high seas, and all persons and cargo on board..... the exclusive jurisdiction of a State over its ships and aircraft on and above the high seas may be limited by other rules of international law as, for instance, those governing the principle of self-defence" (11),

and one may add the crime of piracy, and also the limitations imposed by way of treaty arrangements (12). This type of jurisdiction is quasi-territorial in character in that it extends not only to the ships and aircraft of the flag State, its own nationals and their property on board, but also to all foreigners and their property aboard the ships and aircraft concerned (13). The exclusive jurisdiction of the flag State is codified in Article 6 of the 1958 High Seas Convention:

"1. Ships shall sail under the flag of one State only and, save in exceptional cases provided for in international treaties or in these articles, shall be subject to its exclusive jurisdiction on the high seas. A ship may not change its flag during a voyage or while in a port of call, save in the case of a real transfer of ownership or change of registry" (14).

The 'nationality of ships' concept constitutes further the necessary link and basis for the exclusive jurisdiction of the flag State. Article 5 of the 1958 High Seas Convention provides that:

"1. Each State shall fix the conditions for the grant of its nationality to ships, for the registration of ships in its territory, and for the right to fly its flag. Ships have the nationality of the State whose flag they are entitled to fly. There must exist a genuine link between the State and the ship; in particular, the State must effectively exercise its jurisdiction and control in administrative, technical and social matters over ships flying its flag" (15).

With regard to ships on the high seas which are not shown to have national character, it is argued that the assertion of jurisdiction by any State is not a violation of international law.

Indeed, there would appear to be no clear policies which might
protect stateless ships from "very summary treatment" (16).
That view was taken by the British Privy Council in the case
of Naim Molvan v. Attorney-General for Palestine (The Asya) (17).
In this case, the vessel Asya, sailing in 1946 from France
towards Palestine with several hundred illegal immigrants
aboard, was sighted by a British destroyer when on the high seas,
and at that time was flying no flag. She later hoisted the
Turkish flag, but made no reply to a signal asking her destin-
ation. The Turkish flag was soon replaced by the Zionist flag.
The destroyer escorted Asya to Haifa where it was found that none
of her passengers had passports, or travel documents or visas.
There was no passenger-list nor did the ship have any of the
usual ship's papers with which to prove her national character.
Eventually, Asya was ordered by a court to be forfeited to the
Government of Palestine. On appeal the British Privy Council
affirmed the judgment of the Supreme Court of Palestine and
rejected the contention that the seizure of the vessel was a
violation of international law, saying :

> "..... the freedom of the open sea, whatever those words
> may connote, is a freedom of ships which fly, and are
> entitled to fly, the flag of a State which is within the
> comity of nations. The Asya did not satisfy these
> elementary conditions. No question of comity nor of
> any breach of international law can arise if there is no
> State under whose flag the vessel sails. Their Lordships
> would accept as a valid statement of the law the following
> passage from Oppenheim's International Law (6th ed.),
> Vol I p.546: 'In the interest of order on the open sea,
> a vessel not sailing under the maritime flag of a State
> enjoys no protection whatever, for the freedom of navigat-
> ion on the open sea is freedom for such vessels only as
> sail under the flag of a State.' Having no usual ship's
> papers which would serve to identify her, flying the
> Turkish flag, to which there was no evidence she had a
> right, hauling it down on the arrival of a boarding party
> and later hoisting a flag which was not the flag of any
> State in being, the Asya could not claim the protection of
> any State nor would any State claim that any principle of
> international law was broken by her seizure" (18).

It is true, on the other hand, that although the 1958 High
Seas Convention appears to assume, as already indicated, that
in order to enjoy protection under the doctrine of the freedom
of the high seas a vessel must have a certain nationality
(Articles 4-6), it does not further specify the consequences of
a ship's having no legitimate flag, and does not necessarily
make the vessel a complete outlaw or hostis humani generis.
To conclude, however, "it is clear that absence of sufficient

proof of national character may raise doubt as to the existence
of a right to protection under the principle of the freedom
of the high seas" (19).

2.   Artificial Islands

The absence of territorial sovereignty upon the high seas
was asserted earlier to be the dominant principle of the
international law of the sea.   This does not, however, mean
that persons and their property are not subject to any legal
order upon the high seas.   Thus, with regard to ships, as has
already been seen, a legal order is secured through the recognition of the exclusive jurisdiction of the flag State (quasi-
territorial jurisdiction).   As regards further persons and
their property, other than ships, such as installations or any
other floating craft not qualifying as a 'ship' under international law, a legal order is again secured on the high seas
by the extension of the 'personal' jurisdiction of each State
over its nationals and their property.   Hall, the eminent
English jurist of the nineteenth century, has pointed out that
"unless complete lawlessness is to be permitted to exist", in
providing a legal order for the high seas, "jurisdiction must
be exercised either exclusively by each State over persons and
property belonging to it, or concurrently with the other members
of the body of States over all persons and property, to whatever
country they may belong."   He asserted further that it was the
former principle which was adopted by the international community, and he added :

> "....and although jurisdiction cannot be founded on
> non-territorial property so as to exclude or diminish
> territorial jurisdiction, the possession of an object
> as property at least forms a reasonable ground for the
> attribution of exclusive control to its owner when no
> equal or superior right of control can be shown by
> another.... It is consequently the settled usage that
> as a general rule persons belonging to a State community,
> when in places not within the territorial jurisdiction of
> any power, are in the same legal position as if on the
> soil of their own State, and that, also as a general
> rule, property belonging to a State or its subjects,
> while evidently in the possession of its owners, cannot
> be subjected to foreign jurisdiction" (20).

Following the above principle enunciated by Hall, Sir Humphrey
Waldock has further stated that :

> "..... A State which takes action on the high seas against
> persons or property with which or with whom it has no legal
> link of nationality violates international law, unless

either it has the consent of the national State or the case
falls under one of the recognised exceptions to the
general rule such as piracy, hot pursuit, or contiguous
zone jurisdiction. The onus is always upon a State to
establish the basis of its right to act against the
nationals of another State or their property upon the
high seas. Admittedly, the law on this point has developed
primarily in connection with ships. But the same principles appear to operate in connection with lighthouses,
light beacons, submarine cables and fish traps installed
in the high seas, as well as in regard to wrecks lying
there....
      Any State, it seems to me clear, is authorised under
international law to apply its law and jurisdiction to its
own nationals on an installation owned by them on the
high seas. Accordingly, so far as international law is
concerned, there cannot be said to be a total legal vacuum
with respect to such an installation" (21).

It would thus appear that de lege lata only the national
State is authorized under international law to exercise jurisdiction and control over its own nationals and their property
on the high seas (22). No other State may do so unless it
has the consent of the national State or it shows that its action
is based on an exception recognised either by international
customary law or treaty arrangement. Professor D.H.N. Johnson
also supported in the R.E.M. station case a similar view. He
was of the opinion that what the P.C.I.J. said in the Lotus
case with regard to foreign vessels is "equally relevant to the
case of artificial islands erected on the high seas by foreigners"
(23). There is further one well-known precedent in international
practice which would appear to confirm the rule with regard to
jurisdiction exercised by a State over artificial islands erected
on the high seas by its own nationals. In 1918, surely long
before there was any talk on the continental shelf doctrine, a
United States national asked the State Department what would
be the position of an artificial island erected by him on
the high seas, some 40 miles off the coast in the Gulf of
Mexico, for extracting oil. The State Department replied that
the United States had no jurisdiction over the ocean bottom of
the Gulf of Mexico beyond the territorial sea and could not,
therefore, grant any leasehold or other property rights to
United States nationals. It then went on:

"The Department further informs you that, unless the
erection of an artificial island interfered with rights
of the United States or of its citizens, or formed the
subject of a complaint made upon apparently good grounds,
by a foreign government, it is not likely that this
Government would object to the erection by American

citizens of such an island as you suggest. The Department
is not in a position to procure information from other
nations as to their attitude toward such a project, but
it would seem that no foreign government would interfere with the erection of an artificial island in the
Gulf of Mexico unless its interests or the rights of its
citizens were injuriously affected thereby.

It may also be observed, although the Department
can give no assurances on the subject, that it would seem
possible that, if an island were constructed 40 miles
from the coast of the United States by the efforts of
American citizens and inhabited and controlled by them in
the name of the United States, this Government would
assume some sort of control over the island. However, it
would seem that some special action by the President and
Congress would be necessary to this end. If the
island were erected, and if the United States assumed
control over it, it would then be possible to take such
steps as were necessary to protect the rights of the
occupants" (24).

Accordingly, the occasionally advanced contention that
there exists a legal vacuum with respect to fixed installations
on the high seas would not appear to be accurate and in
accordance with the above enunciated principle. The legal
vacuum theory, which was first publicly advocated by Professor
J.P.A. Francois, was, for example, advanced by the Dutch
Government in justifying its claim to jurisdiction over the
R.E.M. broadcasting station erected on the high seas beyond
the Dutch territorial sea (25).

"Basically, the legal vacuum theory relates that if there
is an occurrence that is not covered by existing international law, then the State affected by this transpir-
ation is free to formulate rules to meet the problems
thus created" (26).

Under the legal vacuum theory, therefore, the only
question that remains is which State is primarily called upon
to fill the vacuum. According to Professor Francois this
must be the nearest coastal State. In the R.E.M. station
case, consequently, the Netherlands should be called upon to
fill the vacuum and thus exercise its jurisdiction upon it, as
the nearest coastal State (27).

It is interesting to note that the 'legal vacuum theory'
was fiercely criticized by the legal advisers of the R.E.M.
station. Their main argument was that there is no legal
vacuum at all, since, in the absence of any territorial
jurisdiction upon the high seas, States are authorized under
international law to apply their law and jurisdiction to their

own nationals on installations owned by them on the high seas (28).
It is, also, interesting to note further than in 1955 the
Permanent United States Delegation denied the existence of a
legal vacuum on the high seas, through the following statement
made at the United Nations:

"It must be pointed out that the high seas are an area
under a definite and established legal status which
requires freedom of navigation and use for all. They
are not an area in which a legal vacuum exists, free to
be filled by individual States, strong or weak" (29).

Undoubtedly, the question may further be raised as to
whether the State which owns, or whose nationals own, an artificial
island on the high seas would be entitled to exercise jurisdiction over foreigners upon the island. "But even if the view
is taken that the owner-State would not be so entitled, the
foreigners would still be subject to the jurisdiction of their
own national State. It could not properly be said that there
was an actual legal vacuum" (30).
Apart from the legal vacuum theory, however, the Dutch
Government further advanced the notion of contiguity in justifying its claim to jurisdiction over the R.E.M. station (31).
Thus, the Dutch Government claimed that this notion gave it the
right to take steps to protect its legal order up to an unspec-
ified distance contiguous to its coasts. Accordingly, both
the continental shelf doctrine and the contiguous zone concept
could be used as a basis for the notion of contiguity.
The notion of contiguity has been advanced in the past
as a basis of territorial sovereignty over natural islands and
"there exists a tendency to consider islands situated on the
continental shelf adjacent to a State as pertaining for that
reason to that State" (32). However, as Judge Huber decided
in his arbitral award in The Island of Palmas case, "the title
of contiguity, understood as a basis of territorial sovereignty,
has no foundation in international law. It is wholly lacking
in precision and would lead to arbitrary results" (33).
With regard now to the continental shelf doctrine, as has
been emphasised time and again, the "sovereign rights" granted
to the coastal State over the continental shelf are strictly
limited to the exploration and exploitation of its natural ·
resources, and do not affect the legal status of the superjacent
waters as high seas (Article 3 of the 1958 Continental Shelf
Convention). The continental shelf doctrine, therefore,
would appear to have no application to the case of artificial
islands or installations, unless used for the limited purposes
of exploration and exploitation.
As regards the old notion of the "contiguous zone", which
was also referred to, it is perfectly clear in present international law that under Article 24 of the 1958 Geneva Convention

on the Territorial Sea and the Contiguous Zone, this zone is
"a zone of the high seas" which "may not extend beyond twelve
miles from the baseline from which the breadth of the territorial
sea is measured," and the powers of the coastal State in that
zone are powers of a restricted nature, limited only to "customs,
fiscal, immigration or sanitary" matters, none of which would
appear to be relevant to the case of a broadcasting station
erected therein.

It is thus clear that the Dutch Government could not find
support, either in the continental shelf doctrine or in the
contiguous zone concept, for its claim to jurisdiction over
artificial islands erected for purposes other than for exploration and exploitation of the shelf resources or not falling
within the powers prescribed by the contiguous zone doctrine.
As has been stated:

> "The mere contiguity of an artificial island to a given
> coast, permanently above water on an elevation of the
> sea-bed, does not confer, under the rules of positive
> international law, any title of sovereignty to the
> coastal State if it is situated or erected outside its
> territorial waters. The same rule applies to the
> property existing on the island if it is owned by foreign
> nationals or companies" (34).

However, as has already been indicated above, and will
be elaborated further below, coastal State jurisdiction upon
artificial islands erected on the continental shelf for purposes unconnected with exploration and exploitation purposes,
could now be based on different legal grounds, amounting in
fact to an emerging new rule of international law, beyond the
controversial doctrines of the "legal vacuum" and the "notion
of contiguity".

As was said earlier, the European Nations in particular have
witnessed since the early sixties the phenomenon of the so-called
"pirate" broadcasting stations, moored or installed either on
board ships or on structures fixed on the sea-bed, outside the
limits of the territorial sea so as to avoid the control of the
coastal States. Indeed, since 1958 there have been at least
eleven such stations operating in the Baltic, Irish and North
Seas (35). It would, therefore, be of particular significance
in the present context of extra-territorial jurisdiction to
consider briefly the legislative measures taken by a number of
European States with regard to broadcasting stations established
on the high seas (36).

United Kingdom. The British Government has consistently
refused to take unilateral action and insisted that the problem
could only be solved by an international agreement. Indeed,
such an agreement has now materialized under the auspices of

the Council of Europe.

(a) Broadcasting Stations operating from structures fixed on
     the sea-bed.

     Radio Sutch and Radio Invicta were established on derelict
     War Department forts (Martello towers) in the Thames
     Estuary outside the British territorial sea.   Despite
     the fact that the structures had originally been Government
     property, and despite pressure from the Opposition in
     Parliament, the Government apparently considered that
     it had no jurisdiction to take action against the stations
     on the high seas. ˙This particular problem was finally
     solved by the British Government through the adoption of
     bay-closing lines under the 1958 Geneva Convention on the
     Territorial Sea, the effect of which was to bring the
     forts within the United Kingdom's territorial sea (37).
     "No suggestion was ever made that the United Kingdom, as
     the nearest coastal State might be entitled to exercise its
     jurisdiction over installations on the continental shelf
     not connected with the exploitation of its natural resources"
     (38).

(b) Broadcasting stations operating on board ships.

     Radio "Caroline" started broadcasting in March 1964, and
     it was followed by Radio "Atlanta" (May 1964) and Radio
     "London" (December 1964) (39).   "Caroline" and "Atlanta"
     were both registered in Panama while "London" was registered
     in the Republic of Honduras.   The British Government reacted
     very cautiously and once again it refused to take unilateral
     action against the radio ships on the high seas.   However,
     it made representations to Panama and to Honduras, and,
     indeed, the Government of the former cancelled the registra-
     tions as soon as the broadcasting was reported to it.   It
     should, in any case, be noted that "despite the cancella-
     tion of Caroline's right to fly the Panamanian flag, the
     United Kingdom Government did not deem it appropriate to
     take action against that ship on the high seas" (40).
         Finally, the United Kingdom Government enacted in
     1967 the Marine and Broadcasting (Offences) Act, whose
     purpose is "to suppress broadcasting from ships, aircraft
     and certain marine structures" (41).   The main provisions
     of this Act are as follows: S.1 (1) prohibits broadcasts
     from any ship or aircraft while it is in or over the
     United Kingdom or the territorial sea, as well as broad-
     casts from a ship or aircraft registered in the United
     Kingdom while it is elsewhere than in or over the United
     Kingdom or the territorial sea.   Under S.1 (2) if a
     broadcast is made from a ship or aircraft in contravention

of S.1 (1), the owner of the ship, the master of the ship
and every person who operates, or participates in such an
operation, as well as the operator of the aircraft, the
commander of the aircraft and every person who operates,
or participates in such an operation, shall be guilty of
an offence.   S.2 prohibits further broadcasts made from:
(a) a structure affixed to, or supported by, the sea-bed
erected in the territorial sea or in tidal waters in the
United Kingdom, and is not a ship, or (b) any other object
in the territorial sea or tidal waters, being neither a
fixed structure nor a ship or aircraft.   Here again
every person who operates, or participates, or assists
the making of a broadcast in contravention of the above
provision shall be guilty of an offence.   Under S.3,
United Kingdom citizens, British subjects and British
protected persons, who operate, participate or assist the
making of a broadcast from the following structures shall
be guilty of an offence: (a) from a foreign ship while
it is on the high seas; (b) from a foreign aircraft while
it is on or over the high seas; (c) from a fixed structure
erected on the high seas and not being a ship; and
(d) from any other object on the high seas, being neither
a fixed structure nor a ship or aircraft.   Sections 4 and
5 further render illegal any form of supply or assistance
to "pirate" broadcasting stations by enabling the British
Government to exercise its jurisdiction over its own
subjects anywhere and any other persons within the United
Kingdom territory.   The practical effect would thus be
to cut off the "pirate" broadcasting stations from all
their practicable sources of supply from the land.
Under S.6, finally, a person guilty of an offence under
the Act shall be liable, (a) on summary conviction, to
imprisonment for a term not exceeding 3 months or to a
fine not exceeding £400, or to both; and (b) on conviction on indictment, to imprisonment for a term not exceeding 2 years or to a fine, or to both.

   It is thus clear that British extra-territorial
jurisdiction is provided by this Act only for British
citizens or subjects, ships and aircraft anywhere, while
no direct measures of jurisdiction and control are
prescribed by it as regards foreigners outside British
territory or foreign ships, aircraft and artificial
islands situated on the high seas.

France. The French Government, by the Decree of 27 October
1965, prohibited "pirate" broadcasts by all French ships,
whatever their position.   "Besides, the French Government
has accepted the principle of refusing all telephone calls of
commercial character to foreign ships eventually affecting
radio broadcasts outside territorial waters, if the Government

appertaining to that particular ship request such intervention"
(42).

Belgium. The relevant Belgian Act is explicitly confined
to mobile stations such as ships or aircraft (43). This Act
does not contemplate direct action against off-shore broadcasting
stations but restricts itself to making punishable within the
territory of Belgium certain acts which, whether committed in
that territory or abroad, amount to the establishment and use
of such mobile broadcasting stations, as well as acts of assistance or complicity. As regards criminal jurisdiction over
foreigners it is stipulated that they may only be prosecuted
if they have committed a punishable offence in Belgium or on
board Belgian ships or aircraft, or if they have acted in
concert with persons of Belgian nationality. In both cases a
foreigner can only be prosecuted after being apprehended within
Belgian territory.

Netherlands. Radio Veronica began broadcasting from the
Santa Veronica, a ship of unknown registry, in 1959. The
ship was anchored just outside the Dutch territorial sea, close
to the R.E.M. fixed station, and although the latter was closed
down under specially enacted legislation – The North Sea
Installations Act, 1964 – no legislative or administrative
action was taken against Radio Veronica, due to the Dutch
Government's distinction between an 'installation' and a
'ship' in international law.

The Scandinavian countries. The relevant laws enacted
by these States were the outcome of concerted action within
the Nordic Council in the early sixties, and they all came
into force on 1 August 1962 (44). Therefore, although the
exact terms of each Statute varied, essentially they followed
a common basic pattern. Thus, whereas the relevant Norwegian
statute is explicitly confined to mobile stations such as ships
or aircraft (45), the laws enacted by Sweden, Denmark and
Finland use a rather broader language, which does not in itself
exclude stations on fixed installations, although it is doubt-
ful whether their authors really intended this wider scope (46).
The four statutes under consideration do not contemplate direct
action against off-shore broadcasting stations established on
the high seas, but they make punishable within the territory of
the State concerned any form of supply or assistance to stations.
For the purpose of these statutes the territories and citizenship
of other Scandinavian countries are equated in the law of each
country, with the territory and citizenship of the country
concerned. In one case, however – the "Lucky Star", of
Guatemalan Registry – Denmark took direct action against the
ship, seizing it and obtaining a confiscation order in a Danish
court. The legal view of the Danish Government apparently was

that it was not precluded from taking such action against the "Lucky Star" on the high seas because the Guatemalan flag had been flown by the ship simply as a flag of convenience.

The Council of Europe Agreement on "Pirate" Broadcasting 1965

On 20 January 1965, the European Agreement for the Prevention of Broadcasts Transmitted from Stations Outside National Territories, was opened for signature by the Council of Europe (47). The Agreement closely follows the pattern of the Nordic legislation (and also of the corresponding Belgian law), but it takes a much more cautious approach to the question of jurisdiction over aliens.

Under the Agreement the Contracting Parties have undertaken to make punishable as offences the establishment or operation of broadcasting stations on board ships, aircraft, or any other floating or airborne objects which, outside national territories, transmit broadcasts intended for reception or capable of being received within the territory of any Contracting Party, or which cause harmful interference to any radio communication service operating under the authority of a Contracting Party, (Arts. 1 and 2 (1)). Acts of collaboration, such as the provision and maintenance of equipment, the provision of supplies or services etc., are also made punishable under Article 2. Although Article 1 does not certainly cover stations established on fixed installations, it is further stipulated in Article 4 (b) that nothing in the Agreement shall be deemed to prevent a Contracting Party from applying its provisions "to broadcasting stations installed or maintained on objects affixed to or supported by the bed of the sea." Such a provision, however, indicates nothing as to the conditions under which action against fixed installations is allowed under international law. It is worth noting in the present context that in a Resolution, adopted on 29 January 1965, the Consultative Assembly of the Council of Europe recommended an examination of the possibility of extending the provisions of the Agreement to fixed installations or, alternatively, the preparation of a separate convention for the prevention of broadcasts from such stations (48).

The Agreement, which is conceived as an implementation of the International Telecommunication Union Radio Regulations of 1959 (49), does not provide for any direct action against broadcasting stations established on the high seas. As regards the extent of jurisdiction, Article 3 of the Agreement distinguishes between nationals and non-nationals. Thus each Contracting Party shall apply the provisions of the Agreement in regard to:

    (a)   its nationals who have committed any punishable offence under Article 2:(i) on its territory, ships or aircraft; and (ii) outside national territories on any ships, aircraft or any other floating or airborne object;

(b) non-nationals, who have committed any punishable offence under Article 2, on its territory, ships or aircraft, or on board any floating or airborne object under its jurisdiction.

In other words, it may be concluded that with respect to nationals the traditional principle of personal jurisdiction has been adopted, while with respect to non-nationals the traditional principle of territorial or quasi-territorial jurisdiction has again been adopted.

IMCO. IMCO, as an organization primarily concerned with matters of maritime safety, has shown a keen interest in the prevention of broadcasts from stations established on the high seas, due to the danger which these broadcasts represent to life at sea through likely interference with radio-communications contributing to the safety of life at sea (50).

In the present context of legislative measures taken by States in their battle against off-shore broadcasting stations, it is interesting to note that the IMCO Assembly in its Resolution A.117 (V), adopted on 25 October 1967, after noting that,

".....(b) the remedy for the situation lies in the form of national legislative measures preventing the supply by any country of food, fuel and advertise-ment material, and services necessary to maintain such stations in operation,

it requests Member States:

"(a) to continue taking the necessary steps to deny facilities to such stations,
(b) to refrain from registering ships used for such purpose or, if already registered, to take steps to cancel the registration" (51).

It is worth noting further that the International Telecommunication Union (I.T.U.) has also adopted a similar view: ".....the attempts which have been made...... to secure the suppression of broadcasts from such stations by the cancellation of ·their registration, will not succeed in suppressing the broadcasts; and that the only real remedy lies in the form of national legislative measures which would prevent the supply, by any country of food, fuel, advertise-ment material and other auxiliary services which are necessary

to maintain the station in operation and to provide.it with
a source of revenue from the sponsors of its programmes" (52).

Once again, a very cautious attitude towards artificial
islands constructed on the high seas is demonstrated and
neither IMCO nor I.T.U. have alluded to the exercise of
extra-territorial jurisdiction as regards aliens and their
property on the high seas.

In the writer's opinion what emerges clearly from the
above brief analysis of the legislative measures taken by
certain European States against the "pirate" broadcasting
stations established on the high seas, is that the former have
been very reluctant to extend their jurisdiction over foreigners
and their property on the high seas. With the exception of
the Netherlands, they have more or less followed the traditional
safe principles of international customary law as regards
extra-territorial jurisdiction. Undoubtedly such a restrained
attitude could only be explained by the fact that States are
extremely reluctant in surrendering their jurisdiction over
their nationals and their property to foreign States. As has
been observed, "States are extremely jealous of their jurisdiction over their nationals and adverse to this jurisdiction
being exercised by foreign States" (53). Neither the 'legal
vacuum theory' nor the 'notion of contiguity' have further
attracted much attention or favourable comments from either
the Governments concerned or eminent publicists in international
law. It is true on the other hand that States have not
protested against the Dutch North Sea Installations Act of 1964,
enacted against the R.E.M. Station, but this could be explained,
as will be shown later, on grounds other than those suggested
above.

It would appear, therefore, that prima facie there is
overwhelming evidence to support the view that de lege lata
only the national State is authorized under international law
to exercise jurisdiction and control over its own nationals
and their property on the high seas, be it a fixed or a floating artificial island, or any other object no qualifying as
a 'ship'. If, on the other hand, a floating structure does
qualify as a 'ship' in international law, it will, of course,
be subject to the jurisdiction of the flag-State.

Having thus accepted in principle the jurisdiction of
the national State over artificial islands erected on the
high seas, two questions arise further. The first is concerned with the jurisdictional status of installations which
are not shown to have a certain national character, while
the second question is whether proof of the national character
of the installations under consideration, is subject to any
particular requirements.

As regards the first question, persons or objects on the
high seas which are not shown to have a certain national
character would probably be assimilated to stateless ships.

It is then arguable that the assertion of jurisdiction by any State is not a violation of international law, according to the principles laid down by the British Privy Council in the case of Naim Molvan v. Attorney-General for Palestine (1948).

With regard to the second question, whether proof of the national character is subject to any particular requirements or whether it is enough simply to prove ownership by the State itself or by its nationals, Sir Humphrey Waldock has suggested that in the case of lighthouses, light-beacons and submarine cables ownership by itself certainly appears to suffice (54). On the other hand, installations erected on the continental shelf for the exploration and exploitation of its natural resources form a separate and quite special category. These are subject to the exclusive jurisdiction of the coastal State independently of the nationality of their owners, by virtue of the sovereign rights enjoyed by the coastal State over the continental shelf resources. With regard to any other installations erected on the high seas, prima facie "it is the State which owns them, or whose nationals own them that has the exclusive right to exercise jurisdiction on the high seas; and it would be a usurpation of the right of the national State if another State were to do so without obtaining its consent" (55). It is quite clear further that particular provisions of national laws of individual States may affect the question "whether a given installation on the high seas is to be considered in international law as possessing the national character of that State and as subject to its jurisdiction. In principle, however, ownership by a national would appear to create a right of jurisdiction unless the national law requires something more or the national State declines to acknowledge the national character of the installation" (56).

However, it should be emphasized that a wide agreement seems to exist for the adoption of a new and quite different approach de lege ferenda, as regards jurisdiction over artificial islands and installations constructed on the high seas. Thus, a 'flag State' regime, similar to that applying to ships, has been advocated by an increasing number of writers. Professor Riphagen, for example, has suggested that:

"..... the obvious starting point - in a functional approach - is, that the State, which introduces the immovable - or under whose auspices it is introduced - exercises "jurisdiction over" the immovable. Indeed the introduction itself should only be permissible under the "flag" of some State which, then, should be responsible for the observance of the rules of international law relating to such introduction and to the subsequent activities "on board." The counterpart of such responsibility is that the "flag"-State has jurisdiction over the persons engaged in the introduction and subsequent activities" (57).

Another commentator has further suggested, in the context of marine resources exploitation, that,

"until enough international competition and friction develop to justify creation of some advance licensing scheme for administration by the United Nations, recognition of the flag of the craft or other surface mechanisms from which the exploration is controlled, sufficiently identifies the jurisdiction which ought to have plenary control over that exploration and over the exploitation of the resources so discovered" (58).

In other words, the flag-nation approach would permit the entrepreneur to operate under the protection of, and subject to the jurisdiction of, the State whose flag his "craft or other surface mechanism" flies. "The flag nation approach appears" further "to be simply an intermediary step between no regime and some form of international regime" (59).

As regards in particular jurisdiction and control over ships, installations and other devices used for the exploration and exploitation of sea-bed resources, the following points have been emphasized by the United Nations Secretary-General in his Report on the International Machinery (60):

"The normal rule is that when ships are on the high seas the State under whose flag the ship sails has sole jurisdiction. So far, the same rule has been applied in the case of vessels, installations and other devices engaged in sea-bed exploration and exploitation. In the case of ships the normal rule has been applied and in the case of fixed installations jurisdiction has been exercised by the coastal State under whose authority they were installed. Having regard, however, to the possibility of establishing a system of international registration or licensing, or of direct exploitation by an international body, the question of jurisdiction and control requires further examination in order to set out the range of possibilities.

If a registration or licensing system were to be adopted whereby activities might be registered by, or licences granted to States, ships might operate under the flag of the State which registered the activity or received the licence. In this case, no change would be required in the standard rule according to which vessels while on the high seas are subject, save in exceptional circumstances, to the exclusive jurisdiction of the flag State in respect of civil, criminal and administrative

matters.   The same rule might be applied also to the
installations and other devices used for the exploration
and exploitation of sea-bed resources in the particular
areas concerned.   In each instance, however, the
content of national jurisdiction might need to reflect
the fact that, under the establishing instrument, the
registration or licensing authority might possibly be
given power to make regulations concerning sea-bed
activities (for example, working practices and safety
regulations) or that international agreements might be
concluded dealing with such matters.   In the case where
a State permitted activities registered in its name, or
a licence granted to it, to be utilized by a non-
national enterprise which employed a vessel or installation
operating under the flag of another State, difficult
questions might arise;   in such circumstances either the
normal rule, whereby the flag State has sole jurisdiction,
might apply, or special provision could be made for a
system of concurrent jurisdiction.

In the event that activities might be registered by,
or licences granted to, entities other than States, it
would be necessary to decide whether the normal rule
should apply, or some form of "international" jurisdiction should be devised, or whether some other solution
should be adopted.....

In the event that direct exploration and exploitation
activities were undertaken by an international body, it
is possible that ships, installations and other devices
might be operated by the international agency concerned.
Reference may be made in this connection to Article 7 of
the Convention on the High Seas, which refers to the
question of ships employed on the official service of an
inter-governmental organization flying the flag of that
organization.   The possibility that ships might be
operated by an international organization was referred
to during the discussions by the International Law
Commission when the Law of the Sea Conventions were
being prepared.   The question was raised whether a
maritime code would have to be prepared to cover the
situation or whether the international organization would
apply the relevant laws of the State where it registered
the ship.   The same choice would thus present itself in
the event that an international body were established to
operate ships, installations and other devices as part
of the exploration and exploitation of sea-bed resources"
(61).

It will be remembered that in Chapter 2, dealing with
the right to construct artificial islands on the high seas a
multilateral approach to the problem of artificial islands

was advocated as best serving the general interest. It was there stated that this multilateral approach should ideally culminate in the establishment of international supervision and control over all types of artificial islands erected in the international ocean space.   Moreover, it was further said that this could best be achieved within the context of the International Regime for the ocean resources exploitation, by placing artificial islands under the effective jurisdiction and control of the International Machinery for the sea-bed. Naturally, the International Authority may authorize a partic- ular State to construct such islands and installations in the international ocean space and delegate jurisdiction over such structures to that particular State.

Already in 1952, M.W. Mouton discussed extensively the idea of international control and he proposed an international body for certain limited purposes, even though he had earlier concluded that "international exploitation would be difficult to realise."   Accordingly, the international organization "should be given the power to approve the erection of oil- installations in connection with shipping interests and could also be given the power to decide in case of conflicts." He would, however, "prefer to have a special Maritime Court to adjudicate conflicts between oil and shipping interests or fishery interests" (62).

Another commentator has recently proposed that "beyond the area of primary coastal State jurisdiction the construction and use of artificial islands should be under the exclusive control of the international community for the benefit of all States, especially the landlocked, the shelf-locked, and the under-developed" (63).

A similar proposal, contained in a Working Paper Concerning Artificial Islands and Installations, was submitted by Belgium to the Sea-Bed Committee in 1973 (64). A distinct- ion between floating islands and permanent islands fixed on the sea-bed is made in the said working paper. With regard to jurisdictional status it was submitted that floating islands could be treated as vessels in view of their notional mobility. As regards "permanent islands, supported on the sea-bed or the ocean floor..... erected beyond the limits of national jurisdiction," these "might be placed under the juris- diction of the international machinery for the sea-bed, whose establishment is contemplated; since they would be supported on the internationalised subsoil or the sea-bed or ocean floor, they would fall within the jurisdiction of the future inter- national body" (65).   It was further submitted that, naturally, "the international authority may authorize a State to erect such islands or installations and delegate jurisdiction over such structures to that State" (66).

Finally, it should be noted that Provision X of Informal Working Paper No. 12, concerning artificial islands and installations, provides as follows (67):

> "Any construction of an artificial island or immovable
> installation on the high seas beyond the limits of
> the continental shelf shall be subject to the authority
> and jurisdiction of the international machinery for
> the sea-bed. The International Authority may authorize
> a State to erect such islands or installations and
> delegate jurisdiction over such structures to that
> State."

However, even at this stage of UNCLOS III it is not yet
known when, if at all, the International Regime for the
deep sea-bed will come into force. Neither the form it will
ultimately take, nor the function or powers of the International
Authority are further known. Considerable work is still
required, despite the fact that a wide agreement has already
been reached at the Conference on certain crucial issues, such
as the territorial sea breadth and the EEZ concept.

On the assumption that a comprehensive International
Regime, including an effective Authority, will be much further
delayed, or that it will not simply materialize, it can rather
safely be said that the 'flag-state' principle will be adopted by
States. This principle will thus supersede the traditional
rule of the 'national-state' jurisdiction over persons and
their property on the high seas.

In other words, with regard to jurisdiction over
artificial islands erected on the high seas beyond the limits
of national jurisdiction, principles similar to those presently
applying to ships will probably be adopted by the international
community, and quasi-territorial jurisdiction will gain further
to the detriment of personal jurisdiction. Indeed, the
construction of an artificial island itself should only be
permissible following its registration in a certain State
and under the 'flag' of that State, which should be responsible
for the observance of the relevant rules of international law
and the activities on the artificial island. "The counterpart
of such responsibility is," as has already been said, "that
the 'flag'-State has jurisdiction over the persons engaged in
the introduction and subsequent activities" (68). This is
the attitude adopted by the Preliminary Draft Convention on
ODAS, Articles 5, 6 and 7 of which make detailed provisions
with regard to registration and jurisdictional matters concerning ODAS. The attendant problem of the "flags of convenience"
phenomenon will, of course, have to be faced and attempts will
have to be made so that future difficulties and disputes similar
to those which have been experienced in the parallel situation
involving ships, will be largely avoided.

If, on the other hand, a comprehensive International
Regime for the deep sea-bed were to be established, it is the

writer's view that, de lege ferenda, artificial islands and
installations, erected beyond the limits of national jurisdiction,
should be subject to international control and supervision.
Naturally, what this means in practice is that the International
Authority may authorize a State to construct such islands and
installations and delegate jurisdiction over them to that
State.

Unfortunately, however, the existing draft Convention
on the International Regime covers only stationary and mobile
installations relating to exploration and exploitation of the
deep sea-bed resources (69). Thus draft Article 16 refers
to "stationary and mobile installations relating to the
conduct of activities in the Area", which under draft Article 1
"means all activities of exploration for, and exploitation of,
the resources of the Area." It follows that artificial
islands and installations erected in the Area for purposes
other than for exploration and exploitation of the Area
resources fall outside the scope of the International Regime.
As one commentator has observed:

"..... free exchange of the products of marine
technology is more difficult to envisage. Only those
products that are relatively inexpensive and non-
strategic in character are likely to be widely distributed among maritime users. It is not fanciful to
expect, however, that the leading technological powers,
moved by hypertechnical logic rather than the spirit
of altruism, will find it advantageous to provide
navigation, weather forecasting and other systems for
general use. There may be a tendency for permanent fixed
installations to be made subject to widely shared
administrative authority, if hypertechnical logic
dictates that these installations form part of a world-
wide system which can only operate at maxiumum efficiency
through universal co-operation" (70).

The last question which arises in the present context
concerns the jurisdiction of the flag-State within the safety
zones established around artificial islands and installations.
Undoubtedly, the flag-State must be entitled to take all
measures necessary for their protection, but how extensive
should its powers be in this respect?

Should, for example, the power to take the necessary
measures within the safety zones be more or less the same as
the jurisdiction enjoyed upon the artificial island, or should
a distinction be drawn between them? Should the rights
enjoyed within the safety zones extend further to penal sanctions for unauthorized entry into these by foreign ships, and
what powers of interference with foreign shipping should
generally be recognized and granted to the flag-State? The

problem has already been faced with regard to installations
and other devices necessary for the exploration and exploit-
ations of the natural resources of the continental shelf.
Thus, it will be remembered that Article 5 (2) of the
Continental Shelf Convention 1958, lays down that, subject to
the provisions of paras 1 and 6, the coastal State is entitled
to establish safety zones around the said installations and
devices "and to take in those zones measures necessary for
their protection," while para 3 provides further that ships
of all nationalities must respect the safety zones. The
same questions as above arise in relation to these installations and devices, and as will be seen later a more extensive
interpretation of the said Article 5 is advocated, so that
penal sanctions would be included in the rights of the coastal
State for the effective protection of the installations
and other devices (71).

Accordingly, a similar extensive jurisdiction is generally
proposed for the safety zones established around artificial
islands anywhere, and penal sanctions are probably necessary
for the effective protection of such structures. In the
words of Professor Riphagen:

> "It would seem that de lege ferenda 'protective juris-
> diction' generally with respect to all immovables
> introduced in the marine environment is, in principle,
> acceptable" (72).

The same author has further suggested that "rather more
'protection' could be allowed in respect of immovables
assimilable to 'land' and rather less in respect of
immovables assimilable to 'ships' " (73).

III.   JURISDICTION OVER ARTIFICIAL ISLANDS
CONSTRUCTED ON THE CONTINENTAL SHELF

As has already been pointed out the exclusive "sovereign
rights" accorded to the coastal State over the continental
shelf are strictly limited to the exploration and exploitation
of its natural resources, and do not affect the legal status
of the superjacent waters as high seas (Articles 2 and 3 of
the Continental Shelf Convention 1958).   Under Article 5
of the same Convention the coastal State is entitled to
construct and maintain or operate on the continental shelf
installations and other devices necessary for the exploration
and exploitation of the shelf resources, and such structures
shall be under the jurisdiction of the coastal State (paras
2 and 4).   As has also been pointed out further, the continental
shelf doctrine would have no application to the case of
artificial islands or installations unconnected with the
limited purposes of exploration and exploitation of the shelf

resources. Indeed, the coastal State could neither construct or operate, nor subject to its jurisdiction, artificial islands and installations erected on the shelf for any other purposes, by virtue of the continental shelf doctrine - either under international customary law or under the Geneva Convention on the Continental Shelf 1958.

Thus, with regard to the jurisdiction exercised over structures deployed or constructed in the continental shelf area the situation would appear to be as follows :

(a) Ships. In view of the fact that the rights of the coastal State over the continental shelf do not affect the legal status of the superjacent waters as high seas (Article 3 of the Continental Shelf Convention 1958), ships are subject to the exclusive jurisdiction of the flag-State (74). However, ships which directly participate in exploration and exploitation activities on the continental shelf, should be covered by the term "installations and other devices," thus subject to the jurisdiction of the coastal State, and not the flag-State, during the time of such exploration and exploitation activities.

(b) Installations and other devices constructed for the exploration and exploitation of the natural resources of the continental shelf.

Such structures, whether floating, mobile or permanently fixed, are subject to the jurisdiction of the coastal State, by virtue of its sovereign rights over the shelf resources, (Article 5 (4) of the Continental Shelf Convention 1958).

(c) Artificial islands constructed for purposes other than for exploration and exploitation of the shelf resources.

As was seen earlier such structures are not covered either by the Continental Shelf Convention 1958, or the continental shelf doctrine under international customary law. Jurisdiction over such islands should, therefore, be based elsewhere.

(i) Floating Installations. These are subject to the regime of the high seas, and as such come under the jurisdiction of the national State which de lege lata is authorized under international law to exercise jurisdiction and control over its own nationals and their property on the high seas.

Floating structures which may qualify as, or are assimilable to, 'ships' in international law, will naturally be subject to the jurisdiction of the flag-State, as is the case with ships.

(ii) Artificial islands fixed on, or otherwise supported by, the bed of the continental shelf.

    As was seen earlier in the chapter dealing with the right to construct artificial islands in the continental shelf area, two arguments may.be advanced in relation to fixed installations. According to the first view, based either on the doctrine of the freedom of the high seas or on the sea-bed title argument, artificial islands may be constructed on the continental shelf by any State, and not only the coastal State, subject, of course, to the rules of reasonable regard to the interests of other States and non-interference with the exploration and exploitation activities of the coastal State. With regard to the question of jurisdiction it would appear that only the national State or flag-State would have the requisite jurisdiction to regulate activities on such structures.

The Belgian delegate at the U.N. Sea-Bed Committee (1971), for example, speaking about the problems involved in using part of the shelf for constructing an off-shore port facility, said in relation to the problem of jurisdiction:

"In Belgium, bills introduced into parliament were first submitted to the Conseil d'Etat for a legal opinion on their content. The bill, which had become the law of 13 June 1969 on the Belgian continental shelf, had therefore been studied by that authority. The opinion of the Conseil d'Etat was that an installation which was not used for the exploration or exploitation of the natural resources of the continental shelf did not come under Belgian jurisdiction. Belgium could take legal action against its own nationals, who could always be brought before the court of their place of domicile for an offence committed outside the territory. That, however, was not the case for foreigners, who might well be numerous among the staff of an artificial port" (75).

An earlier version of the Belgian law of 13 June 1969, embodying many of the principles of the Continental Shelf Convention 1958, (to which Belgium is not a party), "was modified to make it clear that Belgium was only asserting jurisdiction over structures on the continental shelf designed for the exploration or exploitation of its natural resources and not for any broader purpose. This change....., was made in order to delete language which would have literally given Belgium jurisdiction over all permanent installations situated on the high seas on the Belgian continental shelf" (76).

    According to the second view, consideration of coastal

security as well as the paramount importance of the
continental shelf for exploitation purposes, make it necessary to recognize exclusive coastal authority and control over
any use of the continental shelf which would require the
construction of fixed, or permanent installations.   It was
also submitted that embryonic State practice would appear
to confirm such a view.   Accordingly, it could be supported
further that such fixed or permanent installations erected
on the continental shelf should be subject to the jurisdiction
of the coastal State.   Undoubtedly in practice, and in the
absence of an international agreement or an established rule
of international law on this matter, only unilateral declarations of jurisdiction unprotested by other nations, could
initiate such a new legal regime, which could gradually
ripen into accepted international law.   There are unfortunately
certain dangers inherent in, and a great deal of controversy
surrounding the, unilateral declarations, which are too well-
known and discussed to be extensively reiterated here (77).
It is true, however, that "needed change in the law has
often been achieved only by the initiative of interested States.
The special rights of coastal States (including the territorial
sea) began as unilateral assertions: in our days, for particular example, the contiguous zone, the Truman Proclamation on
the Continental Shelf, the United States (and Canadian) Air
Defence Zones.   Special rights at sea have been claimed also
on bases other than coastal proximity, for example United
States (and other) nuclear testing areas" (78).
     In the writer's opinion, therefore, it would appear that
the Dutch action taken against the R.E.M. station in 1964,
embodied in the North Sea Installations Act 1964, could only
be justified upon the grounds of a unilateral declaration of
jurisdiction "as part of a process whereby the customary
international law itself was changed, e.g. by the other
States affected not protesting against the Netherlands law,
and even copying that law" (79).   Indeed, the Dutch action
could hardly be justified on the grounds of the legal vacuum
theory, the notion of contiguity, or the protection of legal
interests, none of which could securely rest on existing
international law.   And even Professors Van Panhuys and Van Boas,
supporters of the Dutch action have concluded that the action
taken was in fact based upon a new rule of international law:
"There is, therefore, every reason to conclude that the action
taken was based upon a new rule of international law, which
may be summarized as being that a coastal State may exercise
jurisdiction over all installations erected on the soil of its
continental shelf, no matter for what purpose" (80).
     It is, of course, arguable whether such a new rule of
international law exists today, let alone that it existed in
1964, as the above writers have suggested.   What the present
writer proposes de lege ferenda is simply the necessity of

recognition of exclusive coastal authority and control over
artificial islands and permanent installations constructed in
the shelf area.   Moreover, certain developments since 1964
and embryonic State practice, as explained above, would appear
to confirm this view, but this is certainly different from
asserting the existence of an established relevant rule of
international law.   It can further be seen that recognition
of coastal State jurisdiction over artificial islands erected
on its continental shelf, is not so much a case of a legal
vacuum being filled by the legal order of the coastal State,
as of one legal order, i.e. the legal order of the national
or flag-State, being replaced by another legal order, i.e. the
legal order of the coastal State, through a legitimate initia-
tion of a new rule of international law, that is by international
agreement or by the process of international customary law.

Certain recent proposals for international action would
also seem to recommend the recognition of coastal jurisdiction
and control over fixed or permanent structures erected on the
continental shelf.   Mr. Margue, for example, in his Report
on artificial islands to the Council of Europe has concluded
that:

> "..... exclusive occupation of portions of the high
> seas is bound to increase, and it would be advisable
> to seek a multilateral solution which might be based
> on the following principles:
> 1.   The coastal State to have functional powers
>   with a view to safeguarding the use of the
>   sea and protecting its national interests
>   (possibly by an authorization and control
>   procedure under the aegis of an international
>   organization).
> 2.   The action of the coastal State to be a
>   temporary extension of its legal order (forum
>   prorogatum ad hoc)" (81).

Belgium has proposed in its Working Paper Concerning
Artificial Islands and Installations, submitted to the Sea-
Bed Committee in 1973 that, (82):

> "..... artificial islands supported on the continental
> shelf could be made subject either to the jurisdiction
> of the coastal State or to that of the State which
> authorized their construction.   It should be recalled
> in this connection that Article 5 of the Convention on
> the Continental Shelf, done at Geneva on 29 April 1958,
> entitles the coastal State only to construct artificial
> installations necessary for the exploration and
> exploitation of the natural resources of the continental
> shelf, and places only those installations under the

jurisdiction of the coastal State.   In the case of
artificial islands which could be used as ports, or for
the deposit of noxious waste, or for any other purpose,
there is a gap to be filled in the law of the sea, and
it would be sufficient to provide that installations of
that kind will in future be placed under the jurisdiction
of the coastal State or of the State which is responsible
for their construction."

A number of commentators on the subject have also called
for coastal State jurisdiction.   One writer, for example,
has advanced some good arguments to support such a view:

"A more simple solution to the jurisdictional problems
of artificial sand islands in the waters of the high
seas would be a unilateral extension of the jurisdiction
of the State on whose continental shelf the island would
be located.   Several consideration support such a solution:
1.   Existing rules of law give coastal States jurisdiction
      over certain categories of islands;
2.   Coastal States are most directly affected by such
      islands and their activities;
3.   They cannot be constructed without the consent of
      the coastal State; and
4.   Coastal State jurisdiction over artificial sand
      islands constructed on their continental shelf avoids
      the complexities of a nationality-based approach" (83).

Furthermore, the draft Convention prepared by the Second
Committee of UNCLOS III provides for coastal State jurisdiction
essentially over all artificial islands and installations
constructed on the continental shelf.   Thus, under Article 68
of the Revised Single Negotiating Text, Part II, which must
be read in conjunction with Articles 48 and 44 in Chapter III
dealing with the EEZ, the coastal State shall have exclusive
jurisdiction, "including jurisdiction with regard to customs
fiscal, health, safety and immigration regulations" over:
   (a)   Artificial islands;
   (b)   Installations and structures for :
            (i)   the exploration and exploitation of the
                  natural resources of the shelf;
           (ii)   economic purposes in general;
          (iii)   scientific research;   and
   (c)   Installations and structures which may interfere with
         the exercise of the rights of the coastal State on
         the shelf.
Finally, the first national instrument assuming coastal jurisdiction over all structures erected on the continental shelf,
i.e. the Dutch North Sea Installations Act 1964, will be
briefly considered in the present context.

As has already been seen, the North Sea Installations Act of 3 December 1964 was specifically enacted against the R.E.M. broadcasting station (84). However, it is not concerned only with measures against 'pirate' broadcasting stations, but has a much broader scope: to provide a legal order for all fixed installations erected on the bed of the Dutch continental shelf, no matter for what purpose, including installations used for the exploration and exploitation of the natural resources of the continental shelf. The Act deals exclusively with fixed installations, leaving, therefore, outside its scope floating installations.

The application of the Act ratione loci is defined in Section 1:

"In this Act the term 'sea installation' shall mean an installation erected outside territorial waters on the bed of that part of the North Sea the boundaries of which correspond with that portion of the continental shelf which appertains to the Netherlands."

Section 2 provides that "the criminal law of the Netherlands shall apply to all such persons as commit any offence on a sea installation." From the international law point of view this appears to be the most crucial provision: it extends Dutch extra-territorial jurisdiction to all persons, nationals and foreigners alike, who commit a punishable offence on a sea installation.

Section 2 must further be read in conjunction with Section 3, which provides that "Provision may be made by Order in Council that any provisions of the statutory law of the Netherlands shall apply on and with respect to sea installations." It should be noted here that Van Panhuys and Van Boas have observed that the Dutch Government has indicated its intention not to apply Section 3 to drilling platforms and similar installations (85).

The Act provides also for the protection of the various uses of the seas from any unreasonable interference by the erection of installations. Thus, Section 7 provides for the promulgation by Order in Council of regulations applying to installations erected on the Dutch continental shelf, and intended to prevent unreasonable interference with shipping, fisheries, the conservation of the living resources of the sea, scientific research, the laying and maintenance of submarine cables and pipelines, the prevention of pollution, and in general the protection of any other interests recognized by international law. Any contravention of regulations made under Section 7 shall be a punishable offence (Section 8).

IV.   JURISDICTION OVER ARTIFICIAL ISLANDS
       CONSTRUCTED IN THE EXCLUSIVE ECONOMIC
       ZONE (EEZ)

As was seen earlier in Chapter 2, the coastal State has
in the EEZ sovereign rights over all resources, both living
and non-living, as well as jurisdiction with regard to
scientific research and preservation of the marine environment.   It was pointed out further that under the draft
Convention prepared by the Second Committee of UNCLOS III,
in the EEZ the coastal State shall have the exclusive right
to construct or authorize the construction, operation and use
of:
  (a) Artificial islands;
  (b) Installations and structures for:
       (i)   the exploration and exploitation of the
             resources of the zone;
      (ii)   economic purposes in general;
     (iii)   scientific research;   and
  (c) Installations and structures which may interfere
       with the exercise of the rights of the coastal
       State in the zone (86).

Article 48, para 2, provides further that:

"The coastal State shall have exclusive jurisdiction over
such artificial islands, installations and structures,
including jurisdiction with regard to customs, fiscal,
health, safety and immigration regulations."

In short, the coastal State shall have exclusive jurisdiction not only over all resource and other economic
installations constructed in the EEZ, but also over all
artificial islands and, in effect, over non-economic installations.   As has been stated elsewhere "if the exclusive right
to authorize the construction and operation of artificial
islands and installations in the Economic Zone will be
conferred on the coastal State, it is only logical to provide
that the structures fall under the exclusive jurisdiction of
the coastal State" (87).

    CONCLUSIONS

1. The coastal State has exclusive jurisdiction and control
    over artificial islands and installations constructed
    in its own internal waters and/or territorial sea by
    virtue of its sovereignty over these areas.
2. Artificial islands and installations situated in the high
    seas are de lege lata, subject to the jurisdiction of
    the national State.   This is so in view of the fact

that under international customary law only the coastal
State has the necessary authority to exercise jurisdiction and control over its own nationals and their
property on the high seas, be it a fixed or floating
structure or any other object not qualifying as a 'ship'.
However, it would appear that de legé ferenda, the
'flag-State' regime is preferable to the traditional
'national-State' rule, under the control and supervision
of the International Sea-Bed Authority.

3. Artificial islands and installations constructed on the
    continental shelf for the exploration and exploitation
    of its natural resources are, de lege lata, subject to
    exclusive coastal jurisdiction and control.   With
    respect to artificial islands and installations con-
    structed in the shelf area for other purposes, in
    theory a distinction must be made between floating and
    fixed installations.   Thus, whereas the former are
    subject to the legal regime of the high seas, the
    latter would be subject to exclusive coastal jurisdiction.
    In practice, however, coastal States will most probably
    tend to assume jurisdiction over all artificial
    islands and installations erected and/or deployed in
    the shelf area.   The relevant provisions of the Revised
    Single Negotiating Text, which essentially confer on the
    coastal State exclusive jurisdiction over all such
    structures, constitute a clear indication of this trend.

4. The coastal State has exclusive jurisdiction over all
    artificial islands and over all resource and other
    economic installations constructed in the EEZ. In practice,
    non-economic installations would also, most probably, be
    subject to exclusive coastal State jurisdiction.

NOTES

    1. "So far as the criminal law is concerned, the
United Kingdom exercises criminal jurisdiction over all persons
whatever their nationality, within the territorial waters
of the United Kingdom," United Kingdom Report to the IOC
as requested by UNESCO Circular Letter NS/9/89E dated
23rd November 1962, in IOC, Technical Series, No.5, Legal
Problems Associated with Ocean Data Acquisition Systems (ODAS),
at p.26.
    2.C.W. Walker, Jurisdictional Problems Created by
Artificial Islands, 10 San Diego Law Review (1973) pp.638-663
at p.646.

3. See the Margue Report, at p.13.

4. "State sovereignty in international customary law is an essentially negative concept. State jurisdiction is its positive complement," G. Schwarzenberger, A Manual of International Law, fifth edition, 1967, p.90. On State Jurisdiction in general see ibid., Chapter 4, pp.90-119. Professor Bin Cheng in distinguishing between the international competence of States to adopt and to enforce rules of criminal law has introduced two new terms: " "jurisfaction" and "jurisaction". The former denotes the legislative power of a State, as well as the competence of its courts to apply such rules. The latter describes the actual administration of justice and the enforcement of such laws, such as powers of arrest, passing sentence, imprisonment and so forth," Bin Cheng, Crimes on Board Aircraft, 12, C.L.P. (1959), pp.177-207, at pp.181-182.

5. J.L. Brierly, The Law of Nations, sixth edition, 1963, p.299.

6. Ibid.

7. Sir Humphrey Waldock on the R.E.M. Broadcasting Station, see in RECHTSGELEERDE ADVIEZEN, at p.28.

8. Ibid., J.L. Brierly, supra, at pp.299-300. The existence of this objective territorial jurisdiction has been recognized frequently by English and American courts; see for example, Rex. v. Godfrey, 1932, 1 K.B.24 and Ford v. United States, 1927, 273 U.S. 593. This principle has further been especially developed by the United States in an attempt to secure observance of its anti-trust laws by foreign corporations, hence the two leading American cases, United States v. Aluminium Co. of America (1945), 148 F.2d 416 (known as the Alcoa case), and American Banana Co. v. United Fruit Co. (1909), 213 U.S. 347; see also N.M. Hunnings, Pirate Broadcasting in European Waters, 14 I.C.L.Q. (1965), pp.410-436, at p.432. The objective territorial principle was the effective basis of the judgment of the P.C.I.J. in the Lotus case (1927), P.C.I.J. Series A 10.

9. Sir Humphrey Waldock, supra; J.L. Brierly, supra.

10. Sir Humphrey Waldock, supra; J.L. Brierly, supra, at p.300.

11. G. Schwarzenberger, supra, at p.96; on the doctrine of the freedom of the high seas in general see ibid., p.133 et seq; J.L. Brierly, supra, p.304 et seq.

12. See in general, Bin Cheng, General Principles of Law as Applied by International Courts and Tribunals, 1955, p.77 et seq.

13. In assessing the hierarchical order of the main forms of sovereignty, Professor Bin Cheng has observed that if they clash, territorial sovereignty overrides the others, while quasi-territorial sovereignty overrides personal sovereignty, Bin Cheng, supra, note 4, at p.183.

154

14.   Paragraph 2 of the same Article provides further that
"A ship which sails under the flags of two or more States,
using them according to convenience, may not claim any of
the nationalities in question with respect to any other State
and may be assimilated to a ship without nationality".   Of
identical formulation is also the corresponding Article 80 of
the R.S.N.T. Part II, entitled, "Status of Ships".
15.   See also the relevant Article 79 of the R.S.N.T. Part
II, entitled "Nationality of Ships".
16.   M.S.McDougal and W.T. Burke, The Public Order of
the Oceans, 1962, at pp.1084-1085.   See also Sir Humphrey
Waldock in RECHTSGELEERDE ADVIEZEN, at pp.35-36.
17.   (1948), A.C.351.
18.   Ibid., pp.369-370.
19.   Sir Humphrey Waldock in RECHTSGELEERDE ADVIEZEN,
at p.36.
20.   Hall's International Law, 8th edition, 1924, at
pp.300-301.
21.   Sir Humphrey Waldock in RECHTSGELEERDE ADVIEZEN, at
p.31.
22.   Even in relation to ships Hall has supported the view
that "Putting aside the fiction of territoriality as untenable,
it may be taken for granted that the jurisdiction exercised
by a State over its merchant vessels upon the ocean is conceded to it in virtue of its ownership of them as property
in a place where no local jurisdiction exists," Hall, supra,
p.306.   See further N.M. Hunnings, Pirate Broadcasting in
European Waters, 14 I.C.L.Q. (1965), pp.410-436, at p.427.
23.   D.H.N. Johnson in RECHTSGELEERDE ADVIEZEN, p.5
at p.8.
24.   Hackworth, Digest of International Law (1941), Vol. II.
p.680.
25.   For a disucssion on the legal vacuum theory see in
general H.F. Van Panhuys and M.J. Van Boas, Legal Aspects of
Pirate Broadcasting: A Dutch Approach, 60 A.J.I.L. (1966),
pp.303-341, at pp.322 and 332-333;   Sir Humphrey Waldock
in RECHTSGELEERDE ADVIEZEN, p.27 et seq; and C.W. Walker,
Jurisdictional Problems Created by Artificial Islands, 10
San Diego Law Review (1973), pp.638-663, at pp.657-658.
26.   C.W. Walker, supra, at p.657.
27.   To determine the 'nearest' coastal State the
criteria employed for the delimitation of the continental
shelf would seem to be most appropriate, Van Panhuys, supra,
at p.322.
28.   See, for example, C.J. Colombos in RECHTSGELEERDE
ADVIEZEN at p.4;   D.H.N. Johnson, ibid., at p.8;   and
Sir Humphrey Waldock, ibid., at p.31.
29.   Quoted in 4 M. Whiteman, Digest of International
Law, para 2, at pp.54-55.
30.   Sir Humphrey Waldock in RECHTSGELEERDE ADVIEZEN,

at p.31.

31.   Indeed, the claim to jurisdiction and the subsequent North Sea Installations Act, 3 December 1964, were in essence based on the three distinct legal grounds of (a) the legal vacuum theory; (b) the protection of legal interest; and (c) the notion of contiguity, see in Van Panhuys, supra, p.331 et seq.

32.   M.W. Mouton, The Continental Shelf, 1952, p.240.

33.   Award reported in 22 A.J.I.L. (1928), p.867 at p.910.

34.   C.J. Colombos in RECHTSGELEERDE ADVIEZEN, at p.4. Of the same opinion were also Prof. D.H.N. Johnson, ibid., p.9 and Sir Humphrey Waldock, ibid., p.38.

35.   N.M. Hunnings, supra, note 22, at pp.410-412.   See also IMCO DOCS. MSC XII/23/Add. 3-5, 1966 and MSC XV/9/Add.1, 6 February 1967.

36.   See in general Sir Humphrey Waldock in RECHTSGELEERDE ADVIEZEN, at pp.34-35; N.M. Hunnings, supra, note 22, at pp.417 -424; Van Panhuys and Van Boas, supra, note 25, at pp.323-324; and J.C. Woodliffe, Some Legal Aspects of Pirate Broadcasting in the North Sea, 12 Netherlands International Law Review (1965), pp.365-384.

37.   Territorial Waters Order in Council, 1964; see E.D. Brown, Delimitation of Maritime Frontiers: Radio Stations in the Thames Estuary, 2 Australian Yearbook of International Law (1966), pp.99-113.

38.   Sir Humphrey Waldock in RECHTSGELEERDE ADVIEZEN, p.34.

39.   IMCO DOC. MSC XII/23/Add.1, 10 December 1965, p.2.

40.   Sir Humphrey Waldock in RECHTSGELEERDE ADVIEZEN, p.34.

41.   1967 Chapter 41, 14 July 1967; see also in U.N. Leg. Ser. ST/LEG/SER.B/15, 1970, at p.294.

42.   IMCO DOC. MSC XII/23, Annex I, 30 November 1965, p.2.

43.   Art. 2 (bis) of the Belgian Act of May 14, 1930, as amended on December 18, 1962; see Van Panhuys and Van Boas, supra, note 25 at pp.323-324, and N.M. Hunnings, supra, note 22 at pp.420-421.

44.   On the Scandinavian States' legislation on "pirate" broadcasting, see in general, N.M. Hunnings, supra, note 22, at pp. 417-420, and Van Panhuys and Van Boas, supra, note 25, at pp.323-324.

45.   Article 1 of the Norwegian Act of .22 June 1962.

46.   Article 1 of the Swedish Act of 27 July 1962 (No.400); S.1 (3) of the Danish Telecommunications Act of 12 April 1949 (No. 188), as amended on 22 June 1962; and Article 1 of the Finnish Act promulgated on 27 July 1962.

47.   The Agreement came into force on 19 October 1967. For the text see Cmnd 2616; European Treaty Series, No. 53; reprinted also in 59 A.J.I.L., 715; 14 I.C.L.Q., 434; and 4 I.L.M., 115, (1965).   See in general Van Panhuys and Van Boas, supra, note 25, pp.324-326; N.M. Hunnings, supra, note 22, p.433; and J.C. Woodliffe, supra, note 36, pp.381-384.

48.   Council of Europe, Consultative Assembly,
Recommendation 422; see also in 59 A.J.I.L. (1965), p.719
and in 14, I.C.L.Q. (1965), p.436.
49.   See the Preamble to the Agreement and also Regulation
422 of the I.T.U. Radio Regulations.
50.   See, for example, the IMCO Assembly Resolution A.107
(IV), adopted on 28 September 1965.
51.   IMCO DOC. A.V/Res. 117, 25 October 1967.
52.   Memorandum by the International Frequency Registration
Board (I.F.R.B.) of the International Telecommunication Union
(I.T.U.) on Broadcasting Stations Operated on Board Ships,
Aircraft or Other Floating or Airborne Objects Outside
National Territories, in IMCO DOC. MSC XII/23/Add. 2,
21 December 1965, p.10.
53.   C.J. Colombos in RECHTSGELEERDE ADVIEZEN, at p.3.
54.   Sir Humphrey Waldock in RECHTSGELEERDE ADVIEZEN, at p.36.
55.   Ibid.
56.   Ibid., at p.37.
57.   W. Riphagen, International Legal Aspects of
Artificial Islands, IV International Relations (1973), pp.327-
347, at p.343.
58.   North Cutt Ely, The Laws Governing Exploitation of
the Minerals Beneath the Sea, in Exploiting the Ocean, Transactions of the 2nd Annual Marine Technology Society Conference,
Washington D.C., 1966, cited in F.T. Christy, Alternative
Regimes for Marine Resources Underlying the High Seas, 1
Natural Resources Lawyer, (1968), No.2, pp.63-77, p.72.
59.   Ibid.
60.   See in the 1969 Report of the Sea-Bed Committee,
pp.81-161, at pp.148-150.
61.   For a relevant discussion, see further N.M. Hunnings,
supra, note 22, at pp.427-430 and B.S. Murty, The International
Regulation of the Uses of Sea-Bed and Ocean Floor, 9 Indian
J.I.L. (1969) pp. 72-77 at p.76.
62.   M.W. Mouton, The Continental Shelf, 1952, pp.309-312.
63.   C.W. Walker, supra, note 2, at p.663.
64.   U.N. DOC.A/AC.138/91, 11 July 1973.
65.   Ibid.
66.   Ibid.
67.   20 August 1974, UNCLOS III, Caracas Session,
Committee II.
68.   W. Riphagen, supra, note 57, at p.343.
69.   See R.S.N.T., Part I.
70.   D.M. Johnston, Law, Technology and the Sea,
55 California Law Review (1967), pp.449-472, at p.451.
71.   For a detailed analysis of these provisions see
further below, chapter 5.
72.   W. Riphagen, supra, note 57, at p.345.
73.   Ibid.
74.   There is no doubt that the same principle holds true

and under international customary law.   See Matson Navigation
Co. and Union Oil Co. of Calif. v. United States, U.S. Court
of Claims, 5 June 1956, in International Law Reports, 1956,
at p.128.

75.   U.N. DOC. A/AC.138/SC.II/SR.4-23 at p.66 et seq.

76.   Ibid.

77.   For a relevant discussion see, for example, in
C.W. Walker, supra, note 2, at p.262.

78.   L. Henkin, Arctic Anti-Pollution: Does Canada Make
- or Break - International Law? 65 A.J.I.L. (1971), pp.131-136,
at p.132.

79.   D.H.N. Johnson in RECHTSGELEERDE ADVIEZEN at p.10.
See also Sir Humphrey Waldock, ibid, at pp.31 and 39.

80.   Van Panhuys and Van Boas, supra, note 25, at p.337.

81   See in Margue Report, supra, at p.15.

82.   U.N. DOC. A/AC.138/91, of 11 July 1973; see
also in the 1973 Report of the Sea-Bed Committee, Vol. II,
pp. 9-11, at p.9.

83.   A.W. Koers, Artificial Islands in the North Sea,
in J.K. Gamble and G. Pontecorvo (eds), Law of the Sea:
The Emerging Regime of the Oceans, Proceedings, Law of the
Sea Institute, Eighth Annual Conference, June 18-21, 1973,
ch.11, p.223, at p.229.   See also H.G. Knight, Law of the Sea
Negotiations 1971-1972, From Internationalism to Nationalism,
9 San Diego Law Review (1972), p.383, at p.389.

84.   For an English translation of the Act see in Van
Panhuys and Van Boas, supra, note 25, at pp.340-341, (an
extensive discussion of the contents of the Act may be found
at pp.326-330); see also in IOC, Technical Series, No.5, at
pp.23-24.

85.   Van Panhuys and Van Boas, supra, note 25, at p.329.

86.   See Ch. III, Articles 44 and 48, R.S.N.T. Part II.

87.   A.H.A. Soons, Artificial Islands and Installations
in International Law, July 1974, Law of the Sea Institute,
University of Rhode Island, Occasional Paper No 22 at p.23.

Part two

Chapter 5

INSTALLATIONS FOR THE EXPLORATION AND EXPLOITATION OF
THE NATURAL RESOURCES OF THE CONTINENTAL SHELF UNDER
THE GENEVA CONVENTION, 1958

Industrial exploration and exploitation of the sea-bed and
subsoil of the high seas has so far been restricted to the
continental shelf resources due to economic and technological
reasons.   The Geneva Convention on the Continental Shelf (1958)
remains, accordingly, the only existing international treaty
which currently regulates the exploration and exploitation of the
sea-bed resources.   Naturally, therefore, any examination of
the legal regime of the installations and structures used for
such exploration and exploitation must be based on the said
Convention, which moreover, largely reflects international
customary law.   However, the exploration for the resources
of the deep sea-bed has already started while exploitation is to
begin soon.   Thus, reference will be made to the relevant
provisions of the Revised Single Negotiating Text concerning
installations constructed or operated in the international sea-
bed area for exploration and exploitation purposes.   In addition,
the relevant Articles covering economic activities in the
exclusive economic zone will also be reviewed in the appropriate
context.   First, however, the existing resources and the
present state of technology will be considered briefly.

I.   RESOURCES AND TECHNOLOGY

1.   Resources

The term 'natural resources' is defined as follows by
Article 2(4) of the 1958 Geneva Convention on the Continental
Shelf:

"The natural resources referred to in these articles

consist of the mineral and other non-living resources of the
sea-bed and subsoil together with living organisms belonging to sedentary species; that is to say, organisms
which, at the harvestable stage, either are immobile on
or under the sea-bed or are unable to move except in constant physical contact with the sea-bed or the subsoil" (1).

With respect to the international sea-bed area, the term
'resources' in Part I of the Revised Single Negotiating Text
covers only "mineral resources in situ" (Article 1 (iii)).
The mineral resources may be divided into :
(a)   marine hydro-carbons;   (b)   superficial deposits; and
(c)   minerals extracted from sea-water.

(a)   Marine Hydro-carbons

This term refers to crude oil, natural gas and gas condens-
ate.   Oil and gas are by far the most important marine minerals
accounting for almost 90 per cent of the value of minerals
recovered from the sea-bed.   Off-shore production now stands at
about 3.3 billion barrels of oil and 50 billion cubic feet of
gas per year.   This represents 18 per cent of the world petroleum production and 10 per cent of total gas production (2).
Moreover, 172.8 billion barrels of recoverable oil are estimated
to lie off shore, while world proved reserves under 200 meters
of water amount to 128.4 billion barrels of oil (3).
It is generally assumed that marine hydro-carbons are
associated with thick sedimentary layers which occur for the
most part in proximity to land masses rather than far from
shore in deep ocean basins.   According to a report of the
U.N. Secretary-General, "little if any economically exploitable
oil or natural gas is likely to be found in the deep sea-bed in
the next few decades" (4).   However, according to an expert
petroleum geologist, "opinion of the potential of the world's
deep ocean areas may well undergo significant re-evaluation.
And it is possible that the deeper ocean may be a potentially
larger area than was underestimated" (5).   The same expert believes
further that: "Excluding Russia, China and the Middle East,
most of the world's undiscovered oil resources, 71%, underlie
the oceans and their continental margins - the shelf, slope
rise and deep marginal basins with water depths up to 1,770
meters (6000 feet) (6).

(b)   Superficial Deposits

Superficial deposits refer to all unconsolidated sediments
lying on the sea-bed and include sand and gravel, tin, heavy
mineral sands, iron sands and diamonds.   Phosphorite nodules
also exist on the outer continental shelf and in some areas, they
may be found in commercially significant quantities (7).

Current exploitation of these hard minerals is limited to those deposits on the continental shelf that can be recovered by dredging at moderate depths. Sand and gravel continue to be the most important, with an estimated annual production volume of more than 45 million tons, compared to nearly 20 million tons of calcium carbonate (shells) and less than one million tons for all other dredged minerals (8).

Offshore deposits of tin are dredged mainly off the coasts of Malaysia, Thailand and Indonesia in waters up to 40 meters in depth. These operations account for over 10% of the world's tin production. Alluvial deposits of tin exist also off Cornwall, in England, and consolidated deposits are under investigation in the Laptev and East Siberian Seas in the Soviet Union, off Tasmania and in the Philippines (9).

Heavy mineral sands (bearing chromite, limenite, rutile and platinum) are being developed by the Soviet Union in the Black, Baltic and Azov Seas, and also in the Sea of Japan. Gold-bearing sands have been found off Nome and Junean (Alaska), in Sakhalin and Tinkan Bays (Soviet Union), and exploration continues in the United Kingdom (Mawddach tidal estuary, Wales) and in Australia (mouth of Burdekin River). Diamonds have been dredged from the continental shelf of South-West Africa since 1961 (10).

However, for the next two or three decades, manganese nodules are expected to be the main minerals of economic interest in the international sea-bed area. Nodule deposits have been found on the floor of every ocean, while the richest deposits are apparently lying in the central-east Pacific. Estimates may vary considerably, but all seem to be agreed that there are immense quantities of these deposits in the deep sea-bed. According to a specialist, there are 1,500,000 million tons of nodules on the floor of the Pacific alone, to which a further 10,000 million tons are added every year (11). On the other hand, a Soviet source has estimated that there are 90 trillion tons of manganese on the floor of the Pacific alone (12), while an IOC report puts the total reserves of nodules of possible economic interest, at one trillion tons (13).

The value of manganese nodules lies in the metals which they contain, principally nickel, copper, cobalt and manganese. These nodules undergo a cycle of constant renewal and most scientists believe that they begin as tiny metal grains that precipitate from chemical solutions, e.g. salt water (14). Extensive work has been carried out over the last decade to locate the most attractive nodule deposits and to develop nodule mining and processing systems. More than $100 million has been spent in surveys and exploratory work by firms and other institutions of Australia, Canada, Federal Republic of Germany, France, Japan, the Soviet Union, the United Kingdom and the United States (15). However, at present, "there is not a single commercial nodule mining operation functioning and none is

expected before 1977 at the earliest and probably not until
1980" (16). Moreover, in view of "the highly sophisticated
nature of nodule mining and processing, the stiff cost of the
entrance fee and the complexity of operating on a multinational
scale under novel legal rules to be established by the international regime and machinery", it would seem certain that
the nodule industry will be a very restricted club indeed, at
least for the near future (17). Thus, according to a report
by the U.N. Secretary-General, "fewer than ten ventures are
likely to become operational within the next decade" (18). In
fact, there has been an increasing tendency towards the merging
of the individual firms in the western countries, and at present
there are only five consortia actively engaged in nodule
prospecting and sample mining. These are headed by Tenneco,
Inc., (it owns Deepsea Ventures which does the actual work
under a service contract); Kennecott Copper Corp. (this
consortium includes Noranda Mines from Canada, Rio Tinto Zinc
and Gold Fields of the United Kingdom, and Mitsubishi of Japan);
International Nickel Co (it heads Deepsea Mining Co., a group
of Japanese companies, and A.M.R., a group of German firms);
Ocean Resources Inc.; and Summa Corporation, the well-known
venture launched by H. Hughes and the CIA (19).

(c)   Minerals Extracted from Sea Water

Many of the minerals contained in solution in sea water
are necessary to the world's chemical industry. Sea chemical
plants in a number of countries already extract sodium chloride
(in the form of common salt) potassium chloride, magnesium
chloride, sodium sulphate, magnesium metal and bromine.
Active research and development for dissolved chemical extraction is continuing in Idia, while the Government of Iceland
is planning the development of a sea chemical plant in
Reykjanes to extract minerals from sea water and from geo-
thermal brine.

The desalination of sea water has continued to find
increasing application over the past few years. The first
economically working desalination plants were installed in
1953 in Kuwait. Another plant with a capacity of 18,800
cubic metres per day is under construction in Hong Kong. The
use of nuclear energy for desalination continues to be under
consideration. An experimental plant, which has been in
operation in the Soviet Union since 1973, provides for dual
purpose application an output of 200 megawatts of electricity
and 1.2×10^8 litres of water per day. Evidently, the use
of desalinated water is particularly important for industrial
purposes in arid areas. Oil producing countries in arid
climates, for example, are important users of desalinated
ocean water (20).

However, it should be made clear that this last category

of minerals is not covered by either the term 'natural resources' as the latter is defined in Article 2 (4) of the 1958 Continental Shelf Convention, or the term 'resources' in Part I of the Revised Single Negotiating Text concerning the international sea-bed area. On the other hand, such·minerals extracted from sea-water in the exclusive economic zone clearly fall under Article 44 (1) (a) of R.S.N.T.,Part II, which provides that the coastal State has in the exclusive economic zone, "sovereign rights for the purpose of exploring and exploiting, conserving and managing the natural resources, whether living or non-living, of the bed and subsoil and the superjacent waters."

2.   Technology

Generally speaking, the installations and structures used for the exploration and exploitation of the mineral resources may be divided into : (a) installations fixed on the sea-bed; (b) mobile installations or units; and (c) floating craft.
    Contemporary fixed platforms used for off-shore oil and gas production are rather elaborate structures using three or more structural towers with a platform on top. Steel structures for oil production are secured by driving piles from the legs deep into the sea-bed. Concrete platforms, on the other hand, rest on the sea-bed by virtue of their own weight, and thus require no piling. The base of the platform can be used as an oil storage facility. A third type of production platform is a combination of the two former types, consisting of a concrete base resting on the sea-bed, with a steel superstructure. These structures provide living quarters for the work crew, a helicopter landing pad, storage space for supplies, and room for the drilling and production equipment. Production platforms, which cost around £45 million, including the equipment modules, are already feasible in 600 to 800 feet of water under moderate weather conditions. Exxon oil company is currently testing a model of a 24-well platform, with an overall height of about 1,800 ft. for the 1,500 ft. deep waters of the North Sea (21). Fixed platforms, however, are economically and technically limited in applicability in deep waters. There is an exponential rise in cost as depth increases. The greater the distance from the shore, the more likely it is for the industry to use mobile units as opposed to fixed structures that rest on the ocean bottom.
    For oil and gas exploration, three types of drilling rigs, all of them mobile, have been developed. The first type of mobile rig is the jack-up rig which rests on legs on the sea-bed and can only be used in relatively shallow waters, for example up to 300 ft. in moderate seas. On arrival at site, the legs are lowered to the sea-bed and the drilling platform is raised above the surface of the sea by jacks acting on the legs. Next in line are the semi-submersible drilling rigs,

which are suitable for deep waters and more severe climatic
conditions. They rest on floats or pontoons which are submerged beneath the surface of the water and are anchored
to the sea-bed. They cost between £15 and £25 million to
build and in the region of £20,000 to £25,000 a day to hire.
They can operate in depths of up to 500 meters, although 200
meters is more common. However, dynamically positioned
semi-submersibles, which obviate the use of anchors, will be
used at even greater sea depths. Such a semi-submersible that
will drill in 4,000 ft. water has already been developed by
Forex Neptune (22).

Still deeper waters require drilling ships. These can be
used in very deep waters, i.e. beyond the continental shelf, and
are kept in position over the well by a complex system of
computer controlled thruster motors enabling them to maintain
an exact and stable position on the well, whatever the direction
of wind and current. The best known drilling ship, the Glomar
Challenger, has worked in 3,710 meters of water and has found
traces of oil at a depth of 4,000 meters of water in the Gulf
of Mexico. Recently, it bored to a record depth of 1,412 meters
in explorations conducted on the Atlantic Continental Shelf (23).
About 350 rigs and drilling ships are in operation around the
world, while 146 rigs were reported in 1975 to be under construction in various parts of the world (24).

The tremendous cost and difficulties of installing
fixed production platforms in deep waters have led oil companies
to develop undersea production systems. Indeed, as the oil
industry moves further from shore, the installation of subsea
production systems is increasing rapidly. According to one
survey there are more than 60 such systems, operating around
the world (25). The main advantage of these systems is, of
course, their ability to produce in much deeper waters than
the conventional production platforms. Although petroleum
exploration has been carried out in depths of over 5,000 ft. and
wells have been drilled in up to 2,000 ft. of water, commercial
production has so far been limited to depths of around 400 ft.
Undersea systems, on the other hand, will permit production
in several thousand feet. Their use is also expected to be
considerably cheaper than platform systems in deeper waters,
particularly in depths beyond 600 ft. At its simplest level,
an undersea system consists of underwater well heads which
are completed from the surface. At their highest technical
level, they involve a large underwater chamber or base, which
is in effect an underwater production platform. The largest
group in the field is Subsea Equipment Associates Limited
(SEAL), which has developed three new systems of undersea oil
and gas production (26).

With regard to superficial deposits, sea-bed mining in
shallow waters utilizes dredging technology to obtain such
minerals as gold, tin sands, iron sands, titanium, and calcium

carbonate as well as sand gravel (27). The technological principles of dredging are comparatively simple and involve sea-bed
excavation by mechanical digging or suction with equipment
mounted on a barge or vessel. Thus, the wire line method
utilizes a "drag bucket" or "clamshell dredge" to scoop sea-bed
material and is capable of operating in relatively rough wave
conditions. The continuous bucket ladder system has a great
digging capacity and the hydraulic (suction) dredge with a
cutting head has a high production capacity. However, both
systems are restricted to sheltered sea conditions. The capital
investment for dredging systems is generally less than 5 million
dollars per system.

In contrast to shallow water mining, which employs
existing technology for dredging, mining operations on the deep
sea-bed require large scale and capital intensive technological
innovations. As regards in particular mining of manganese
nodules, which, as was said earlier, are expected to be the
main minerals of economic interest in the deep sea-bed, several
methods have been suggested. However, only two nodule collection system concepts have progressed so far from the drawing
board stage and are now being tested at an overall pilot-plant
level (28).

The first concept is the continuous line bucket system
(CLB). This consists of dredging the sea-bed by means of
buckets arranged on a long continuously rotating cable loop
and which carry out the collecting and raising functions in
sequence.

The second concept concerns a hydraulic system which has
been developed by Deepsea Ventures, Inc. The nodules are
collected by a bottom dredger which moves along the ocean
floor, pushing away obstructions and gathering up nodules to a
suction inlet where the moving water carries them up the
dredge pipe. Deepsea Ventures have operated such a system on
the Blake Plateau off the coast of Georgia and South Carolina
in 3,000 ft. depth. They are confident that this system will
also work at a depth of 18,000 ft.

In the long term, the uses of ocean space associated
with the exploitation of the resources of the sea will grow and
intensify. Indeed, there is no technological limit to such
exploitation given the necessary motive and financial resources.
As has been observed elsewhere, "one point is clear: the
ultimate brake on exploitation will arise from economic factors
rather than the limits of production systems or exploratory
drilling technology" (29).

II.   THE OUTER LIMIT OF THE CONTINENTAL SHELF

The open-endedness of the definition of the term
'continental shelf' in the 1958 Geneva Convention (exploitability criterion), has given rise to an endless discussion on
the correct interpretation of that term and to a voluminous
literature on the subject (30).   A similar discussion is,
of course, beyond the scope of the present study.   It need only
be emphasized that, irrespective of where the seaward limit of
the continental shelf is drawn, the legal regime contemplated
by the Geneva Convention on the Continental Shelf applies to
installations and other devices constructed and operated landward of the outer limit.

However, the Revised Single Negotiating Text has now
abandoned the exploitability criterion.   Article 64 of Part
II, defines the continental shelf as extending either to the
outer edge of the continental margin, or to a distance of 200
nautical miles where the outer edge of the continental margin
does not extend up to that distance.

With respect to the exclusive economic zone, Article 45
of the R.S.N.T. (Part II) lays down that its breadth "shall
not extend beyond 200 nautical miles from the baselines from
which the breadth of the territorial sea is measured."

It follows that the new Convention for the deep sea-bed
shall apply "to the sea-bed and ocean floor and subsoil thereof
beyond the limits of national jurisdiction, hereinafter called
the 'Area'" (31), i.e. beyond a distance of 200 nautical miles
from the territorial sea baseline or beyond the outer edge of
the continental margin when the latter exceeds the 200-mile
distance.   It is assumed, of course, that continental margin
areas beyond 200 miles will ultimately be included in the
definition of the continental shelf, an issue unresolved so
far.

III.   RIGHTS OF THE COASTAL STATE OVER ITS
CONTINENTAL SHELF

Article 2 (1) of the Geneva Convention confers upon the
coastal State sovereign rights to explore the continental shelf
and exploit its natural resources.   The formula 'sovereign
rights' rather than 'sovereignty' was chosen because the I.L.C.
wanted to make clear the decisive importance of safeguarding
the full freedom of the superjacent sea and the air space above
it (32).   Furthermore, Article 3 lays down explicitly that
these sovereign rights of the coastal State over the continental
shelf do not affect the legal status of the superjacent waters
as high seas, or that of the airspace above these waters.   The
sovereign rights referred to in Article 2 (1), are exclusive in
the sense that they can be exercised only by the coastal State
and nobody else, without the express consent of the coastal

State.   It is further provided that these rights do not
depend on occupation, effective or notional, or on any express
proclamation (Article 2, paras 2 and 3).

It should also be mentioned in the present context that
Articles 65 (coastal State rights) and 66 (superjacent waters
and airspace) of the Revised Single Negotiating Text, Part II,
repeat verbatim the provisions of Articles 2 and 3 respectively
of the 1958 Geneva Convention.

As regards the legal status of the superjacent waters of
the continental shelf, the question arises whether the coastal
State may take action against foreign shipping in that area
to protect its exclusive rights in the continental shelf.
Bearing in mind the purpose of the Continental Shelf Convention,
which is to safeguard and make effective the exclusive rights
granted to the coastal State, it is submitted that the latter
would be entitled to exercise a limited degree of jurisdiction
and control over foreign shipping in the waters superjacent to
the shelf for this purpose.   Professor Brown, for instance,
has suggested that :

"Whilst it has to be admitted that the question is
not free from doubt, the most reasonable conclusion
would seem to be that, in the interests of a functionally
effective interpretation of the coastal State's sovereign
rights, a limited degree of jurisdiction and control over
foreign vessels in the high seas above the shelf must be
admitted" (33).

Professor Shigeru Oda, on the other hand, has proposed that,
for the effective exercise of the coastal State's jurisdiction,
the superjacent waters of the continental shelf be given the
same status as the contiguous zone (34).   The importance
of the recognition of the right of interference with the
freedom of navigation above the continental shelf will be seen
more clearly in the section dealing with the problem of
jurisdiction over installations and safety zones.

With respect to the exclusive economic zone, it will be
remembered that the coastal State enjoys therein: "Sovereign
rights for the purpose of exploring and exploiting, conserving
and managing the natural resources, whether living, or non-
living, of the bed and subsoil and the superjacent waters."
It also enjoys exclusive jurisdiction with regard to:
"Other activities for the economic exploitation and exploration
of the zone, such as the production of energy from the water,
currents and winds" (35).   It will be noted that unlike the
continental shelf, the coastal State enjoys within the
exclusive economic zone sovereign rights and exclusive
jurisdiction not only over all mineral and living resources,
but also over all economic activities.

1.   Right of the Coastal State to Construct
       Maintain or Operate Installations and
       other Devices

As has been stated elsewhere, "In the present state of
technology, it would be illogical to recognise these rights (i.e
rights of exploration and exploitation) without also recognising the corollary - the right to exploit these resources by
means of structures or devices situated in, or extending
into, the superjacent high seas" (36).   Indeed, Article 5,
para. 2 of the Continental Shelf Convention 1958, spells out
clearly this corollary right of the coastal State, as regards
the continental shelf:

> "Subject to the provisions of paragraphs 1 and 6
> of this article, the coastal State is entitled to
> construct and maintain or operate on the continental
> shelf installations and other devices necessary for
> its exploration and exploitation of its natural
> resources, and to establish safety zones around such
> installations and devices and to take in those zones
> measures necessary for their protection."

Two points have to be emphasised in relation to the said
Article 5, para. 2.   First, paragraph 2 covers only installations connected with the exploration and exploitation of the
natural resources of the continental shelf.   The coastal
State, therefore, is not entitled to construct or operate
installations for the recovery of 'other resources' lying on
the sea-bed of the continental shelf, such as archaeological
relics, sunken ships or other lost objects, by virtue of
the Continental Shelf Convention 1958.   Such 'other resources'
do not fall within the 'natural resources', according to
Article 2, para. 4, of the Convention.   Thus, installations
constructed on the continental shelf for the recovery of
these 'other resources' will not be placed under the jurisdiction of the coastal State by virtue of Article 5 of the
Continental Shelf Convention (37).   It is equally clear that
Article 5 does not cover artificial islands and installations
erected on the continental shelf for any other uses.   Secondly,
following the principle enunciated in Article 2 of the
Convention - exclusiveness of sovereign rights over the continental shelf resources - it is clear that only the coastal
State is entitled to construct installations and other devices
for exploration and exploitation purposes.   No-one else may
do the same without the express consent of the coastal State.
Thus, in the United Kingdom,for instance, the Crown is vested
with "any rights exercisable by the United Kingdom outside territorial waters with respect to the sea-bed and subsoil and their
natural resources...." (38).   Similar provisions are contained

in the United States Outer Continental Shelf Lands Act, 7 August 1953, S. 1332 (39), and in the Soviet Union Continental Shelf Act, S.3 (40).

In relation to the safety zones referred to in para. 2 of Article 5, paragraph 3 of the same Article provides further that they "may extend to a distance of 500 meters around the installations and other devices which have been erected, measured from each point of their outer edge. Ships of all nationalities must respect these safety zones."

On the other hand, the coastal State enjoys exclusive rights and jurisdiction with regard to the establishment and use of all artificial islands, installations and structures in the exclusive economic zone (41). Article 48, para 5, of the R.S.N.T., Part II, provides further for safety zones which "shall not exceed a distance of 500 meters" around artificial islands, installations and structures erected in the said zone.

Provision for safety zones around stationary and mobile installations relating to the exploration and exploitation of the resources of the international sea-bed area, is also made in Article 16, para 2 (iii) of the R.S.N.T. Part I.

2. Obligations of the Coastal State During the Construction, Maintenance or Operation of Installations and other Devices

(a) To Give Due Notice of the Construction of any Installations

According to Article 5 para. 5, of the Geneva Convention, "Due notice must be given of the construction of any installations, and permanent means for giving warning of their presence must be maintained." The primary purpose of this provision is to protect the right of navigation, and to a lesser degree fishing, in the area under consideration. For that purpose all interested parties and not only Governments, (that is, any groups interested in navigation and fishing), should be duly notified of such constructions, so that they may be marked on charts (42). Installations should be suitably equipped with warning devices, such as lights, radar, buoys, audible signals, etc.

Paragraph 5 provides further that "Any installations which are abandoned or disused must be entirely removed." Here again, the over-riding principle is the protection of the other users of the seas. Interference with navigation and fishing-interference with trawling and likely damage to nets - can be avoided by obligations imposed upon the coastal State to completely remove abandoned installations.

Municipal legislation of States parties to the Convention contains similar provisions aimed at safeguarding other users

of the high seas and balancing conflicting interests (43).
     Similar provisions are also contained in Part II of the
R.S.N.T., concerning artificial islands, installations and
structures erected in the EEZ, and in Part I, covering installations constructed in the international sea-bed area for
exploration and exploitation purposes (44).

(b) Not to Interfere Unjustifiably with
     Navigation, Fishing or the Conservation of
     the Living Resources of the Sea

     Article 5 of the Continental Shelf Convention attempts
to apply "the basic principle of the unaltered legal status of
the superjacent sea and the air above it", pronounced in the
preceding Article 3 of the Convention, to "the main manifestations of the freedom of the seas, namely, freedom of navigation
and of fishing" (45).   Thus, Article 5 (1) lays down that :

> "The exploration of the continental shelf and the
> exploitation of its natural resources must not
> result in any unjustifiable interference with navi-
> gation, fishing or the conservation of the living
> resources of the sea......"

It will be noted that what is prohibited by this Article
is not any kind of interference but only unjustifiable interference.   The ILC, in introducing this qualification, commented
that:

> "The extent of that modification must be determined
> by the relative importance of the needs and interests
> involved...... The case is clearly one of assessment
> of the relative importance of the interests involved.
> Interference, even if substantial, with navigation
> and fishing might, in some cases be justified.   On
> the other hand, interference even on an insignificant
> scale would be unjustified if unrelated to reasonably
> conceived requirements of exploration and exploitation
> of the continental shelf......" (46).

These general rules offer no easy solutions to conflicting
interests on the continental shelf, except, maybe, in extreme
cases, where the discrepancy between the competitive interests
is only too obvious.   When, however, these interests are more
evenly balanced, the solution would be much more difficult.
It would then be "a question of making a value judgment on
the basis of the best available economic and social data, which
would include - but not over-emphasise - the economic
and social consequences of the priority in time of the establishment" of the navigation, fishery or conservation interest (47).

Admittedly then "... current international law has little
to offer to the solution of such conflicts beyond the general
concepts of reasonableness and equity" (48).   However,
bearing this in mind, it has to be emphasised that in the case
of competing interests, assessment of the relative importance
of the interests involved carried out in good faith may prove
a very useful guideline.   As has been observed elsewhere :

> ".....In evaluating allegedly unjustifiable interference
> there should be taken into account such factors as the
> relative economic importance of the competing interests
> to each State;   the impact of any change in the economy
> and society of the affected States;   the availability
> of alternative fishing grounds, fishing techniques, or
> navigation channels;   the possibility of employing other
> and less disruptive exploitation methods;   and the
> long-range benefits or detriments to be expected not
> only for the States concerned but also for the region
> as a whole.   Proper evaluation of such elements would
> require the combined attention of statesmen, jurists,
> economists, social scientists, fishery experts, mariners,
> and engineers;   but it would not seem beyond the limits
> of human ingenuity to reach tolerable adjustments in
> most instances" (49).

As regards navigation, Article 5 (6) prohibits the
establishment of installations and other devices, and safety
zones around them, where interference may be caused to the
use of recognised sea lanes essential to international
navigation.   Unfortunately, problems of interpretation and
practical application arise here as well.   What is a "recognised
sea lane"?   And what is considered to be "essential to international navigation"?   Can there be such a lane where only a
handful of ships pass through it?   Again, how wide should such
a lane be?   This clearly involves the problem of navigational
safety and efficient exploitation.   The problem of warning
arrangements suitable for installations situated on the
edges of the sea lanes has also to be faced.
    In relation to conservation of the living resources of the
sea Article 5 (7) provides further that the coastal State is
obliged to take all appropriate measures in safety zones around
installations for the protection of the living resources of
the area from harmful agents (50).

      (c)   Prohibition of Any Interference with
            Fundamental Oceanographic or Other Scientific
            Research Carried out with the Intention of
            Open Publication

According to the formulation in Article 5 (1) of the 1958

Continental Shelf Convention, the freedom of scientific
research seems to enjoy a relatively greater degree of protection
than the freedoms of navigation, fishing or conservation of
living resources, all of which are merely protected from
unjustifiable interference. This provision must, however, be
read in the light of Article 5 (8) which subjects scientific
research concerning the continental shelf to the condition of
the prior consent of the coastal State (51).

(d) Not to Impede the Laying or Maintenance of
Submarine Cables or Pipelines

The freedom to lay submarine cables and pipelines is
codified in Articles 2 and 26-29 of the Geneva Convention on
the High Seas 1958 (52).   This freedom, in common with other
freedoms, must, of course, be exercised with reasonable
regard to the interests of other users of the seas.
Under Article 4 of the 1958 Continental Shelf Convention
and Article 26 (2) of the High Seas Convention, the coastal
State may not impede the laying or maintenance of submarine
cables or pipelines on the continental shelf, subject, however,
to its right to take reasonable measures for the exploration
of the continental shelf and the exploitation of its natural
resources.
Thus, the coastal State is clearly forbidden either to
remove arbitrarily a pre-existing cable or pipeline on its
shelf, or to prohibit in general the laying of new cables
or pipelines by others.   However, in order to avoid unjustif-
able interference with exploitation activities, it may impose
conditions concerning the route to be followed (53).   Requirements as to construction standards and minimum depths would not
appear to be beyond the competence of the coastal State either,
provided they are reasonable and non-discriminatory.   Prior
consultation between the coastal State and the owners of the
cables and pipelines to be laid on the continental shelf is,
normally, to be expected.   Conflicts would, thus, by and large
be avoided and a reasonable accommodation of the competing users
achieved.

IV.   LEGAL STATUS OF INSTALLATIONS AND OTHER
DEVICES

There are two methods used for exploration and exploitation
of the natural resources of the submarine areas adjacent to a
coastal State:

1.   Exploration and exploitation by means of tunnels
driven from the coast, that is tunnelling from
terra firma;   and

2. Exploration and exploitation in the sea by means
of structures located on or above the continental
shelf.

1. Tunnelling from Terra Firma

Article 7 of the 1958 Continental Shelf Convention provides that, "The provisions of these Articles shall not
prejudice the right of the coastal State to exploit the
subsoil by means of tunnelling irrespective of the depth of
water above the subsoil."
It is, thus, quite clear that such exploration and
exploitation is outside the scope of the Continental Shelf
Convention and so far as international regulation is concerned,
it is still governed by international customary law. The
reason, of course, is that the purpose of the Convention is
to minimise interference with the freedom of the high seas,
and the exploitation of the subsoil of the high seas by
tunnelling from terra firma does not result in any such
interference (54).

2. Exploration and Exploitation by Means of Structures
Located on or Above the Continental Shelf

As has been seen, Article 5 (2) of the 1958 Continental
Shelf Convention provides that the coastal State, in order
to explore and exploit the natural resources of its continental
shelf, is entitled to construct and maintain or operate thereon
"installations and other devices" necessary for that purpose.
A definition of "installation and other devices" is not
provided in either the Convention or the ILC's Commentaries.
It is very difficult to draw a line between installations or
devices and ships pure and simple. Indeed, many of the
'devices' used for exploration and exploitation are 'ships'
in every sense of the word, such as drilling ships. Many
of the installations also, when transported from one site to
another, behave like ships, and semi-submersible, self-
propelled drilling rigs, could be held by a judge to be 'ships'.
The Convention, in any case, does not treat the installations
and devices as though they were ships and this becomes clear
if one reads Article 5 carefully. The same Article 5 lays
down, moreover, in para 4, that such installations and devices
are under the jurisdiction of the coastal State. We also find
in the ILC's Commentary to Article 71 (now Article 5) that,
".....the installations are under the jurisdiction of the
coastal State for the purpose of maintaining order and of
the civil and criminal competence of its courts" (55). The
clarification of the term 'installations and devices' is of
crucial importance in view of these provisions. Take, for
instance, a drilling ship carrying out exploratory work above

the continental shelf, which is registered as a ship and flies
the flag of a State other than the coastal State.   How could
such a ship, which surely is a "device necessary for the
exploration and exploitation", be subjected to the jurisdiction
of the coastal State, and especially "for the purpose.....
of the civil and criminal competence of its courts"? (56).
It follows from the principle of freedom of navigation,
sanctioned by both international customary law and the High
Seas Convention 1958, that, unless in accordance with exceptional
rules, such as those on piracy or permissive rules provided by
treaty, a State cannot interfere with a ship of foreign
nationality on the high seas, (the waters above the continental
shelf are certainly high seas - Article 3 of the Continental
Shelf Convention).   Indeed, much of the remainder of the
High Seas Convention spells out this rule in detail (57).

    It is, therefore, quite clear that the drilling ship in
question is either a 'ship' or a 'device' used for the
exploration and exploitation of the natural resources, but
it cannot be both in the legal sense of the terms used.
Assuming, thus, that a certain type of maritime craft will
be held by a judge to be a ship in international law, it
will be subject to the exclusive jurisdiction of the flag
State on the high seas above the continental shelf, whereas if
it is an 'installation or device' it will be under the
jurisdiction of the coastal State.   Unfortunately both the
Continental Shelf Convention and subsequent municipal legislation
of either States parties to the Convention or of non-parties
fail to make the necessary distinctions, thereby causing
confusion.   Article 3 of the French Law No. 68 - 1181 of
30 December, 1968 relating to the continental shelf, however,
expressly includes sea-going vessels which directly participate
in exploration and exploitation activities on the continental
shelf under the term "installations and devices" (58).

    Regarding the legal status of "installations and devices",
the Convention does, however, provide in Article 5 (4), that
these do not possess the status of islands, even though they
are under the jurisdiction of the coastal State.   It is
further provided in the same paragraph that these installations
and devices have no territorial sea of their own, and their
presence does not affect the delimitation of the territorial
sea of the coastal State (59).

    It is submitted that for the purposes of the Continental
Shelf Convention the notion of 'installations and other
devices' must be interpreted in the widest possible sense,
because the installations and devices used are of a vast
variety.   Prima facie, of course, it includes ships participat-
ing in exploration and exploitation activities above the
continental shelf.   These are subject to the jurisdiction of
the coastal State and not the flag State whilst in operation.

    Thus, as regards the legal status of installations and

other devices used for exploration and exploitation of the
natural resources of the continental shelf, it is clear that
these cannot be assimilated to ships or islands.   The Geneva
Convention on the Continental Shelf has, more or less, created
a distinct legal category of maritime structures.   It should,
of course, be added that attempts have also been made elsewhere
to gain recognition for the existence of such a separate legal
category of maritime structures.   This is already the case with
the devices collecting scientific data in the seas (ODAS).
During the preparations for the Draft Convention on ODAS the
idea was put forward that ".... platforms and installations
for the exploration and exploitation of the continental shelf..."
should be covered by the legal regime contemplated for ODAS.
However, it was decided in the end to delete these from the
definition of ODAS (60).

At the IMCO Maritime Safety Committee, on the other hand,
the American Delegation has supported the view that a new
breed of vessel has been created, as a result of the exploitation of sea-bed resources.   Unlike the conventional passenger
and cargo vessel, they have argued, these new vessels,
".....do not carry persons or goods from port to port.   Rather
they are intended to be an operating platform, factory, laboratory and hotel for undertakings at sea.   Many of these craft
have little resemblance to conventional vessels and may rest
on the sea-bed while in the operating mode.   These craft
come in a variety of shapes, configurations and operation
conditions.   There are often great numbers of individuals -
neither seamen nor passengers, who are employed and living
aboard these craft round the clock.   This combination of
conditions has led the United States to conclude that there
should be considered a third category of vessels, besides the
passenger and the cargo vessel, called "industrial vessels" "(61).
The novel concept of the "industrial vessel" has, thus, been
introduced by the United States.   Corresponding changes in
U.S. Regulations reflect this development :

"Industrial Vessel
This term means every vessel which by reason of its
special outfit, purpose, design, or function engages
in certain industrial ventures.   Included in this
classification are such vessels as drill rigs.....
dredgers, cable layers, derrick barges, pipe laying
barges, construction and dredging barges.....

Industrial Personnel
This term means every person carried on board an
industrial vessel for the sole purpose of carrying
out the industrial business or functions of the
industrial vessel.   Examples of industrial personnel
include tradesmen, such as mechanics, plumbers,

electricians and welders; labourers, such as wreckers and construction workers; and other persons, such as supervisors, engineers, technicians, drilling personnel, and divers" (62).

It would appear from the above definition of industrial vessel that this includes in principle mobile installations or units and floating structures. The United States delegation did not propose that this novel concept should at present be adopted internationally. It was merely pointed out that such a category could facilitate "....an overall approach to safety problems not constrained by configurations and consider- ations which were developed for other purposes." Indeed the need for uniformity in safety measures applicable to these new special purpose vessels is necessitated by the fact that many off-shore mobile units may operate from time to time on the continental shelves or in the territorial seas of various countries. Operating personnel, moreover, are employed from different countries and the owners are of different nationalities. It would appear, therefore, necessary and desirable to adopt as many common rules as possible, so that a drilling rig approved in one country will not be rejected for drilling in another country (63).

As regards fixed installations, such as production platforms, the United States delegation observed that, when manned, they have many of the same characteristics as a bottom bearing industrial vessel. Since, however, most of the fixed platforms are unmanned, regulations concerning safety measures for these should be left to the discretion of the individual country (64).

The United States has, finally, proposed that a revised SOLAS (International Convention for the Safety of Life at Sea, London, 17 June 1960), Convention should also include provisions for the industrial vessels (65).

V.   JURISDICTION OF THE COASTAL STATE OVER INSTALLATIONS OR DEVICES AND SAFETY ZONES

It was noted earlier that the coastal State is entitled to exercise a limited degree of jurisdiction and control over foreign shipping in the waters above the continental shelf to protect its exclusive rights to continental shelf resources.

Indeed, as regards installations and safety zones, the jurisdictional rights of the coastal State are quite clearly spelt out by Article 5 of the 1958 Continental Shelf Convention. Paragraph 4 makes it clear that installations and other devices constructed or operated for exploration and exploitation purposes, are under coastal State jurisdiction. Paragraph 2 lays down that, subject to the provisions of paragraphs 1 and 6, the coastal State is entitled to establish safety zones

around installations and devices, and to take in those zones
measures necessary for their protection.   Paragraph 3
provides further that ships of all nationalities must respect
the safety zones.

With regard to installations and other devices, the
position is clear and no further comment is necessary.   Any
act or omission which takes place on, under or above them will
be under the competence of the coastal State's courts.   They
are subject to any regulations and orders issued by the
coastal State authorities, such as those concerning maintenance
of order on the installations, safety measures, registration,
etc.   Thus para. 6 of the ILC's Commentary on Article 71,
(now Article 5), provides that,

> "...the installations are under the jurisdiction
> of the coastal State for the purpose of maintaining
> order and of the civil and criminal competence of
> its courts" (66).

The same, however, cannot be said for the safety zones,
where the position is not clear and certain questions arise.
In relation to these, it is only stated that coastal States
may take the measures necessary for the protection of the
installations and devices.   What kind of measures could come
under such a classification? Is the power to take necessary
measures within the safety zones more or less the same as the
jurisdiction enjoyed upon the installations, or should a distinction be drawn between them? Do the rights enjoyed within
the safety zones extend to penal sanctions for unauthorized entry
into these by foreign ships, and what powers of interference
with foreign shipping are generally implied in these provisions?
In view of Article 3 of the Convention, which preserves the
legal status of the superjacent waters of the shelf as high
seas, there is prima facie, a strong presumption in favour of
a restrictive interpretation of the coastal State's powers to
interfere with foreign shipping.   Bearing in mind, however,
the need for an effective protection of the coastal State's
exclusive rights over exploration and exploitation, a more
extensive interpretation is advocated.   A foreign vessel, for
instance, which strikes an installation after entering the
safety zone must, surely, be liable to seizure and punishment
by the coastal State.   According to the latter interpretation,
therefore, penal sanctions are deemed necessary for the
effective protection of installations and other devices (67).

A brief·examination of the municipal legislation of a number
of State parties to the Continental Shelf Convention 1958, will
illuminate further these provisions and the suggested interpretation.

United Kingdom.   The Continental Shelf Act was

enacted by the British Parliament in April 1964 (68). Its
purpose is to bring English law into line with the provisions
of the Continental Shelf Convention 1958, and also to regulate
exploration and exploitation activities carried out in the
North Sea (69). The United Kingdom, by enacting this legislation, has certainly adopted the more extensive interpretation
and, indeed, it has been argued that Section 2 of the Continental Shelf Act 1964 goes further than the Convention, and
that it is contrary to the fundamental rule of international
law concerning the freedom of the high seas. Section 2
reads as follows :

> "2. (1) The Minister of Power may for the purpose of
> protecting any installation in a designated area
> by order made by statutory instrument prohibit
> ships, subject to any exceptions provided by
> the order, from entering without his consent
> such part of that area as may be specified in
> the order (70).
>
> (2) If any ship enters any part of a designated
> area in contravention of an order under this
> section its owner or master shall be liable –
> (a) on summary conviction, to a fine not
> exceeding one hundred pounds or to imprisonment
> for a term not exceeding three months, or to
> both;
> (b) on conviction on indictment, to a fine or
> to imprisonment for a term not exceeding one
> year, or to both; unless he proves that the
> prohibition imposed by the order was not, and
> would not on reasonable inquiry have become,
> known to the master."

Prima facie, this appears to go too far (71). Section 2
refers potentially to the whole or any part of the United
Kingdom's continental shelf (by reason of the definition of
"designated area")(72). As has been pointed out, however,
the purpose of any such prohibitory order would be the protection of installations in 500 meters "specified areas" around the
installations, and, indeed, in practice the orders so far
issued under Section 2 are restricted to such 500-meter safety
zones. In view of the Geneva Convention provisions any
attempt to prohibit navigation anywhere outside the 500-meter
safety zones would certainly appear to be illegal.
It is thus clear that the sanctions provided for in Section
2 of the Act may be imposed upon foreign shipping entering the
safety zones, since foreign vessels are not included in the
exceptions to the scope of the orders promulgated according to
the Act. This might appear to be a far-reaching interference

with the freedom of navigation on the high seas to the
advocates of such an absolute freedom, but it is, nevertheless,
a reasonable interpretation of the coastal State's power,
recognised in the Convention, to take measures necessary for
the protection of installations and other devices on its
continental shelf.

Section 3 provides for the application of the criminal
and civil law with respect to -

"Any act or omission which -
(a)   takes place on, under or above an installation in
      a designated area or any waters within five hundred
      meters of such an installation; and
(b)   would, if taking place in any part of the United
      Kingdom, constitute an offence under the law
      in force in that part;"
any such act or omission "shall be treated for the purposes of
that law as taking place in that part" (73).

The same Section provides further for the exercise of
jurisdiction by United Kingdom courts with respect to questions
arising out of acts or omissions taking place in a "designated
area", or in any part of such an area, ".....in connection
with the exploration of the sea-bed or subsoil or the exploitation of their natural resources....." (para.2).

The importance of Section 3, thus, clearly lies in the
extra-territorial application of the English criminal law.
This confers jurisdiction on English courts over criminal
offences committed within the relevant areas.   According to
Article 11 (1), further, proceedings for any offence under
this Act, including of course offences under Section 3 (1),
may be taken, and the offence may for all incidental purposes
be treated as having been committed, in any place in the
United Kingdom.   A constable has on any installations in
a designated area all powers, protection and privileges as if
he were on the mainland (Section 11, para 3).

United States.   In the United States the legal
regime of the continental shelf is regulated by the Outer
Continental Shelf Lands Act 1953 (74).   Section 4 of the
Act extends the "Constitution and laws and civil and political
jurisdiction of the United States.... to all artificial islands
and fixed structures which may be erected thereon for the
purpose of exploring for, developing, removing and transporting
resources therefrom, to the same extent as if the outer
Continental Shelf were an area of exclusive Federal jurisdiction
located within a State" (75).

It is clear from the wording of this Section that artificial
islands, structures, and installations erected for exploration
and exploitation purposes on the continental shelf, are treated,

for jurisdictional purposes, as though they were part of the
mainland.   The same Section further adopts as "the law of
the United States for that portion of the subsoil and sea-bed
of the outer Continental Shelf, and artificial islands and fixed
structures erected thereon" the "civil and criminal laws of
each adjacent State" as of the effective date of the Act, 7 August, 1953, to the extent the State laws are not inconsistent
with the Act or other federal laws and regulations.

Soviet Union.   Section 4 of the Russian Decree of
6 February 1968 relating to the Continental Shelf, provides
that "installations and devices and the safety zones around
them shall be under the jurisdiction of the Union of Soviet
Socialist Republics.   Foreign ships may enter the safety
zones only with special permission of the competent Soviet
authorities" (76).

Clearly, then, as regards jurisdiction, no distinction
whatsoever is made between installations and safety zones.
Both the criminal and civil jurisdiction extend to installations
and safety zones.   Foreign shipping is prohibited from entering the safety zones unless special permission is granted.
Since the reference is only to foreign shipping, does that
mean that Russian ships may enter without the special permission
of the authorities? (77).   Section 6 prescribes rather severe
penalties for violations of the Decree, including of course
foreign shipping (78).

France.   Article 4 of the French Continental Shelf
Act 1968 (79), provides for the establishment of safety
zones to a distance of 500 meters around installations and
other devices used for exploration and exploitation of the
shelf resources.   The same Article provides further that
entry into these safety zones for reasons unconnected with
the exploration or exploitation activities is prohibited
without permission (80).

Article 5 lays down that subject to the provisions of
the Act, French laws and regulations shall apply on the installations and devices as though the latter were situated on
French metropolitan territory, for as long as they are
engaged in exploration and exploitation activities.   "These
laws and regulations shall apply under the same conditions to
the safety zones, for the purpose of controlling operations
being carried out there as well as for the maintenance of
public order."

Extra-territorial application of French municipal laws,
is thus explicitly provided for by Article 5, as regards the
installations and safety zones around them.   Here, again, it
can be seen that the French Act adopts an extensive interpretation of Article 5 of the 1958 Continental Shelf Convention,
for an effective protection of the exclusive coastal rights

over exploration and exploitation of the shelf resources.

Australia. According to Article 119 of the Petroleum (Submerged Lands) Act, 1967, the Designated Authority may, for the purpose of protecting a well, structure or any equipment on the continental shelf, prohibit all vessels from entering or remaining in a specified area (safety zone) surrounding the well, structure etc. without the consent in writing of that Designated Authority (81). The safety zone extends to a distance of 500 meters around the installations measured from each point of the outer edge of the well or structure (para.2).

Where a vessel enters or remains illegally in a safety zone the owner and the person in charge of the vessel are each guilty of an offence punishable by a penalty not exceeding a fine of 10,000 dollars, (para.3).

New Zealand. Section 8, entitled 'Regulations', of the Continental Shelf Act 1964 (82) lays down that,

> "(1) The Governor-General may from time to time,
> by order in Council, make regulations for
> all or any of the following purposes:
> (a) Regulating the construction, erection,
> or use of installations or devices.....
> ....
> (c) Establishing safety zones, extending to a
> distance not exceeding five hundred meters.....
> (d) Prescribing such measures..... necessary in any
> safety zone for the protection of the instal-
> lation or device.....
> (e) Regulating or prohibiting the entry of ships
> into any such safety zone;
> ....
> (k) .... (l) Prescribing penalties for
> breaches of the regulations not exceeding a
> fine of five hundred pounds."

Sweden. Article 6 of the Swedish Act No. 314 of 3 June 1966 concerning the Continental Shelf, provides for the establishment of 500 meters safety zones around installations (83). The same Article also provides that unless otherwise provided in that Act or elsewhere, ships shall not be permitted to sail into the safety zones without the consent of the owner of the installation.

Article 10 lays down further that Swedish law shall apply on installations or safety zones established outside Swedish territorial limits. In this connection, the installations and safety zones shall be deemed to be situated within the nearest part of the Swedish territorial sea.

Finland. The construction of installations and establishment of safety zones are provided for by Article 5 of the Law No. 149 Concerning the Continental Shelf, 5 March 1965 (84). It is further stipulated in the same Article that "It shall be unlawful to navigate in a properly marked safety zone.....without the permission of the supervising authority or to contravene any other provision concerning the protection of a safety zone....." Violation of the Act entails punishment by fines and cancellation of the permission granted for the construction of installations and establishment of safety zones (Article 7).

Malta. The Maltese Continental Shelf Act 1966, has in many ways been based on the United Kingdom Continental Shelf Act, 1964 (85). According to Section 4, para 1, "The Prime Minister may for the purpose of protecting any installation or other device in a designated area by order.... prohibit ships..... from entering without his consent such part of that area as may be specified in the order." Violation of this provision entails punishment by fine and/or imprisonment (Section 4, para.2). Section 6 provides for the application of the criminal and civil law with respect to any act or omission which takes place on, under or above an installation or other device in a designated area, or any waters within five hundred meters of such an installation or device and which "would, if taking place in any part of Malta, constitute an offence under the law in force in Malta." It also provides that for jurisdictional purposes "any installation or device in a designated area and any waters within five hundred meters of such an installation or device shall be treated as if they were situated in the island of Malta," (para.2), (86).

Yugoslavia. According to Article 24, of the Law of 22 May 1965, "it is prohibited for the ships to navigate through... safety zones, except when allowed by special regulations" (87). The establishment of installations and other devices necessary for exploration and exploitation operations, and of safety zones (500 meters) around these installations, is provided for by Articles 23 and 24.

Portugal. Article 25 of the Portuguese Decree No.47973 of 1967, provides for the establishment of safety zones, to a distance of 500 meters, around installations and other devices used for the exploration and exploitation of the shelf resources (88). It is further provided in a Sole Paragraph that "unless expressly authorized by the Ministry of Marine, ships, aircraft and other water-borne or air-borne vessels not connected with the operations shall be prohibited from entering the safety zone."

Venezuela. Article 5 of the Act of 27 July 1956 (89) distinguishes between installations and the safety zones around them. Thus, the installations "shall be subject to the sovereignty of the Republic," whereas in the safety zones, it is merely provided, that the Republic shall "take such measures for the protection of these installations as it considers necessary." The same questions, as those with the corresponding Article 5 of the Geneva Convention, arise here. What kind of measures are deemed necessary for such a protection, and do these extend to penal sanctions for unauthorized entry into the safety zones by foreign ships? According to the more extensive interpretation advocated above, the answer should be in the affirmative.

Malaysia. Section 5 of the Continental Shelf Act 1966 (90), provides for the application of the criminal and civil law with respect to every act or omission which takes place on or under or above, or any waters within 500 meters of, any installation or device necessary for the exploration and exploitation of the shelf resources; every such installation or device or safety zones shall be deemed, for jurisdictional purposes, to be situated in the Federation (paras. 1(a) and (b)). Every Court in the Federation which would have jurisdiction (whether civil or criminal) in respect of that act or omission if it had taken place in the Federation, shall have jurisdiction accordingly (para. 1 (c)):

"every power of arrest or of entry or search or seizure or other power..... in respect of any such act or omission..... may be exercised on or in respect of any such installation or device or any waters within five hundred meters thereof as if the installation or device or such waters were in the Federation;" (para 1 (d)).

Section 6 further empowers the Yangdi-Pertuan Agong to make regulations for (a) the construction, erection, or use of installations or devices.....(c) the establishment of safety zones extending to a distance of 500 meters,..... (e) regulating or prohibiting the entry of ships into any such safety zone.....(i) prescribing penalties for breaches of the regulations, not exceeding 5,000 dollars.

In the writer's opinion, it is clear that the preceding, albeit brief, examination of the municipal legislation of a number of State Parties to the Geneva Convention on the Continental Shelf 1958, supports the view that an extensive interpretation of Article 5, as regards jurisdiction over installations and safety zones, is widely accepted. Penal sanctions, therefore, are included as necessary for the effective protection of installations and other devices. Indeed,

only such an extensive interpretation is in accordance with
the need for an effective protection of the coastal State's
exclusive rights over exploration and exploitation, and
the subsequent practice of State Parties to the Convention
confirms this, as demonstrated above.

NOTES

1.   Of identical formulation is also Article 64 (4), in
Chapter IV, concerning the Continental Shelf, of the R.S.N.T.,
PART II.

2.   U.N. DOC.E/5650, 30 April 1975, at p. 7, (Report of
the U.N. Secretary-General on the Uses of the Sea).

3.   Ibid., at p.7 and Annex II, at p.8.

4.   U.N. DOC.A/CONF.62/37, 18 Feburary 1975, "Economic
Implications of Sea-Bed Mining in the International Area", paragraph 1.

5.   Paper presented at the Ninth World Petroleum Congress,
held in Tokyo in 1975, by Mr. J.D. Moody, a retired Mobil Oil
Corp. Senior Vice-President.   See in World Oil, Vol. 181, No.4,
September 1975, pp.47-56, at p.50.

6.   Ibid.   Theoretically oil may be found at a depth
of 62,620 feet in sandstone and 51,300 feet in limestone,
Cloninger, How Deep Oil and Gas may be Expected, World Oil,
Vol. 130, No.6, May 1960, at p.60.

7.   DOC. E/5650, at pp.9-11.

8.   Ibid., at p.9

9.   G. Askevold, Ocean Mining in Perspective, 4 Stanford
Journal of International Studies, 1969, p.115 et seq, at
pp.125 and 129;   DOC. E/5650, at pp.9-10.

10.   G. Askevold, supra, at pp.126-127 and DOC E/5650, at p.10.

11.   T. Loftas, Wealth from the Oceans, 1967, at p.46.

12.   Cited in W.T. Burke, Ocean Sciences, Technology
and the Future International Law of the Sea, 1966 at p.38.

13.   Draft of a General Scientific Framework for World
Ocean Study, prepared by IOC, UNESCO, Paris 1965, at p.22.

14.   A recent hypothesis is that manganese nodules owe their
existence to microscopic marine organisms which participate in
their formation, DOC. E/5650, at p.10.

15.   Ibid.

16.   M.I. Glassner, The Illusory Treasure of Davy Jones'
Locker, 13 San Diego Law Review 1976, p.533 et seq, at p.537.

17.   DOC. A/CONF/62/37, supra, note 4, para. 4.

18.   Ibid.

19.   Ibid.   See also M.I. Glassner, supra, at pp.537-538, and
13 San Diego Law Review, 1976, at p.656.

20. See in general DOC. E/5650, at p.11, and 10C Draft 1965, supra, note 13, at pp.21-23.

21. Ocean Industry, December 1975, Vol. 10, No.12, at p.35.

22. Ibid., at p.40.

23. 13 San Diego Law Review 1976, at p.656.

24. INVESTORS CHRONICLE - Offshore Oil Worldwide, A Survey of September 5, 1975, at p.15.

25. DOC. E/5650, at p.19.

26. See A. Jaffe (Vice-President of SEAL), SEAL's Subsea Petroleum Productions Systems, 16 March 1973. The original parent companies of SEAL were British Petroleum, Compagnie Francoise des Petroles, Westinghouse Electric Corporation, and Groupe DEEP. Mobil Oil became later the fifth partner in SEAL.

27. See in general Document A/CONF.62/C.3/L.22, 27 February 1975, Description of some Types of Marine Technology and Possible Methods for their Transfer: Report by the U.N. Secretary-General, paragraphs 34-40.

28. See in general DOC. A/Conf. 62/25, 22 May 1974, Economic Implications of Sea-Bed Mineral Development in the International Area: Report of the U.N. Secretary-General, at p.9 et seq; M. Gauthier and J. Marvaldi, The Two-Ship CLB System For Mining Polymetallic Nodules, Oceanology Internationa 75, 16/21 March 1975, Brighton, England, at pp.346-349; and J.E. Flipse, Deep Ocean Mining Technology and Its Impact on the Law of the Sea, in Law of the Sea Institute, Ninth Annual Conference, January 6-9, 1975, Law of the Sea: Caracas and Beyond, 1975, at pp.325-332.

29. M.M. Sibthorp (ed), The North Sea: Challenge and Opportunity, 1975, at p.56.

30. See, in general, B.H. Oxman, The Preparation of Article 1 of the Convention on the Continental Shelf, 3 Journal of Maritime Law and Commerce 1971-72, at pp.245-305, 445-472 and 683-723; E.D. Brown, The Legal Regime of Hydrospace, 1971, esp. at pp.3-40; L.F.E. Goldie, Where is the Continental Shelf's Outer Boundary? 1 Journal of Maritime Law and Commerce 1970, at pp.461-472; L.W. Finlay, The Outer Limit of the Continental Shelf, A Rejoinder to Professor Louis Henkin, 64 A.J.I.L. 1970, at pp.42-61; and Sh. Oda, Proposals for Revising the Convention on the Continental Shelf, 7 Columbia Journal of Transnational Law 1968, at pp.1-31.

31. Article 2 (1) of the R.S.N.T., Part I.

32. II ILC Yearbook 1956, at p.297.

33. E.D. Brown, supra, at p.94; for an extensive discussion on the protection of the exclusive rights on the continental shelf, see ibid., at pp.90-96.

34. Sh. Oda, The Geneva Conventions on the Law of the Sea: Some Suggestions for their Revision, 1 Natural Resources Lawyer (1968), pp.103-113, at pp.106-107.

35. See Article 44, para. 1 (a) and (c), of the R.S.N.T., Part II.

36. E.D. Brown, supra, at p.99.

37. See further the ILC's Commentary to Draft Article 68 (now Article 2), para 5, in II ILC Yearbook (1956) at p.298.

38. Continental Shelf Act, 1964, S.1 (1).

39. "U.S. Code" (1964 ed), Title 43 (Public Lands); see in U.N. Leg. Ser. DOC/ST/LEG/SER.B/15, 1970, at p.462 et seq. See Also S. 1333 (a) (1).

40. Decree of the Presidium of the Supreme Soviet of the U.S.S.R. dated 6 February 1968, entitled "On the Continental Shelf of the U.S.S.R." See in U.N. Leg. Ser. DOC/ST/LEG/SER. B/15, 1970, pp.441-443. All three countries have ratified the Continental Shelf Convention, 1958.

41. See Articles 44, para. 1 (b) and 48 para. 1 (a), (b) and (c), of the R.S.N.T., Part II.

42. See the ILC's Commentary to draft Article 71 (now Article 5) paras 4 and 5, in II ILC Yearbook (1956), at p.299.

43. See, for instance, § 1333 (e) of the U.S. Outer Continental Shelf Lands Act of 1953, concerning marking and equipment of artificial islands and structures, supra, note 39; S.4 of the U.S.S.R. Continental Shelf Act, supra, note 40; New Zealand, Continental Shelf Act 1964, (No. 28 of 1964; 3 November, 1964), U.N. Leg. Ser. DOC.ST/LEG/SER.B/15, 1970, at p.389 et seq., section 8 (1), (h) and (i) at p.391.

44. See Articles 48 (3), Part II, and 16, para. 2 (i), Part I, of the R.S.N.T.

45. See the ILC's Commentary to draft Article 71 (now Article 5), para. 1, in II ILC Yearbook (1956) at p.299.

46. Ibid.

47. E.D. Brown, supra, at p.96.

48. Ibid. For an excellent analysis of the conflicting uses and their reconciliation under the Geneva Convention on the Continental Shelf, see esp. at pp.87-103.

49. R. Young, Off-shore Claims and Problems in the North Sea, 59, A.J.I.L. (1965), pp.505-522, at p.521. On the competing interests, see esp. at pp.507-508 and 517-522.

50. See also the relevant Articles 48 (7), Part II, and 16, para. 2 (ii), Part I of the R.S.N.T. concerning installations and structures in the EEZ and the international sea-bed area respectively.

51. See further Chapter 7 in the section dealing with the deployment of ODAS in the shelf area.

52. As regards the protection of submarine cables, see also the Submarine Cables Convention 1884, in N. Singh, International Conventions of Merchant Shipping, 1973, second edition, at p.378.

53. See the ILC's Commentary to Article 70 (now Article 4), para. 1, in II ILC Yearbook (1956), at p.299. See further Article 67 of the R.S.N.T., Part II.

54. See also Article 74 (tunnelling), of R.S.N.T.,Part II.

55. See the ILC's Commentary to Article 71 (now Article 5),

para 6, in II ILC Yearbook (1956), at pp.299-300.

56. See Arts. 6 and 11 of the 1958 High Seas Convention
under which ships, save in exceptional cases, are subject
to the exclusive jurisdiction of the flag State on the
high seas.

57. See, for instance, Arts.8 and 9; which provide for
the complete immunity of warships·and public non-commercial
vessels from the jurisdiction of other States; Article 13,
which provides that, even in a case of the slave trade,
jurisdiction lies with the flag State; see further Article
22 - on boarding and search of foreign vessels; 23 - hot
pursuit; 24-29 - on pollution, submarine cables and pipelines,
etc.

58. See in U.N. Leg. Ser. Doc. ST/LEG/SER.B/15, 1970, at
p.356.

59. The same provision is also repeated in the Revised Single
Negotiating Text. See Arts. 48 (8) of the R.S.N.T., Part II
(concerning installations in the economic zone and the
continental shelf), and 16, para 2 (v), Part I (concerning
installations in the international sea-bed area).

60. Doc. SC-72/CONF.85/8, Paris, 30 March 1972, at p.6,
item 13; see also Draft Article 1 (2) on the definition of
ODAS, ibid., Annex III, p.4.

61. See IMCO Doc. MSC XVIII/7/1, 8 October, 1968; see
further Docs. MSC XXV/16, 15 March, 1972 and MSC XXV/16/1,
16 March 1972.

62. Doc. MSC XVIII/7/1, 8 October, 1968. For further
discussion and definitions of "special purpose ships" see IMCO
DOCS.MSC XXVIII/ 16, 7 August 1973, with Annexes thereto I-IV;
MSC.XXVIII/16/1, 30 August 1973; MSC XXVIII/SR.5, 1 March
1974, pp. 10-12; and MSC XXVIII/SR.6, 1 March 1974, pp.2-11.

63. IMCO DOC.MSC XVIII/7/1, 8 October, 1968.

64. IMCO DOC. MSC XVIII/7/1, 8 October, 1968.

65. The same delegation also noted that the U.S.S.R.
Government has submitted similar proposals, see IMCO DOC. XXV/16,
15 March 1972.

66. II ILC Yearbook (1956), para. 6, at pp.299-300.

67. See also E.D. Brown, supra, note 30, at pp.89, 100;
Sh. Oda, supra, note 34, at p.107.

68. 1964, Chapter 29.

69. For an extended analysis of the United Kingdom
Continental Shelf Act, 1964, see Colombos, International Law
of the Sea, 6th ed., 1967, at pp.78-81; L. Gombos, Continental
Shelf Act, 1964, 61 Law Society's Gazette (1964), pp.475-479;
C. Thornberry, Continental Shelf Act, 1964 (U.K). 27 M.L.R.,
(1964), pp. 573-576; J.C. Woodliffe, The Continental Shelf Act,
1964 - A Comment, The Solicitor Quarterly, Vol. 3 (1964),
pp.339-348; Alec Samuels, The Continental Shelf Act, 1964, in
Developments in the Law of the Sea 1958-1964 (published by the
British Institute of International and Comparative Law,

International Law Series, No. 3, 1965), pp.155-167;
J.W. Morris, Oil and Gas Legal Problems on the North Sea
Continental Shelf, 1 Natural Resources Lawyer, No.1, (1968),
pp.1-23.

70. The Continental Shelf (Protection of Installations)
(No.5) Order 1972 (S.I.1972, No.883) lays down that the
prohibition does not apply, in relation to a specified area,
to a ship engaged: (a) in the repair of any submarine
cables; (b) services for, or inspection, or the transport of
goods to and from an installation in that specified area;
(c) to a ship carrying out movements with a view to saving or
attempting to save life or property at sea; (d) to a ship
which enters that specified area owing to stress of weather; and
(e) to a ship in distress.

71. Alec Samuels, for instance, has supported the view
that Section 2 "is plainly contrary to the general rule of
international law, because penal or disciplinary proceedings
may only be instituted before the judicial or administrative
authorities either of the flag State or of the State of which
such person is a national", (see Article 11 of the Geneva
Convention on the High Seas, 1958), A. Samuels, supra, at p.162;
for a similar view see also Woodliffe, supra, at p.143, where he
favours a more restrictive interpretation.

72. Section 1 (7) of the Act provides that her Majesty may
from time to time by Order in Council designate any area within
which the rights mentioned in the Act are exercisable and such
area shall be referred to as a "designated area."

73. For the interpretation to be attached to this
terminology see the decision of the House of Lords in the case
of Cox v. The Army Council (1963), A.C.48, where similar
terminology was considered. (This case concerned the
interpretation of the Army Act 1955, S. 70 (in relation to
an offence arising out of careless driving in Germany).

74. Public Law 212 - 7 August 1953; "U.S. Code" (1964
ed) Title 43. For an extensive analysis of this Act see
R.B. Krueger, The Background of the Doctrine of the
Continental Shelf and the Outer Continental Shelf Lands Act,
10 Natural Resources Journal (1970), pp.442-514, and 763-810.

75. 43 U.S.C., S.1333 (a) (1).

76. Decree of the Presidium of the Supreme Soviet of the
U.S.S.R., dated 6 February 1968, entitled "On the Continental
Shelf of the U.S.S.R.", see in U.N. Leg. Ser. Doc. ST/LEG/SER.B/
15, 1970, pp.441-443; or in 7 I.L.M. (1968), pp.392-394.
See also the Decision of the Presidium of the Supreme Soviet of
the U.S.S.R. concerning the Application of the Decree of the
Presidium of the Supreme Soviet of the U.S.S.R. concerning
the Continental Shelf of the U.S.S.R., 13 August 1969, in
U.N. Leg. Ser. Doc. ST/LEG/SER.B/16, Vol.II, 8 May 1972,at p.159.

77. Such an interpretation would be illogical in view of
the purpose of the safety zones, which is to protect the
installations from any ships and not only from the foreign ones.

The more reasonable interpretation is that an additional
requirement is provided for foreign ships, but that navigation
within the safety zones is prohibited in general for all ships.

    78. Fines up to 10,000 roubles or imprisonment up to
one year or both are prescribed by this Section.

    79. Loi No. 68-1181 Du 30 Decembre 1968 Relative A'
L'Exploration du Plateau Continental et a L'Exploration
de Ressources Naturelles; see in U.N. Leg. Ser. DOC.ST/LEG/SER.
B/15, 1970, pp.356-358. For an English translation see in
New Directions in the Law of the Sea, edited by S.H. Lay,
R. Churchill and M. Nordquist, 1973, Vol.I, at p.310.

    80. Article 4 also provides that "restrictions may be
imposed on the over-flight of installations and devices and
safety zones to the extent necessary for the protection of
these installations and devices and for the safety of aerial
navigation."

    81 No.118 of 1967; 22 November 1967, see in U.N.Leg. Ser.
DOC.ST/LEG/SER.B/15, 1970, at p.319, et seq.

    82. No. 28 of 1964; 3 November 1964, see in U.N. Leg.
Ser. DOC. ST/LEG/SER.B/15, 1970, p.389, et seq.

    83. Ibid., at p.437 et seq.

    84. Ibid., at pp.354-355.

    85. Act No. XXXV of 1966, see in U.N. Leg.Ser. ST/LEG/SER.B/
16/Add.2, 2 April 1973, pp.82-84.

    86. Section 9, para 2, lays down that "A member of the
Police Force shall on any installation or device in a
designated area have all the powers, protection and privileges
which he has in Malta."

    87. Law of 22 May 1965, on Yugoslavia's Marginal Seas,
Contiguous Zone and Continental Shelf, see in U.N. Leg. Ser.
DOC.ST/LEG/SER.B.15, 1970, at p.473 et seq.

    88. Decree No. 47973 of 30 September 1967, ibid., at
p.423 et seq.

    89. Concerning the Territorial Sea, Continental Shelf,
Fishery Protection and Air-Space, ibid., at pp.472-473.

    90. Act of Parliament No. 57 of 1966, 28 July 1966, see
in U.N. Leg. Ser. DOC. ST/LEG/SER.B/15, 1970 at p.375 et seq.

Chapter 6

OCEAN DATA ACQUISITION SYSTEMS, AIDS AND
DEVICES (ODAS)

INTRODUCTION

Oceanography has been defined as "the scientific study
of that part of the earth which is covered with sea water.
Its objective is to increase human understanding of all
aspects of the oceans - the properties and behaviour of the
ocean waters, the nature of living creatures in the sea,
the interactions between the waters, the air above them, and
the solid earth beneath, and the shape and structure of the
oceans basins" (1).   There are, indeed, many good reasons why
we should study the oceans: Human needs for protein food and
greater knowledge of weather and climate, requirements for
monitoring the pollutants entering and contaminating the
natural environment, our increasing dependence on marine
minerals, and national needs for security can be mentioned.
Ultimately, one of the most important uses of the oceans
may prove to be a source of human protein food.   Since time
immemorial fish has been the staple sea-resource used by man,
yielding high food protein.   Oceanographic research may
result in savings in costs of goods and services, and increases
in production.   Environmental predictions which identify
harvestible populations will substantially aid fishing operations.   Exploration and exploitation of marine mineral
resources is clearly dependent on data as to their location,
quantity, exploitability and relatively accurate estimates of
benefit-cost ratios.
Environmental prediction improvements will contribute
significantly towards the reduction of loss of life and
property resulting from natural hazards - hurricanes, tornadoes,
floods and snow storms.   Effective advance warning can minimize

such losses.   Weather hazards, by conservative estimates, cost
the United States 1,200 lives and 11 billion dollars in
property damage annually (2).   In the long run, perhaps,
technological advances and increased inter-governmental
co-operation may lead from weather prediction to weather control.
Better forecasts of surface environment, (waves, winds and
currents), will also improve the capability to route ships and
lower the costs of freight.
      The dangers posed by pollution to our natural environment
are only too well known to be reiterated here.   Survival and
welfare of the human species depends, ultimately, on our
capability to preserve the environment.   Rational use of
the sea as a dumping ground for the waste products of our
industrialised societies depends largely on environmental
predictions.   There is no doubt that the marine environment
has the capacity to receive a certain amount of waste discharge
without damage to its other uses and to marine life in general.
Yet constant monitoring on the oceans and oceanographic
research of the rate of introduction of pollutants into the
marine environment is necessary so that the former will not
result in the degradation of the latter from the standpoint of
other uses, such as fishing and recreation.
      Finally environmental prediction improves, also national
defence and security interests, especially those of the
technologically advanced states.   Knowledge of the sub-surface
environment, for instance, is particularly significant for the
development of submarine warfare strategy and the permanent
establishment of habitats on the sea-bed.
      This much needed information is obtained through a great
variety of vessels, devices, automatic buoy stations, meteorological and communication sstellites, tools and systems.   A
multiplicity of international, national, local and private
programmes of oceanographic data acquisition are currently
under way and a major increase in this activity has already
been noted during the present International Decade of Ocean
Exploration (IDOE).   For example, programmes related to the
development of air-sea interface observational networks of
global dimensions have been undertaken and planned by the
Intergovernmental Oceanographic Commission (IOC) and the World
Meteorological Organization (WMO)   Regarding weather prediction
and communications instrumentation, global systems are represented by the Integrated Global Ocean Station System (IGOSS) and
the World Weather Watch (WWW).   Operationally, the WWW makes
use of buoys, ships, airplanes and satellites to cover the
ocean areas as well as existing and additional land-based
observation stations (3).
      The introduction of certain of these new research, data-
gathering devices creates novel legal problems concerning
inter alia: the legal status of Ocean Data Acquisition Systems
(ODAS);   the right of deployment of ODAS in the various

jurisdictional zones in the seas;   safety rules for the use
of ODAS and safety of navigation;   registration and jurisdictional problems concerning ODAS;   illegal acts and collision
liability.

It is accordingly the purpose of this and the following
chapters to examine mainly the international law aspects of
these new research instrumentalities operating in the marine
environment.

I.   THE WORK BY IOC/IMCO ON THE LEGAL STATUS
     OF, AND THE PREPARATORY CONFERENCE ON,
     ODAS (1972)

Prior to 1960, there was not one single organization
taking full responsibility for international co-ordination of
oceanographic research in the widest possible sense.   A
number of international organizations were dealing either with
regional or applied oceanographic problems.   In F.A.O. we
find, for instance, the Biology Branch of the then Fisheries
Division, and the two regional Fishery Councils, dealing with
marine science problems.   After the mid-1950's an International
Advisory Committee on Marine Science was formed in UNESCO.   In
the same period the Oceanographers organized themselves better
internationally at the non-governmental level, and the Special
(later Scientific) Committee on Ocean Research (SCOR) was
formed in ICSU (4).

By the end of the late 1950's the idea of an Intergovernmental Commission had been clarified.   Thus, the
Intergovernmental Oceanographic Commission (IOC) was established
under the aegis of UNESCO, at its Eleventh General Conference
in 1960, in order, "..... to promote scientific investigation
with a view to learning more about the nature and resources
of the oceans through the concerted action of its members,"
(Article 1 (2) of the Statues of IOC).

The main work in IOC is carried out by the many Working
Groups set up within that organization, which are bodies of
a technical character.   Two of these groups, however, are
of particular importance for the purposes of the present study.
They are the IOC Working Group on Legal Questions Related to
Scientific Investigations of the Ocean, and, primarily, the
IOC Group of Experts on the Legal Status of ODAS (5).   Indeed,
the legal problems associated with ODAS have been a subject of
study within the IOC for the past fifteen years.   During that
period close collaboration has been maintained with the IMCO.
As early as its first session in 1961 the IOC adopted Resolution
I - 7 asking its member States to provide information and
details on ODAS, requesting the establishment of a Working
Group of Experts to study "Fixed Stations", and recommending to
UNESCO "that steps be taken in consultation with IMCO to clarify
the legal status of unmanned and manned observing buoys" (6).

Pursuant to this Resolution, UNESCO entered into consultation
with IMCO and eventually a "Proposed Plan of Study" evolved.
The IOC Working Group on Fixed Oceanographic Stations considered in 1962 the Plan of Study and drafted a report for the
IOC (7).   IOC, in turn, recommended IMCO collaboration and
adopted Resolution II-18 requesting that the legal study be
continued by considering further relevant international maritime conventions with a view to defining in a new international
convention the legal status of fixed oceanographic stations;
requesting IOC members to report on domestic laws, regulations,
orders etc., concerning such stations, and regulations and
practices concerning the marking and identification of these
stations; and to suggest legal problems they would wish to
be considered in a new international convention concerning such
stations together with possible solutions that might be adopted
in an international convention (8).

The response from member States indicated that while
there was some awareness of the problems created by ODAS,
hardly any legislation existed specifically covering ODAS (9).
For example, Argentina, the United Kingdom and the Soviet Union
answered that they had no special legislation dealing with
Fixed Oceanographic Stations or regulations relating to the marking and identification of these (10).

In short, the existing state of affairs as regards ODAS
was perhaps best summed up in the following passage from the
reply of the United States:

"The international law as it presently stands is not
so free from obscurity that one can say what the
settled law with regard to this subject may be.   Since
these meteorological and oceanographic 'observing buoys'
are a relatively new development and in most cases
will not readily fit into established concepts, their
status and treatment probably could be most effectively
determined by an international convention" (11).

As a result of further consideration the IOC Group of
Experts on the Legal Status of ODAS prepared a Preliminary
Draft Convention at their fourth session held in London from
15-26 June 1970 (12).   This Draft was circulated to the
member States and the United Nations Organizations for comment.
The same Preliminary Draft Convention together with the four
Technical Annexes attached to it and the Comments and proposals
for amendments submitted by Member Governments and Organizations,
formed the basis of discussion for the Preparatory Conference
of Governmental Experts to Formulate a Draft Convention on the
Legal Status of ODAS.   The Preparatory Conference was held
in Paris under the auspices of UNESCO/IOC and IMCO from
31 January to 11 February 1972 (13).   It was attended by
delegates from 37 countries and representatives from seven

international organizations. An examination of the Report of
the Preparatory Conference and the Draft Convention shows that
the Conference did not intend to produce a final document and
one of its recommendations was that a second Preparatory
Conference be convened (14). Indeed, due to lack of time
the Conference examined approximately only half of the draft
Articles plus the Technical Annexes (15). The Conference did,
however, recommend the advance implementation of the Safety
Provisions for ODAS contained in Technical Annexes by Member
States without waiting for the adoption of the main Convention
which may take a number of years (16).

A number of preliminary questions proved quite controversial at the beginning of the discussion. The main question
was whether the Conference on ODAS or the U.N. Conference on the
Law of the Sea should come first and whether the Convention
should be allowed to encroach upon wider issues related to
the Law of the Sea and expected to be tackled at the U.N.
Conference. However, despite the fact that certain delegations
wished to widen the area of discussion it was noted that "There
was a general consensus of opinion that this Convention should
not be allowed to encroach upon wider issues basic to the Law
of the Sea, as this could prejudice decisions possibly to be
taken elsewhere" (17). It seems that there was a dichotomy
between those who wanted a broad discussion of all the major
problems in the Law of the Sea and those who wished to
keep the subject as narrow as possible. Thus, the President
was forced to emphasize, in response to comments, that
".....issues such as the legal regime of scientific research or
the limits of national jurisdiction would not be dealt with
in the Convention and were, therefore, not within the competence
of this Conference" (18). Indeed, the subsidiary issue of
the freedom of scientific research was one of the legal questions
which proved highly controversial. Other such issues were those
concerning the jurisdictional questions and matters relating to
private law such as civil liability.

As regards the latter in particular, a Group of Experts
on Private Law Aspects of ODAS has been set up for the purpose
of preparing draft articles to be included in the proposed
Convention on the Legal Status of ODAS. The first session of
this Group of Experts was convened by IOC, with the assistance
of IMCO, at Paris from 27 to 31 May 1974, and it examined all
basic elements of the problem, that is collision, civil liability
for interference with an ODAS, salvage, and penal responsibility
(19).

Finally, it should be mentioned that a second session
of the Preparatory Conference is hoped to take place after the
Third United Nations Conference on the Law of the Sea, while a
full diplomatic Conference, originally planned for 1973, is now
expected to be convened before the end of the present decade.

II.   THE PRELIMINARY DRAFT CONVENTION:
       DEFINING THE ODAS

ODAS stands for Ocean Data Acquisition Systems, Aids and
Devices, as has already been seen (20).   The original term
used by the IOC to describe the devices under consideration
was "Fixed Stations", later altered to ."Fixed Oceanographic
Stations" and subsequently to "Ocean Data Stations".   However,
difficulty arose from the fact that the term "Ocean Data Station"
was being used to describe both the geographical position at which
data is gathered and the devices used for this purpose.   To
overcome this difficulty the term "Ocean Data Stations" was
adopted to define geographical positions and the term "Ocean
Data Acquisition Systems" (ODAS) was introduced to cover the
ships, platforms, devices, etc., used to gather data (21).

Draft Article 1, para 2 defines an ODAS as follows :

"ODAS means a structure, platform, installation,
buoy or other device, not being a ship, together
with its appurtenant equipment, deployed at sea
((for non-military purposes) (for peaceful
purposes) (in non-military service)) essentially
for the purpose of collecting, storing or transmitting
samples or data relating to the marine environment
or the atmosphere or the uses thereof" (22).

The formulation of Draft Article 1 (2), is a little
unfortunate.   To provide that "ODAS means a structure,
platform, installation, buoy or other device not being a
ship....." is not very helpful in the absence of a definition
of a ship.   However, ships are definitely excluded from
the definition of ODAS, according to the present formulation.
There had been some discussion as to whether or not ships
should be covered and originally the term ODAS in the Proposed
Articles for the Preliminary Draft Convention expressly comprised
ships (23).
It is also clear that installations and other devices used
for the exploration and exploitation of the sea-bed are
excluded from the definitition of ODAS.   Any other platforms,
installations and artificial islands in general, such as floating
docks, floating airports, power stations, etc. are also excluded.
Generally speaking it only covers devices used for the collection of data.   In that context, however, the definition is
purposely wide and the Rapporteur has noted that "the wording
accepted has been developed in an effort to ensure that all
devices used at sea for the collection of data are covered
either by this Convention or by the accepted norms of
International Law relating to vessels" (24).   Thus, the
definition is not limited to ODAS collecting only oceanographic
data but it also covers ODAS collecting meteorological or geo-

biological research.

Another matter discussed was whether the Convention should be restricted to ODAS used for non-military or peaceful purposes. This apparently caused considerable discussion. The Swedish delegation raised this point and suggested the limitation of the Convention to ODAS used for non-military purposes. A number of other delegations found this unacceptable. They argued that it is difficult to distinguish military from non-military uses and deployment by civil as opposed to military bodies. No final agreement on this point was reached and it was similarly undecided whether there should be special rules for nuclear powered ODAS.

It was further suggested that the definition should be restricted to registered ODAS, whereas the Spanish delegation proposed that besides registration "it should be an additional requirement to have international confirmation thereof before ODAS could reap benefits from the Convention" (25). This, however, has to be seen in conjunction with Article 5 of the Draft Convention which proposes the establishment of special registers for ODAS, as is the practice for vessels. In effect only registered ODAS are to be covered by the Convention. Article 5, para 2, provides that "No benefits under the present Convention may be claimed in respect of unregistered ODAS." However, it is further provided that "Nevertheless, with a view to protecting other legitimate uses of the sea and the marine environment, State Parties undertake to apply the provisions of the present Convention to all unregistered ODAS wherever possible." (Para 3).

Draft Article 1 prescribes nine various modifying sub-definitions of ODAS which, according to the Rapporteur, "were developed to circumscribe carefully the application of a given Article to precisely the object in mind". In other words, these various types of ODAS will be treated according to their particular characteristics and structure in the context of certain rules, such as collision liability, salvage etc. Each sub-definition has been based on the functional design characteristics of the ODAS. This distinction was found to be essential "or else an ODAS would change its type and, in consequence, the regulations applying to it, for reasons beyond the control of the operator, e.g. an "anchored" ODAS which has broken adrift should remain subject to the regulations for "anchored" ODAS and should not suddenly become a "drifting" ODAS" (26).

ODAS which can be manned, unmanned, anchored, drifting, surface penetrating, sub-surface, bottom bearing, nuclear and dual mode may be classified as follows for working purposes (27):

A. Manned Systems.

    (i) Fixed structures - attached to the sea-bed,
         i.e. bottom bearing, or anchored -

       (a) Surface penetrating.
       (b) Sub-surface.

    (ii) Buoys and unconventional 'vessels' (FLIP, SPAR.etc)

       (a) Surface.
       (b) Sub-surface.

    (further sub-divided, as required, into moored and
    free floating or drifting systems).

B. Unmanned Systems.

    (i) Fixed structure - as A (i) above.
    (ii) Buoys - as A (ii) above.

Unconventional 'vessels' are covered in the Preliminary Draft Convention on ODAS by the term "dual mode," (horizontal and vertical types), which refers to such devices as FLIP (Floating Instrumented Platform)(28). The distinction regarding the dual mode ODAS is perhaps the most important from the law point of view. A "dual mode" ODAS is "a device an example of which is designed so that when on station and operation it is to float in a vertical or upright mode and when on passage to or from the station, it is to float in a horizontal condition. When in the vertical mode such a device is considered as an ODAS and is subject to this Convention; when in a horizontal mode, it is considered as a ship and will be subject to existing regulations for ships"(29).

The provision of a main definition followed by many modifying sub-definitions may appear to be a complicated and difficult process but, nevertheless, it is deemed to be a necessary and desirable method of classification due to the complexity of the subject matter itself. The appropriate legal rules must apply on the various types of ODAS according to their particular functional characteristics within a flexible framework. As the Rapporteur has commented:

> "The subject matter is sufficiently complex that it
> is difficult to develop a precisely circumscribed
> definition of ODAS that would be applicable to all
> the provisions of the draft convention. Hence a broad
> definition has been employed with suitably modifying
> language to effect the purpose of any given Article" (30).

NOTES

1.   Draft of a general scientific framework for
world ocean study, published by IOC, UNESCO, 1965, at p.8.
2.   Walter Orr Roberts, We're Doing Something about
the Weather, National Geographic, Vol. 141, No.4, April, 1972,
pp.518-555, at p.520.
3.   The WWW also receives support, in addition to that
received from IOC and WMO, from the Global Atmospheric Research
Programme (GARP), jointly organised by the International Council
of Scientific Unions (ICSU) and the International Union of
Geodesy and Geophysics (IUGG), the Committee on Atmospheric
Sciences and the Committee on Space Research (COSPAR) of ICSU.
4.   SCOR initiated the International Indian Ocean
Expedition (1959-1965) in which 23 countries participated (14
of which ship-operating) with 40 research vessels, while
180 research cruises of varying duration and complexity took
place, IOC Technical Series, No.2, UNESCO, 1966, at p.5.
5.   Other Working Groups are the Working Group on
Communications, on Oceanographic Data Exchange, etc., IOC,
Technical Series, NO.2, UNESCO, 1966, pp.32-34.   The two
advisory bodies to the IOC should also be mentioned:
(a)   The SCOR OF ICSU which is also advisory body to UNESCO, and
(b)   The Advisory Committee on Marine Resources Research of
FAO (ACMRR), which is also an advisory body to FAO, ibid., at p.10.
6.   Resolution I-7 - Fixed Stations, reproduced as Annex I
to Legal Problems Associated with Ocean Data Acquisition
Systems (ODAS), IOC, Technical Series, No. 5, UNESCO, 1969,
(hereinafter cited as IOC, Techn. Ser. No.5).
7.   Doc. UNESCO NS/IOC/INF-34, (Subsequently revised to
form Part I of the Document published by IOC, Techn. Ser., No.5).
8.   IOC Resolution II-18, Legal Status of Fixed
Oceanographic Stations, reproduced as Annex II in IOC, Techn.
Ser., No.5.
9.   For the letters and comments received from
Governments see in IOC Techn. Ser., No. 5, Part II at p.19
et seq.
10.   Ibid., at pp. 19, 25 and 29.
11.   Ibid., at p.28.
12.   DOC.SC/IOC.EG-1 (IV)/12, 17 September 1970,
Fourth Session of the IOC Group of Experts on the Legal
Status of ODAS, IMCO, London, 15-26 June 1970.   The
Preliminary Draft Convention may be found in Annex III (and
also in IMCO DOC. LEG. IX/3, 3 September 1970).   The Group
had before it the Documents SC/IOC.EG-1/7, Annex IV, entitled
"Proposed Articles for the Preliminary Draft Convention",
prepared by the Group at their third Meeting in 1969, and the
Comments by the Rapporteur of the Group on the Proposed
Articles which had been distributed as Annex IV to Document
SC/IOC EG -1/7;   it also had the DOC.SC/IOC.EG-1/7, Annex III

entitled "Problems to be resolved in clarifying the legal
status of ODAS and their solutions" (short Title: Legal
Problems Paper).

13. DOC.SC-72/CONF.85/8, Paris, 30 March 1972:
Preparatory Conference of Governmental Experts to formulate
a Draft Convention on the Legal Status of Ocean Data
Acquisition Systems (ODAS), UNESCO, Paris, 31 January –
11 February 1972 (hereinafter cited as DOC.SC-72/CONF.85/8).

14. Resolution 2: Convening of a Second Session of
the Preparatory Conference, DOC.SC-72/CONF.85/8, Annex II.

15. The Conference did not consider Articles 16-27.
These, however, have been reproduced in Annex III of DOC.
SC-72/CONF.85/8 in their original form along with comments
and proposed amendments submitted by Governments and
Organizations, see Summary Report at p.15.

16. To that end it adopted Resolution 1: Advance
Implementation of Safety Provisions, DOC. SC-72/CONF.85/8,
Annex II. It considered it as highly desirable that UNESCO/IOC
and IMCO should re-examine the Technical Annexes with a view
to recommending their voluntary use by Member States, ibid.

17. DOC.SC-72/CONF.85/8, Summary Report at p.2.

18. Ibid., at p.3.

19. See Doc. IOC/ODAS-LEG/3, Paris, 10 June 1974.

20. DOC.SC-72/CONF.85/8, Annex III, Article 1 (1).

21. IOC. Techn. Ser., No. 5 at p.7. Presently a
geographical position is defined by the term "Station" which
"means a geographical location occupied from time to time by
an ODAS," Draft Article 1, para 3.

22. Those Articles, paragraphs, sentences or phrases
enclosed in brackets /̄   /̄are included as items on which
there was a difference of opinion as to the inclusion of the
item, or as to the principle reflected, or as to its wording;
see Explanantory Note to the Preliminary Draft Convention,
DOC.SC-72/CONF.85/8, Annex III, p.1

23. ".....ODAS means a structure, platform, vessel,
craft....." etc., Article 1 (1) Third Meeting, Group of
Experts, DOC.SC/IOC.EG-1/7 Annex IV.

24. DOC.SC/IOC.EG-1(IV)/12, Annex III, p.5.

25. DOC.SC-72/CONF.85/8, Summary Report, p.5.

26. DOC.SC/IOC.EG-1 (IV)/12, Annex III, at pp. 5-6.

27. IOC, Techn. Ser., No. 5, p.7; DOC SC-72/CONF.85/8,
Draft Article 1, (2) (a) – (i).

28. This type of ODAS has been developed by the Office
of Naval Research and the Scripps Institution of Oceanography
(USA). It is 355 ft. in overall length (300 ft. normally
submerged),weighs 600 tons and provides laboratory and hotel
spaces for five people, IMCO DOC. NAV. IX/INF.2, 10 April 1970.
This Document contains illustrations and information on the
various types of ODAS which have been or are in use around
the world.

29. DOC.SC-72/CONF.85/8, Draft Article 1 (2) (i).
30. DOC.SC/10C.EG-1 (IV)/12, Annex III, p.5.

Chapter 7

DEPLOYMENT OF ODAS

INTRODUCTION

According to Article 1 (6) of the draft Convention on
ODAS, " 'Deployment' means placing, siting, using, employing
managing or operating ODAS."

It should, of course, be emphasized that the right of
deploying ODAS in the seas is closely related to the question
of freedom of scientific research.   Indeed, the latter
question was discussed as a subsidiary issue in relation to
the deployment of ODAS during the Preparatory Conference on
ODAS.   The question of the freedom of scientific research
is, however, outside the scope of the present study and it
will be considered incidentally and so far as it is related
to the right to place ODAS in the seas (1).   Assuming that
there exists a freedom of scientific research on the high seas
it would be illogical, in the present state of technology, to
recognise   such a freedom without recognising the corollary
right of placing the necessary means and tools in the seas
to conduct such research.

Moreover, it has to be made clear from the outset that
this study is concerned with the rules of international law
governing the conduct of "fundamental or 'pure' oceanographic
research."   Fundamental research "means any study or related
experimental work designed to increase mankind's knowledge
of the marine environment" (2).   Having said that, however,
it has to be emphasized that the distinction between such
'fundamental' or 'pure' research on the one hand and 'applied',
'commercial' or ' military' research on the other hand, is
purely theoretical and almost impossible in practice.

The same question has also been the subject of an extended

discussion by Sub-Committee III of the U.N. Sea-Bed Committee
and the Third Committee of UNCLOS III, dealing with the issues
of marine pollution, marine scientific research and development and transfer of marine technology.   The idea of distinguishing between types of research has at times dominated
the discussions (3).   In general, a clear distinction between
'fundamental marine scientific research' and 'marine scientific
research aimed at the exploitation of resources' has been
sought by a number of States during these discussions.   The
Working Group on Scientific Research defined as follows the
term 'Marine Scientific Research' in its 1973 Report (4):

> "Marine scientific research is any study and related
> experimental work, excluding industrial exploration and
> other activities aimed at the direct exploitation of
> marine resources, designed to increase mankind's
> scientific knowledge of the marine environment and
> conducted for peaceful purposes."

The distinction between 'fundamental' and 'applied'
research is an important one in terms of State jurisdiction
exercised upon the various maritime zones.   As will be explained
further below, there are certain maritime zones where the
coastal State has exclusive jurisdiction over all forms of
scientific research, pure or applied.   There are, however,
other zones where exclusive jurisdiction is enjoyed only for
limited practical purposes such as exploration and exploitation
of the natural resources of the sea-bed and subsoil.   In such
zones "effective freedom for the scientist to engage in
fundamental research depends upon clear rules limiting the
jurisdiction of the coastal State over scientific research
to the purpose for which its exclusive rights have been
recognised" (5).

The Revised Single Negotiating Text adopts this general
approach.   Scientific research in the EEZ or on the continental shelf would be conducted with the consent of the coastal
State, subject to such requirements as notice to the coastal
State (stating the nature and objectives of the proposed
research, methods and means to be used, precise geographical
areas, etc);   participation by the coastal State;   provision
of data and samples to the coastal State;   assistance to the
coastal State in assessing data, samples and results;   and
international dissemination of results (6).

However, the coastal State may not withhold its consent
unless the research project is related to the exploration and
exploitation of the living or non-living resources or it
involves drilling and construction of artificial islands and
installations.   Moreover, the results of such research "shall
not be published or made internationally available against
the express wish of that State" (7).   The right to conduct

scientific research beyond the EEZ and continental shelf is
now expressly recognised as a freedom of the high seas by
Article 76 of the Revised Single Negotiating Text, Part II.

Article 2 of the Preliminary Draft Convention on ODAS
deals only with the deployment of ODAS on the high seas, while
the Proposed Articles for the Preliminary Draft Convention
did include two separate Articles dealing with the deployment
of ODAS in the internal waters, territorial sea and the
continental shelf (8). The IOC Group of Experts had earlier
concluded that: "The right to place ODAS in the sea can be
analysed from the standpoint of the various possible geographical parts of the sea where the systems might be placed, the
status of the persons using the systems and the application
of international or domestic law" (9). Thus, for the sake
of clarity it may be advisable to consider separately these
"various possible geographical parts of the sea where the systems might be placed." This will be followed by the consideration of who may deploy or authorize the deployment of ODAS
in the sea.

I. MARITIME ZONES

For the purpose of considering the degree of national
jurisdiction exercised by States in the sea, the latter may
be divided into the following six maritime zones :
1. Internal Waters;
2. Territorial Sea;
3. Contiguous Zone;
4. Continental Shelf;
5. Exclusive Economic Zone; and
6. High Seas.

1. Internal Waters

The whole maritime zone on the landward side of the
baseline of the territorial sea is subject to the exclusive
sovereignty of the coastal State and under its full control
as regards scientific research. Subject to one exception,
arising from the provisions of the Geneva Convention on the
Territorial Sea and the Contiguous Zone 1958, foreign shipping
is not even entitled to the right of 'innocent passage' which
is enjoyed in the territorial sea beyond internal waters (10).

Thus, as regards deployment of ODAS, the coastal State
may place or operate whatever ODAS it wishes in its own
internal waters. In the absence of any treaty commitments
to the contrary, a foreign State or national cannot place
or operate ODAS in that zone without the express permission
of the coastal State. The IOC Group of Experts has formulated
this as follows (11):

"Internal waters lie within the exclusive territorial

sovereignty of the State to which they appertain; a foreign State can only place or anchor and/or operate ODAS therein with the express permission of the sovereign State."

2. Territorial Sea

The entire maritime zone lying between the baseline and the outer limit of the territorial sea is under the exclusive sovereignty of the coastal State subject to a right of innocent passage for foreign shipping (12).

Any type of scientific research carried out in this zone is subject to the express consent of the coastal State. This principle is now codified in Article 57 of the Revised Single Negotiating Text, Part III, which lays down that:

"Coastal States have the sovereign right to conduct and regulate marine scientific research in their territorial sea established in accordance with this Convention. Scientific research activities therein shall be conducted only under the conditions set forth by the coastal State."

The right of a coastal State, therefore, to place or authorize others to place ODAS in its territorial sea is clearly established. In the absence of any treaty commitments to the contrary, a foreign State or national cannot deploy ODAS in that zone without the express permission of the coastal State. As has already been said, the Proposed Articles for the Preliminary Draft Convention on ODAS did include a separate Article dealing with the deployment of ODAS in the Territorial Sea and Internal Waters (Draft Article 4) which reads as follows (13):

"A coastal State has exclusive jurisdiction over the deployment of ODAS in its territorial sea and internal waters. No State may deploy ODAS in the territorial sea or internal waters of another State without the express consent of that State."

The Rapporteur had commented then that this formulation is simply a restatement of existing international law (14). For that very reason, the Group of Experts were divided in their views on the desirability of including such an Article in the Convention. The same doubts as to the desirability of incorporating such an Article in the Convention were also expressed by the IMCO Legal Committee at its 8th Session and the Netherlands Delegation (15). It was thus decided to delete Draft Article 4 which does not appear in the final text of the 1972 Preliminary Draft Convention on ODAS.

The placement of ODAS in the territorial sea must be

consistent with reasonable requirements of navigation and maritime safety. It must not hamper innocent passage or hinder
navigation in general. Article 15 of the Geneva Convention
on the Territorial Sea and the Contiguous Zone, provides that:

> "1. The coastal State must not hamper innocent passage
>   through the territorial sea.
> 2. The coastal State is required to give appropriate
>   publicity to any dangers to navigation, of which
>   it has knowledge, within its territorial sea."

Generally speaking, navigation must not be impeded
through deployment of ODAS in recognized sea lanes essential
to international navigation or in narrow channels. According
to Article 73 of the Revised Single Negotiating Text, Part III:
"The deployment and use of any type of scientific research
installations or equipment must not constitute an obstacle
to the established international shipping routes."
    If a coastal State authorizes the deployment of ODAS
in its territorial sea by a foreign State or national, it may
impose any restrictions it deems necessary upon such placement,
e.g. for the safety of navigation. It may also decide upon
the use of which data collected by ODAS in its territorial
sea and internal waters may be put. The foreign State or
national, however, should be entitled to prior notice as to
such restrictions and decision before the ODAS is deployed.
    Finally, the IOC Group of Experts on the Legal Status
of ODAS after noting that:

> "The right of a government to employ or authorize others
> to employ ODAS is clearly established as regards objects
> placed in its territorial sea";

> "There are no known cases where the right of a coastal
> State to place or use ODAS in these waters has been
> questioned on the basis of international law"

has suggested the following tentative conclusions as regards
the territorial sea:

> "1. The coastal State may exercise its sovereign
>   rights respecting the employment of ODAS;
> 2. The coastal State may place such restrictions,
>   limitations or regulations as it deems fit on
>   the placement, purpose or use of ODAS, if these
>   are liable to affect the safety and freedom of
>   navigation;
> 3. No-one may claim an international right to place,
>   anchor and/or operate ODAS in the territorial sea
>   of any State without the express or implied permission

of the government of that State" (16).

3.   Contiguous Zone

Article 24 of the Geneva Convention on the Territorial
Sea and the Contiguous Zone (1958), lays down that in a zone
of the high seas contiguous to its territorial sea, which may
not extend beyond twelve miles from the baseline from which
the breadth of the territorial sea is measured, the coastal
State may exercise the control necessary to (17):

(a)   Prevent infringement of its customs, fiscal
        immigration or sanitary regulations
        within its territory or territorial sea.

(b)   Punish infringement of the above regulations
        committed within its territory or territorial
        sea.

It is clear from these provisions that the coastal
State does not possess any right to control or prohibit
scientific research and/or deployment of ODAS in the contiguous zone by virtue of its status.   The contiguous zone
is a zone of the high seas and as such it falls under the
regime of the high seas de lege lata.   The coastal State
will, however, have certain rights as regards scientific
research and/or deployment of ODAS in cases where the
waters of the contiguous zone are superjacent to the continental shelf.
Under the Revised Single Negotiating Text the contiguous
zone is no longer a zone of the high seas but part of the
exclusive economic zone.   According to Article 75 of the
Text, Part II, the term 'high seas' as used in the Convention
"means all parts of the sea that are not included in the
exclusive economic zone, in the territorial sea or in the
internal waters of a State....."

4.   High Seas

Article 3 of the Geneva Convention on the Continental
Shelf 1958 lays down that, "The rights of the coastal State
over the continental shelf do not affect the legal status of
the superjacent waters as high seas,..."   It may, therefore,
be advisable before discussing the freedom of scientific
research and deployment of ODAS in the area of the continental
shelf, to clarify the legal status of the high seas in
relation to research and deployment of ODAS.

(a) Freedom of Scientific Research

Article 2 of the High Seas Convention 1958 does not mention this freedom.

The United Kingdom delegation reflecting the concern of the scientific community at the absence of specific reference to freedom of research, proposed, during the eighth (1956) session of the International Law Commission, the addition of a fifth freedom to those listed in Article 2, reading: "(5) Freedom of research, experiment and exploration" (18). Unfortunately, the discussion of this proposal was linked with the related question of the legality of atomic tests on the high seas and it was decided in the end not to include this fifth freedom in draft Article 27 (now Article 2). However, paragraph (2) of the ILC's Commentary on draft Article 27 does refer to the freedom of research:

> "The list of freedoms of the high seas contained in this article is not restrictive. The Commission has merely specified four of the main freedoms, but it is aware that there are other freedoms, such as freedom to undertake scientific research on the high seas - a freedom limited only by the general principle stated in the third sentence of paragraph 1 of the commentary to the present article," that is, that "States are bound to refrain from any acts which might adversely affect the use of the high seas by nationals of other States" (19).

It is thus assumed generally that the freedom of scientific research is covered by the doctrine of freedom of the high seas (20). The freedom of research, it is argued, may be inferred from the general concept of freedom of the seas, the language of Article 2 of the High Seas Convention, together with the travaux preparatoires of the International Law Commission, and from the known practice of States.

For example, "the USSR and other socialist States have taken a consistent stand for the principle of freedom of research on the High Seas as a reliable legal basis for co-operation between States in exploring the ocean. It meets the interests of all nations, and needs to be preserved and consolidated" (21).

On the other hand, debates in the United Nations Sea-Bed Committee and the Preparatory Conference on ODAS have revealed that a number of States oppose this view of the law. According to certain delegations, the expression "freedom of scientific research" is not to be "interpreted as one of the freedoms of the high seas and should preferably be replaced by the term "promotion and development of scientific research." It was maintained that it is untenable under this approach to consider such freedom as "a recognised principle of

international law" or as "one of the freedoms of the seas and
oceans generally accepted by international law" (22). The
delegation of Argentina and other delegations also took the
position at the 1972 Preparatory Conference on ODAS that
"the content of the principle of freedom of the high seas was
presently under examination and up to now the deployment of
ODAS had not been included in the principle and neither had
scientific research" (23).

Clearly then, there is still some debate as to whether
there exists in international customary law a freedom of
scientific research. It is, therefore, advisable that the
new Convention on the Law of the Sea expressly recognises the
right to conduct scientific research as a freedom of the high
seas. Indeed, this right is now included in the list of
freedoms of the high seas - enumerated in Article 76 of
R.S.N.T. Part II (24). It must, however, be remembered that
under the draft Convention, the term 'high seas' refers only
to those parts of the seas that extend beyond the outer limit
of the exclusive economic zone.

According to Arts. 68-69 of the R.S.N.T., Part III,
States, irrespective of their geographical location, as well
as competent international organizations, shall have the
right to conduct marine scientific research in the international
sea-bed area and in the water column beyond the limits of the
economic zone.

(b)   Deployment of ODAS

As has already been seen considerable preparatory work
is still required for the completion of the Convention on
ODAS. It is, therefore, advisable, before discussing draft
Article 2 (deployment) of the Convention on ODAS, to clarify
the right of deployment on the high seas and the sea-bed thereof,
under international customary law.

Article 2 of the Geneva Convention on the High Seas
makes clear that the four named freedoms do not exhaust the uses
of the sea and sea-bed covered by the principle of freedom
of the high seas. The view has been supported, therefore,
that freedom of the high seas comprises, apart from the
four named freedoms, and any other uses of the high seas which
are recognised as flowing from the principle that the high
seas are open to all nations. It has further been submitted
that State practice supports such a view. McDougal and Burke,
for instance, have supported the view that any use of the
seas for peaceful purposes is permissible under international
law (25). Thus, the deployment of ODAS on the high seas is
a right which falls within the principle of the freedom of
the high seas. As a freedom of the high seas it has, of
course, to be exercised with reasonable regard to the interests
of other States.

It has to be acknowledged, however, that this view of
the law is disputed. Already in 1965 the Federal Republic
of Germany in its reply to the request by UNESCO/IOC that member
States report on their domestic laws and regulations on ODAS,
after referring to Article 2 of the High Seas Convention and
Article 5 (1) of the Continental Shelf Convention, concerning
the freedom of scientific research, observed that : "The
right..... to lay out independently working Data Stations
is not expressed nor deducible." It asked, therefore, that
the right of all nations to deploy ODAS on the high seas be
expressly stated in the Convention on ODAS (26). A similar
request was also made by the Netherlands Government in its
reply of 3 January 1967: "The Convention should state
explicitly that all nations have a right to establish ocean
data stations on the high seas" (27). It has also been
seen that, "According to the delegation of Argentina and
other delegations, the content of the principle of freedom
of the high seas was presently under examination and up to
now the deployment of ODAS had not been included in the
principle and neither had scientific research" (28).

In the writer's opinion the deployment of ODAS on the
high seas is a freedom sanctioned by the principle of the
freedom of the high seas, (as is the freedom of scientific
research on the high seas), under international customary law.
Indeed, it would be illogical to recognise in the present state
of technology the freedom of scientific research on the high
seas, without recognising the corollary right of placing the
necessary means and tools on the seas to conduct such research.
Deployment of ODAS is already taking place on the high seas
and it is a desirable and necessary development for the
advancement of scientific research. Whenever in the past the
necessity for a new use of the seas has arisen, such as
laying submarine cables and pipe-lines, and flying over the
seas, States have had recourse to such uses without seeking
the consent of other States and without protestation from
the States concerned. This has also been the case with the
construction of lighthouses, navigational aids and installations
constructed on the sea-bed of the high seas for the exploitation
of the natural resources. This is the case today with
construction of off-shore harbours beyond the limits of the
territorial sea and the deployment of ODAS on the high seas
and the sea-bed thereof. The underlying common interest
of all States in such activities makes it unlikely that they
will protest at the engagement of such activities by other
States and their nationals. Indeed, so far as we know, no
such protests have been recorded. In case of doubt,
acquiescence and express or implied recognition legitimize
these acts in international law. Thus, the problem is not
really whether the right to deploy ODAS is a freedom of the
high seas or not. The real problem is how to regulate best

this activity vis-a-vis other legitimate uses of the seas.
It becomes increasingly clear that as the use of the oceans
is intensified, the various freedoms of the seas can only
survive as regulated freedoms.   Herein lies the importance
of the contemplated Convention on ODAS.   The elaboration
of a conventional regime would provide an opportunity for
the transformation of the ambiguities and general guidelines
of international customary law into more precise and definite
rules concerning the legal regime of ODAS.

With regard to the right to place ODAS on the high seas,
the following tentative conclusions have been suggested by
the IOC Group of Experts:

"1.   Freedom of the high seas includes the "freedom
        of research in the high seas;"
  2.   No State may exercise exclusive sovereign rights
        of the high seas for the conduct of research by
        means of ODAS;
  3.   No State may restrict the reasonable conduct of
        such research by other governments or by individuals
        over whom it has no personal jurisdiction;
  4.   States are under a duty to ensure that such
        research undertaken by them or by their nationals
        is conducted with reasonable regard to the inter-
        ests of other States in their exercise of the
        freedom of the high seas;
  5.   A State is permitted by international law to place
        additional restrictions on the conduct of research
        on the high seas for its own nationals and vessels,
        but not for persons over whom the State has no
        jurisdiction" (29).

Turning now to the Preliminary Draft Convention on ODAS,
Article 2 (1) reads as follows :
/   1.   State Parties deploying or authorizing the deployment
        of ODAS in the high seas in accordance with their
        national legislation shall do so in accordance with
        the provisions of the present Convention and relevant
        norms of international law, taking into account the
        rights and interests of coastal States and the rights
        and interests of all States in other uses of the sea.
        In such deployment State Parties shall pay due regard
        to the safeguarding of human life and the preservation
        of the marine environment.   _/
Draft Article 2 contains what the Rapporteur's comments
refer to as restatements of existing international law (30).
Indeed, this is simply a reiteration of the principles contained
in Article 2 of the Geneva Convention on the High Seas 1958.
The safeguarding of human life and the preservation of the
marine environment have been singled out as items of particular
importance.

Since the freedom to deploy ODAS must be exercised with due consideration to other uses of the high seas, particularly navigation and fishing, it is considered that the placement of ODAS on the high seas must be subject to prior notification and may involve consultation with and co-ordination by IOC, WMO and IMCO. Indeed, certain areas of the high seas, such as approaches to ports, fishing grounds, estuaries and straits, and busy shipping areas where sea-traffic separation lanes are in force, need particular attention. Most of these areas have an agreed buoyage authority and it is sensible to accept the requirements of these authorities when placing ODAS in their area (31).

Discussion arose as to whether the Convention (Article 2 (1)) should refer only to high seas or "should encompass also the deployment of ODAS on the sea-bed and ocean floor beyond the limits of national jurisdiction" (32). With an eye on the particularly relevant "bottom bearing" ODAS it is only logical that Article 2 (1) should encompass also the sea-bed of the high seas, and express reference to it should be made. Here again, in view of the likely conflicts between the deployment of ODAS and exploration and exploitation activities in the international sea-bed area, a notification, consultation and co-ordination procedure with the International Authority to be established could certainly be devised. The exploration and exploitation of resources in the international sea-bed area must not result in any unreasonable interference with scientific research and/or deployment of ODAS.

It is also clear that deployment of ODAS should not give rise to any claims of jurisdiction in the adjacent areas of the seas. Draft Article 6 (5) provides that: "In the case of deployment of any ODAS, the Registry State shall not thereby claim or have any jurisdiction in the adjacent or under-lying sea-bed, subsoil or water column and such ODAS shall not possess the status of an island" (33).

5.   Continental Shelf

According to Article 5 (1) of the 1958 Continental Shelf Convention, the exploration and exploitation of the shelf resources must not result in any interference with fundamental oceanographic or other scientific research carried out with the intention of open publication. Scientific research thus seems to enjoy a greater degree of protection than navigation, fishing or conservation of living resources, all of which are merely protected from unjustifiable interference. This provision must, however, be read in the light of paragraph 8 which is certainly of much narrower scope than paragraph 1. Paragraph 8 subjects the research concerning the continental shelf and undertaken there to the condition of the prior consent of the coastal State. The interpretation of this

particular provision is of cardinal importance for the
clarification of the scope of paragraph 8. Regarding the
interpretation States place upon this provision, "It is
unknown whether or not a consensus has developed since 1964
on the scope of the consent requirement in terms of the type
of research affected, but some States apparently adopt a
restrictive interpretation. The United State..... apparently
considers, without objection by other States, that coastal
consent is needed only for research involving physical contact
with the ocean bottom" (34).

On the other hand, during the discussions of the Sea-Bed
Committee (Sub-Committee III) in 1971, "Some delegations
expressed the view that the consent of the coastal State was
required for all research related to the continental shelf
and undertaken there. The opinion was also expressed that
in accordance with the applicable rules of international law,
freedom of scientific research on the continental shelf is
not unrestricted since it is subject to conditions that would
allow the coastal State to verify at any moment the
scientific character of the research" (35).

It is, therefore, essential that the new Convention on
the law of the sea incorporates a clear rule on this point.
In fact, the Revised Single Negotiating Text, Part III,
(Chapter II dealing with the question of marine scientific
research), does attempt a distinction between fundamental
research and research aimed at the exploration and exploitation
of resources in the EEZ or on the continental shelf. However,
these provisions will be examined more closely in the following
section dealing with the exclusive economic zone.

As regards deployment of ODAS in the area of the
continental shelf the following cases may be discerned:

    (a)   Deployment of ODAS for research in and
           concerned with superjacent waters

    Conduct of such scientific research, and deployment of
ODAS, would certainly seem to be beyond the jurisdiction of
the coastal State. This is so under both the Geneva Convention
on the Continental Shelf and international customary law.

The Proposed Articles for the Preliminary Draft Convention
included a separate draft article (Article 5) on deployment
of ODAS on the continental shelf. Paragraph 1 of that Article
was formulated as follows :
    "ODAS may be deployed to detect, sense, sample, store
    or transmit the characteristics of the ocean environment
    and the superjacent atmosphere over the continental
    shelf as these waters form part of the high seas" (36).
The IOC Group of Experts has also observed that: "It
is important to note that the reference to "fundamental oceanographic or other scientific research" which appears in the

Convention on the Continental Shelf is not seen as inhibiting
the use of ODAS for other purposes such as meteorological
and oceanographic observations of the superjacent atmosphere
and subjacent waters over the continental shelf, such as
will be required for the Integrated Global Ocean Station System
(IGOSS) of IOC and the World Weather Watch (WWW) of WMO" (37).

Finally, The United States in its report to IOC has
observed that "With regard to the outer continental shelf....
It would seem that there would be no prohibition to the
establishment of "observing buoys" so long as it is not in
any way inimical to the interests of the nation, and did not
involve the resources of the bottom" (38).

(b) Deployment of ODAS on the Continental Shelf
     for research concerning the superjacent waters

It can be argued, under both the Continental Shelf
Convention and international customary law, that the uncontrolled
emplacement of ODAS on the continental shelf may constitute
an impediment to exploration and exploitation of its natural
resources. Such research, therefore, is subject to the
sovereign rights of the coastal State since that right of
control is necessary for, and connected with, the exploration
and exploitation of the shelf resources. Thus, the IOC Group
of Experts on ODAS has suggested that: "When..... an ODAS
either rests or moves on an area of the sea-bed which
constitutes part of the continental shelf or is moored to
such an area, it does not seem unreasonable to expect the
ODAS operator in question to act on the advice of the
Government of the coastal State concerned" (39).

It would appear, therefore, that the deployment of ODAS
on the shelf for research concerning the superjacent waters
may not in principle be prohibited by the coastal State.
However, in view of the fact that such deployment may constitute an impediment to exploration and exploitation of the
shelf resources, it is only reasonable to assume that the
ODAS operator will act in close co-operation with, and on
the advice of, the coastal State concerned.

(c) Deployment of ODAS on the Continental Shelf for
     research concerning the Continental Shelf but
     unconnected with the exploitation of the
     natural resources of the Shelf, for example,
     submarine geology

Here again the uncontrolled emplacement of research
tools on the continental shelf may constitute a potential
impediment to exploration and exploitation of its natural
resources. Such research, therefore, should be subject to
the control of the coastal State since this right is necessary

for, and connected with, the exploration and exploitation
of the natural resources of the continental shelf. Moreover,
the power to control and regulate research which may not be
intended to provide commercially useful data on the shelf
resources but is incidentally capable of so doing, is within
the legitimate rights of the coastal State.

As regards cases (b) and (c) above, the view has been
supported further that under international customary law a
good case can be made for permitting the coastal State to
protect its exclusive rights by forbidding all research
conducted on the shelf whatever its object. "The argument
is that such uncontrolled research might enable foreign
interests to acquire commercially valuable information about
Shelf resources" (40).

It has also been noted "that at least two States, the
United States and the Netherlands, take the position that
scientific research on the shelf is subject to coastal
authority by virtue of customary law" (41). It follows
that deployment of ODAS on the shelf is also subject to
coastal authority according to this view. Indeed, so far
as the Netherlands is concerned, claim to coastal authority
may rest on an even broader basis since the Dutch North Sea
Installations Act 1964, provides that Dutch legislation
applies, without restriction, to all installations erected on
the Dutch continental shelf (42). In the United States
the Outer Continental Shelf Lands Act 1953, extends the
"authority of the Secretary of the Army to prevent obstruction
to navigation in any navigable waters of the United States.....
to artificial islands and fixed structures located on the
outer Continental Shelf" (43).

    (d) Deployment of ODAS in the superjacent waters for
        fundamental research concerning the continental
        shelf

It would appear that prima facie, such research enjoys
the freedom protected by Article 5 (1) of the 1958 Continental
Shelf Convention. This interpretation is borne out if it
is accepted that according to Article 5 (8) of the same
Convention, the requirement of prior consent is limited
only to research concerning the continental shelf which
involves physical contact with the sea-bed or subsoil of
the shelf. This provision is not, therefore, applicable to
research concerning the continental shelf not undertaken
there but conducted from the superjacent waters and involving
no physical contact with the shelf.

It may, however, be argued under both the Continental
Shelf Convention and international customary law that the
coastal State is entitled to protect its exclusive rights by
controlling all research concerning the shelf, wherever

conducted (44).   Here again, the need for clarification of
the scope of Article 5 (8) is demonstrated.

In short, conventional clarification is needed regarding
the conduct of scientific research and deployment of ODAS
in the area of the continental shelf.   It remains uncertain
whether Article 5 of the Geneva Convention on the Continental
Shelf is declaratory of international customary law;   and
"on the assumption that it is not, the rules of international
customary law are not at all clear" (45).

It is thus to be regretted that the Preliminary Draft
Convention on ODAS does not provide separately for deployment
of ODAS in the area of the continental shelf.   As has already
been seen, the Proposed Articles did include a separate draft
Article on this point.   Paragraph 2 of this Article provided
that: "ODAS deployed in those parts of the high seas superjacent to the continental shelf for research concerning the
shelf itself shall be governed by the provisions of the
Convention on the Continental Shelf" (46).

Even such a provision, however, is unsatisfactory in
view of the ambiguity in the language of Article 5 (8) of
the Geneva Convention on the Continental Shelf.   A new draft
containing separate and clear rules concerning deployment
of ODAS in the area of the continental shelf is highly
desirable.   These rules would, of course, have to be drafted
with an eye on the relevant provisions of the Geneva
Convention on the Continental Shelf and their possible
revision at The Third United Nations Conference on the Law
of the Sea.

Further conflict and difficulties in interpretation
could thus be avoided.   The following tentative conclusions
reached by the IOC Group of Experts, may be used as a basis
for the proposed rules on Deployment of ODAS in the area of
the continental shelf:

"It is by no means clear that the types of exploration
and research governed by this Convention / on the
Continental Shelf _/ are as extensive as the uses
to which ODAS may be employed and it is not therefore
to be assumed that the coastal State has the right to
control the placing and use of ODAS over its continental
shelf.   Nevertheless, if the research concerns the
sea-bed, the potential user of ODAS would, in accordance
with the Convention, be subject to the exercise by the
coastal State of its sovereign rights to explore and
exploit its continental shelf" (47).

6.   Exclusive Economic Zone

The legal regime of the Exclusive Economic Zone (EEZ) is dealt with by Chapter III, Part II, of the Revised Single Negotiating Text.   The rights, jurisdiction and duties of the coastal State in the EEZ are set out in Article 44.   Under that Article, the coastal State enjoys in the EEZ exclusive jurisdiction with regard to, inter alia, scientific research (48).   Article 48 provides further that in the EEZ, the coastal State shall have the exclusive right to construct and to authorize and regulate the construction, operation and use of :

    (a) artificial islands; (b) installations and
    structures for the purposes provided for in
    Article 44; and (c) installations and structures
    which may interfere with the exercise of the rights
    of the coastal State in the zone.

The question of scientific research in the EEZ and on the continental shelf has dominated the work of an informal negotiating group on marine scientific research at UNCLOS III, Committee III.   Apparently, the main issue has been whether such research should be subject to coastal State consent (as proposed by the Group of 77) or whether such research should be subject to a series of treaty obligations and compulsory dispute settlement, obviating thus the need for, and dangers of, consent (as proposed by developed and landlocked countries).
As the Revised Single Negotiating Text stands now, an uneasy compromise has been reached.   Scientific research in the EEZ and on the continental shelf is dealt with by Chapter II, Section III, Articles 58-66, (Part III).   Perhaps the most important provisions are those in Article 60 which establishes a consent regime subject to a series of treaty arrangements.
According to Article 60 (1), "Marine scientific research activities in the economic zone or on the continental shelf shall be conducted with the consent of the coastal State in accordance with the provisions of this Convention".   However, under paragraph 2, the coastal State shall not withhold its consent unless the proposed scientific research project: (a) bears substantially upon the exploration and exploitation of the living or non-living resources; (b) involves drilling or the use of explosives; (c) unduly interferes with economic activities performed by the coastal State; and (d) involves the construction, operation or use of such artificial islands, installations and structures as are referred to in Articles 44 and 48 of Part II.
States and competent international organizations which intend to undertake scientific research in the EEZ or on the continental shelf of a coastal State shall give notice to the latter stating: the nature and objectives of the research

project; the method and means to be used; the precise
geographical areas in which the research is to be conducted;
the time required; deployment of the equipment and its
removal, as appropriate; the name of the sponsoring institution;
and, finally, the extent to which it is considered that the
coastal State should be able to participate in the research
project (Article 58).

Such States and competent international organizations
must also comply with the following conditions: ensure the
right of the coastal State, if it so desires, to participate
in the research project without any financial burden; provide
the coastal State with preliminary reports and the final
results; provide access for the coastal State to all relevant
data and samples, and, if requested, assist the coastal
State in assessing such data, samples and the results thereof;
unless otherwise agreed remove the scientific installations
or equipment once the research is completed; and ensure the
open publication of the research results (Article 59).
However, it should be noted that the results of a research
project related to the resources of the EEZ and the continental
shelf "shall not be published or made internationally available against the express wish" of the coastal State (Article 61).

In conclusion, it would appear that under the existing
draft U.N. Convention on the Law of the Sea, deployment of
scientific installations and structures, such as ODAS, in
the EEZ and on the continental shelf, falls in effect within
the exclusive jurisdiction of the coastal State.

II. DEPLOYMENT OF ODAS BY INTERNATIONAL ORGANIZATIONS

The IOC Group of Experts had earlier decided that
international organizations have the right to deploy ODAS
and this is recognized in Article 2 (2) of the Draft Convention.

There had been some discussion during the Conference
as to whether intergovernmental organizations had such a right,
but it was generally accepted that they could deploy ODAS (49).
The fact that the right of these organizations to own and
operate ships has been accepted on the same principle, was
referred to (50).

In this context, and as regards the international personality of intergovernmental organizations, the Advisory Opinion
of the International Court of Justice on Reparations for
Injuries suffered in the Service of the United Nations, may
be recalled (51). The Court, after it came to the conclusion
that the United Nations Organization is an international
person, continued,as follows :
"This is not the same thing as saying that it is a State,
which it certainly is not, or that its legal personality
and rights and duties are the same as those of a State.....

What it does mean is that it is a subject of international
law and capable of possessing international rights and
duties, and that it has capacity to maintain its rights
by bringing international claims" (52).

However, it was emphasised that international organizations
would probably be unable to fulfil all the obligations of a
contracting State under the Convention, e.g. provisions relating
to criminal matters (53).   Accordingly, as the Rapporteur
had earlier observed, "it is anticipated that the intergovernmental organization will enter into an agreement with
a Registry State whereby that State will exercise the necessary
functions under the convention on behalf of the intergovernmental
organization" (54).   Indeed, Article 2 (2) should be read
in conjunction with Article 5 (5) of the Draft Convention,
which provides that :

> "In the event that an intergovernmental organization
> desires to register ODAS, the organization must register
> such ODAS with a State Party, provided that the
> organization declares its acceptance of and takes the
> necessary measures to apply the provisions of this
> Convention, including entering into an agreement with
> the Registry State for the implementation of the
> relevant provisions thereof."

III.   INTERNATIONAL CO-OPERATION IN THE
        DEPLOYMENT OF ODAS AND EXCHANGE OF
        SCIENTIFIC DATA

Draft Article 3 deals with co-operation in deployment
and exchange of data collected by ODAS.   It provides that
where appropriate, such co-ordination should be conducted
through the competent international organizations.   Such
competent organizations would presumably be the UNESCO/IOC,
WMO and IMCO.

The importance of such a non-mandatory Article lies
in the fact that it underlines the great value of close co-
operation in the deployment of ODAS, so as to avoid wasteful
duplication of effort.   As the Rapporteur has commented :

> "It is not contemplated that there will be an adequate
> number of data gathering devices for a very long time,
> if ever.   Accordingly, it is extremely important that
> the employment of these devices be carefully husbanded
> so as to return the greatest possible value to the
> world.   Co-ordination of efforts by individual States
> through the offices of the intergovernmental bodies
> established for this purpose, is obviously the most
> intelligent method of providing for a rational
> deployment" (55).

During the Preparatory Conference, a number of
delegations expressed the view that the exchange of data
collected by ODAS is one of the most important matters for
international co-operation and wished this to be stated
specifically in the Article.   This matter has also been the
subject of extended discussions during the deliberations of
the Sea-Bed Committee (Sub-Committee III) and Committee III
at UNCLOS III, dealing with scientific research.   It was
pointed out that if mankind were to benefit from marine
scientific research, the participation of all States,
particularly developing countries, in such research must be
encouraged and ensured.   The view was supported further that
scientific data should be part of the common heritage of mankind and consequently available to all members of the international scientific community.   To that effect is was suggested
that competent international organizations and technologically
advanced countries should help the developing countries to
improve the capability of technical personnel to participate
in scientific research and to utilize the results of such
research.   Assistance to developing countries, therefore,
as well as gathering, processing and disseminating scientific
data should be part of any treaty relating to scientific
research in the oceans (56).

However, some delegations felt the Article was unnecessary
altogether and others whilst agreeing on the importance of
international data exchange, opposed such a reference on the
grounds that this is dealt with adequately elsewhere and
is inappropriate to this Convention (57).   Due to these
diametrically opposed views no agreement could be reached
on the Article.

Finally, the IOC Group of Experts had reached earlier the
following conclusions as regards use of information obtained
by ODAS :

"Preliminary research in this area has not disclosed
any clear precedents in supporting an assertion that
the owner may claim exclusive rights to the data
obtained nor for a claim that the devices should be open
to the entire world for inspection and the taking of
scientific data.....It is arguable, moreover, that the
owners' rights in the physical property extend to
afford proprietary rights in the data obtained, in which
case, the owners would be entitled to the exclusive right
of access and use of the resulting scientific data.

On the other hand, there are indications that
the scientific data obtained on the high seas should
be available to all.   In the Convention on the Continental
Shelf, for instance, there is a reference to ".....oceano-
graphic or other scientific research carried out with
the intention of open publication", (Article 5 (1)).

This is an area of the law which is evidently still'

quite uncertain..... these problems might be better
treated in an international convention where provision
would be made for notices, clear and detailed rules,
the requirement of publication of results where indicated
and such further distinctions as might be desirable or
necessary" (58).

NOTES

1. For an excellent analysis of the freedom of
scientific research see E.D. Brown, Freedom of Scientific
Research and the Legal Regime of Hydrospace, 9 Indian J.I.L.
(1969), pp.327-380. W.T. Burke, Scientific Research Articles
in the Law of the Sea Informal Single Negotiating Text, Law
of the Sea Institute, Occasional Paper No. 25, June 1975;
and W.S. Wooster (ed), Freedom of Oceanic Research, N.Y. 1973.
2. See the definition of marine scientific research
in Article 48 of the Revised Single Negotiating Text, Part III
(DOC.A/CONF.62/WP.8/REV.1/Part III, 6 May 1976).
3. See, for example, the 1973 Report of the Sea-Bed
Committee (Supplement No. 21, Doc. A/9021), Vol. I, at p.75
et seq, and J.R. Stevenson and B.H. Oxman, The Third United
Nations Conference on the Law of the Sea: The 1975 Geneva
Session, 69 A.J.I.L. 1975, p.763 et seq., at pp.793-794.
4. See in the 1973 Report of the Sea-Bed Committee,
W.G.3/Paper No.4, at p.103.
5. E.D. Brown, supra, at p.329.
6. R.S.N.T., Part III, Ch.II: Marine Scientific
Research, Arts. 58-59.
7. Ibid., Arts. 60-61.
8. See Arts. 4 and 5 in Doc. SC/IOC.EG-1/7, Annex IV.
9. IOC, Techn. Ser. No.5, at p.8 et seq.
10. See Arts. 4 and 5 of the 1958 Territorial Sea Convention and also Arts. 6 (straight baselines) and 7 (internal
waters) of R.S.N.T., Part II.
11. IOC, Techn. Ser., No.5, p.9, item 11.
12. See Articles 1 and 14-17 of the Geneva Convention
on the Territorial Sea and the Contiguous Zone, 1958. See
also Ch.1, S.1 (Art.1) and S.3 of R.S.N.T., Part II.
13. IOC Group of Experts, Third Meeting, Paris 27 October
- 14 November 1969, DOC.SC/IOC.EG.-1/7.
14. DOC.SC/IOC.WG-4/INF.-1; DOC.SC/IOC EG-1/7 Annex
IV, see in IMCO DOC.LEG. VIII/2/Add.1, 1 April 1970, Article 4
p.5.
15. IMCO DOC.LEG VIII/WP.3, 23 April 1970, at p.7; for
the Netherlands Delegation's comments see IMCO DOC.LEG.VIII/2/

Add. 2, 15 April 1970, at p.3.

16. IOC., Techn. Ser., No.5, at p.9, items 12-14.

17. Article 32 of R.S.N.T., Part II, extends the breadth of the contiguous zone to 24 nautical miles.

18. U.N. DOC.A/CN.4/99/Add.1, in II ILC Yearbook (1956) at p.80.

19. II ILC Yearbook (1956) at p.278.

20. See W.T. Burke, Contemporary Legal Problems in Ocean Development, IV Scientific Research in the Oceans, in W.T. Burke, Towards a Better Use of the Ocean, (A SIPRI monograph), 1969, pp.114-131, at p.121; E.D. Brown, Freedom of Scientific Research and the Legal Regime of Hydrospace, 9 Indian J.I.L. (1969), pp.327-380, at p.346 et seq; 1973 Report of the Sea-Bed Committee, Vol. I, item 28, at p.76; IOC, Techn. Ser., No.5, at pp.10-11.

21. A. Vysotsky and P. Nastin, On Freedom of Research in the World Ocean, International Affairs (Moscow), May 1975, p.74, at p.82.

22. 1973 Report of the Sea-Bed Committee, Vol.I, item 27, at p.76. See also the 1972 Report of the Sea-Bed Committee, item 243, at p.60.

23. DOC. SC-72/CONF.85/8, Summary Report, at p.6. "Customary international law does not recognize the freedom of scientific research in and on the high seas," R.K. Dixit, Freedom of Scientific Research in and on the High Seas, 11 Indian J.I.L., 1971, pp.1-8, at p.7.

24. See also the relevant Article 10 (scientific research in the International Area) of R.S.N.T., Part I.

25. M.S.McDougal and W.T. Burke, The Public Order of the Oceans, 1962, at p.763.

26. IOC, Techn. Ser., No. 5, at pp.21-22.

27. Ibid., at p.24.

28. DOC.SC-72/CONF.85/8, Summary Report, at p.6.

29. IOC, Techn. Ser., No. 5 at p.11.

30. DOC. SC/IOC.WG-4/INF.-1, see in IMCO DOC. LEG VIII/2/Add.1, 1 April 1970, at p.4.

31. IMCO DOC. LEG VII/5, 26 November 1969, Legal Committee, at p.6. See also DOC SC/IOC-VI/INF.H2, Annex I, at p.2.

32. DOC. SC-72/CONF.85/8, Summary Report, p.6.

33. Ibid., Annex III, p.12.

34. W.T. Burke, supra, note 20, at pp.118-119. Professor E.D. Brown has, also supported a similar view: "It would seem reasonable to conclude that the intention was to make clear that the requirement of prior consent was limited to research concerning the Continental Shelf which involved physical contact with the sea-bed or subsoil of the shelf. This is also the interpretation favoured by the U.S. State Department," E.D. Brown, supra, note 20, at p.356.

35. 1971 Report of the Sea-Bed Committee, Item 155, at p.46, See also the 1973 Report of the Sea-Bed Committee, Vol. I,

Item 35, at p.78.

36. DOC.SC/IOC.EG-1/7, Annex IV.

37. DOC.SC/IOC.EG-1/7, Annex II, see in IMCO DOC.LEG VII/5, 26 November 1969, at p.7.

38. IOC, Techn. Ser., No. 5, at pp.27-28.

39. DOC.SC/IOC.EG-1/7, Annex II, see in IMCO DOC. LEG VII/5, 26 November 1969, at pp.6-7.

40. E.D. Brown, supra, note 20 at p.363.

41. W.T. Burke, supra, note 20, at p.120.

42. It will be remembered that the establishment of the R.E.M. T.V. and Radio station on the high seas, beyond the Dutch territorial sea, forced the Dutch Government to pass this Act in 1964, as a result of which the station ceased operating a short period after it started.

43. 43 U.S.C. § 1333 (f) (1964).

44. See also E.D. Brown, supra, at pp.355-357 and 362 and 363.

45. Ibid., at p.363.

46. DOC.SC/IOC.EG-1/7, Annex IV, at p.4

47. IOC, Techn.Ser., No.5, at p.10.

48. Article 44, (1), (c), (ii), of R.S.N.T., Part II.

49. DOC. SC-72/CONF.85/8, Summary Report, p.7.

50. See Article 7 of the Geneva Convention on the High Seas 1958, and also the ILC's Commentary to Draft Article 29 (now Article 5) of the High Seas Convention, II ILC Yearbook (1956) at pp.278-279.

51. I.C.J. Reports, 1949, at p.174.

52. Ibid., at p.179.

53. One delegation pointed out that it was necessary to accept that these organisations were in a position to accept or reject the Convention as they saw fit, DOC.SC-72/ CONF.85/8, Summary Report, p.7.

54. DOC.SC/IOC.WG-4/INF-1, see in IMCO DOC.LEG VIII/2/ Add.1, 1 April 1970, at p.4.

55. Ibid.

56. See, for instance, the 1973 Report of the Sea-Bed Committee, Vol. I, at p.75 et seq; see also the relevant Arts. 10-11 of R.S.N.T., Part I; Section II, Arts. 53-56, and Section III, Arts. 59, 62-63, 66-67 of R.S.N.T., Part III. Presently the exchange of data generally is arranged on a voluntary basis in accordance with the IOC manual on international oceanographic data exchange, with States exchanging data from voluntary declared national programmes (DNP), see DOC.SC/IOC-V1/INF.142, Annex I, at p.6.

57. See Comment to Draft Article 3, DOC.SC-72/CONF.85/8, Annex III, at p.8.

58. IOC. Techn. Ser., No. 5, at pp.14-15.

Chapter 8

JURISDICTIONAL MATTERS CONCERNING ODAS

This chapter is concerned with four aspects of the crucial problem of jurisdiction regarding ODAS: first, that of retrieval of ODAS and personnel found in a maritime zone under the jurisdiction of a foreign State; second, that of the registration of ODAS; third, that of the jurisdiction exercised over ODAS; and, fourth, that of liability for unauthorized interference with ODAS, including intentional illegal interference (i.e. criminal and civil liability), salvage and collision. Naturally, the Preliminary Draft Convention on ODAS is once again taken as the basis for discussion.

I.   RECOVERY AND RETURN OF ODAS FOUND IN MARITIME ZONES UNDER THE JURISDICTION OF A FOREIGN STATE

The purpose of Article 4 of the ODAS Convention, on recovery and return, is to provide some system for the retrieval of ODAS and personnel found in a maritime zone under the jurisdiction of a foreign State, such as territorial sea and internal waters.   It purports "to extend the accepted principles of international law applying to vessels entering a State's territorial sea to the case of ODAS" (1).

Paragraph 1 provides that a State Party shall inform the Registry State of an ODAS which has, owing to wreck, distress or "force majeure", entered a zone under its jurisdiction and shall return it to the owner or operator upon request, or shall permit the owner or operator to recover it.

Paragraph 4 provides further that the owner or operator shall bear all reasonable expenses that may have been incurred in the recovery and return of the ODAS.   This paragraph

provides a degree of protection for the ODAS owner in that
unreasonable expenses or fees shall not be imposed by the coastal
State.   This would certainly cover transportation costs and
actual expenses incurred in the necessary removal of the ODAS.

It will be noted that the coastal State is required,
according to paragraph 1, to inform the State of Registry of
the ODAS and not the owner or operator since it may be
difficult, or even impossible in certain cases, for the coastal
State to identify the owner or operator.   The burden of
informing the Registry State that its ODAS has been found
appears to be a reasonable requirement to place upon the
coastal State.   On the other hand, the view has been supported
during the discussions of the IMCO Legal Committee on ODAS
that "it would be desirable, in order to enable the coastal
State to discharge its obligations in the interest of the
safety of the ODAS and other users of the sea if the State of
Registry or the owner and/or the operator of the ODAS would
in so far as it is possible be required under the convention
to notify the coastal State whenever they had reason to
believe that an ODAS might accidentally enter into the
coastal State's territorial seas or internal waters.   This
would enable the coastal State concerned to take the necessary measures to safeguard the ODAS, prevent damage to other
users of the sea area concerned and take the necessary
measures to return the ODAS or facilitate its recovery" (2).

Paragraph 5 provides for the immediate repatriation of
the personnel of an astraying ODAS.   The coastal State shall
facilitate such repatriation and shall raise no obstacles to
it.   As the Rapporteur has noted this "is intendend to reaffirm
the principle which is clear in the case of vessels and
would probably be applied by any coastal State even in the
absence of this paragraph".   Moreover, this paragraph "is
modelled in substance not only on the existing laws of the
sea but on the provisions of the Convention concerning the
return of personnel from space vehicles" (3).

Indeed, the provisions governing repatriation of personnel
of an astraying ODAS and expenses that may have been incurred
in the recovery and return of the ODAS have obviously been
drafted with an eye on the Agreement on the Rescue of Astronauts and the Return of Astronauts and Space Vehicles, the
relevant provisions of which are as follows (4):

Under Article 2 each Contracting Party shall immediately
take all possible steps to rescue the personnel of a space-
craft landing in territory under its jurisdiction, owing to
distress, accident, emergency or unintentional landing, and
render them all necessary assistance.   Article 4 provides
that astronauts found in the territory of a Contracting Party,
or on the high seas or in any other place not under the jurisdiction of any State, owing to accident, distress, emergency
or unintended landing, shall be safely and promptly returned
to representatives of the launching authority (5).   Under

Article 5, space objects and their component parts found in
the territory of a Contracting State or on the High Seas or
in any other place not under the jurisdiction of any State
shall, upon the request of the launching authority, be recovered
and returned to that authority (6). Expenses incurred in
the recovery and return of the space object or its component
parts shall be borne by the launching authority.

Paragraph 6 provides that a State Party shall take all
reasonable measures for the rescue of personnel of an ODAS
in distress. Here again this is intended "to reaffirm
humanitarian principles and assure equality of treatment with
personnel from vessels" (7). The same paragraph provides
further that:

"Provisions for rendering assistance to persons in
distress at sea and relevant Search and Rescue Agreements that are in force are applicable to personnel
of an ODAS in distress" (8).

In this respect Article 12 of the Geneva Convention on
the High Seas 1958 may also be recalled. According to that
Article a master of a ship is required, in so far as he
can do so without serious danger to the ship, the crew or
the passengers: to render assistance to any person found at
sea in danger of being lost; to proceed to the rescue of
persons in distress; and also, after a collision, to render
assistance to the other ship, her crew and her passengers.
Moreover, coastal States shall promote the establishment and
maintenance of an adequate and effective search and rescue
service regarding safety on and over the sea (9). Clearly,
these provisions are also applicable, where appropriate, to
the personnel of an ODAS distress.

Two new paragraphs covering accidental entry of ODAS
into zones subject to national jurisdiction and the disposal
of data obtained from ODAS in such zones, have been added to
Article 4, following a proposal by the delegation of Brazil.

Paragraph 2 provides that no State Party shall be obliged
to return the data obtained by an ODAS in a zone under its
jurisdiction, while paragraph 3 provides that the operation
of an ODAS in a zone under the jurisdiction of a Party,
even if accidental, shall remain subject to the national
legislation of that Party.

II. REGISTRATION OF ODAS

Article 5 deals with the registration of ODAS. As
the Rapporteur has noted, "The great value of the registry
system for conventional vessels indicates the need to create
a similar system for ODAS" (10). The register of ships "is
used as evidence of the right to fly the flag of the State
as well as of the right of ownership and of mortgages, in much
the same way as in the case with the registration of title

to land" (11). In a similar vein paragraph 8 of Article 5 provides that: "The entry in an ODAS register shall be regarded as proof of nationality and presumptive proof of ownership." However, unmanned registered ODAS are not required to carry on board documents attesting to their nationality.

Discussion on this Article focussed initially on the problem of choosing between compulsory registration systems with permitted exemptions, and voluntary systems. The advocates of voluntary registration felt that the Convention should try to attract the acceptance of as many States as possible, by inducing and not requiring registration through imposition of unnecessary obligations. They also pointed out that not all ships were registered and so there was no reason to establish a compulsory system for ODAS. On the other hand, several delegations were in favour of compulsory registration. They felt that registration would establish a legal link which would be particularly important in liability matters (12).

Paragraph 1 provides that, "State Parties deploying or authorizing the deployment of ODAS within the scope of the present Convention shall establish a special register in which all such ODAS shall be entered....." (13). Compulsory registration is thus adopted by this formulation. But on the proposal of the United States delegation an alternative to the first paragraph was included. This provides that, "Any ODAS that is not subject to a vessel registry system may be registered in an ODAS register of a Registry State." In adopting the compulsory registration system, however, it was considered that it ought to be within the competence of the Registry State to provide for minior exemptions from the registry, such as ODAS of very small size or of short term deployment. Indeed, paragraph 1 allows a Registry State to exempt an ODAS from registration by reason of (a) its small size; (b) its light construction; and (c) because the circumstances of its deployment, such as short duration or area of deployment, render registration unnecessary. In any case, it is further provided that an ODAS cannot be exempted from registration "if it carries on board any hazardous substance or if it may constitute an undue interference with or hazard to other uses of the seas or to the marine environment."

It would appear that the adoption of a registration system with permitted exemptions, such as that provided in Article 5 (1) constitutes a sensible way of tackling the registration problem. It must be remembered that a registry system may serve very useful purposes which could not probably be achieved through voluntary systems. It should also be pointed out that similar registry systems with certain exemptions have been adopted by various municipal legal systems in relation to vessels (14).

Paragraph 2 provides further that, "No benefits under the

present Convention may be claimed in respect of unregistered ODAS." In other words, the Convention will apply only to registered ODAS. This would certainly include ODAS exempted from registration by a Registry State. Nevertheless, it is further stipulated that, "with a view to protecting other legitimate uses of the sea and the marine -environment, State Parties undertake to apply the provisions of the present Convention to all unregistered ODAS wherever possible, " (paragraph 3).

According to paragraph 4 no ODAS may be registered by more than one Registry State. If, however, contrary to this provision, an ODAS is registered in more than one State the first registration in order of time shall be effective under the terms of the Convention.

Paragraph 5 provides that if an international organization wishes to register ODAS, it must register such ODAS with a State Party. The reason for such a provision was given in an earlier section where it was pointed out that Article 5 (5) must be read in conjunction with Article 2 of the Convention.

The weak point of Article 5 is that concerning the publication and notification of ODAS registers: "Each State Party shall publish its ODAS register annually and shall provide a copy to the depository of this Convention. Copies shall also be supplied on request to other appropriate inter-governmental organizations" (paragraph 6).

As the Rapporteur has commented the purpose of any such provision would be "to ensure that registers do not become out of date and thereby diminish their usefulness. It is essential that the appropriate specialized Agencies of the United Nations, in order to exercise their co-ordinating functions, have available timely information concerning ODAS..." (15). However, the requirement for publication of registers annually does not seem adequate since annual publication alone would not ensure that information on ODAS registers is fully up to date. Thus, the delegation of the Federal Republic of Germany, supported by other delegations, suggested that registers should be readily available for inspection by all interested persons. To that effect it proposed a modification to paragraph 6 providing that registers will be open to public inspection (16).

Moreover, in order to achieve proper notification and information on ODAS it would seem possible to require registration with a designated intergovernmental organization, such as IMCO. The designated organization would then provide a central registry and perhaps it could also provide a frequent (monthly?) "ODAS Report."

III. JURISDICTION OVER ODAS

Article 6 dealing with the assignment of nationality to ODAS and jurisdiction over them proved highly controversial during the discussions of the Preparatory Conference. After a full discussion, the Conference was unable to reach agreement on the text of this Article and it was, therefore, agreed to reproduce the preliminary draft Article as prepared by the fourth session of the IOC Group of Experts on the Legal Status of ODAS.

Under Article 6 ODAS are generally assimilated to ships and they are given the nationality of the State in which they are registered (17). Such State (Registry State) shall have the same rights and obligations as have States in matters concerning ships sailing under their flag, (paragraph 1). According to the Rapporteur, this provision identifies the nationality of an ODAS "irrespective of the nationality of the individuals aboard and gives States similar rights and obligations over ODAS as they at present hold for vessels" (18).

Several delegations considered that nationality was the only way to determine ownership and ensure the owner's liability. They emphasized that these provisions were significant in that they clarified the obligations of States in the high seas. On the other hand, some delegations felt that there was no need to attribute a nationality to an ODAS, and that rules in the fields of administrative, civil and penal law would be created outside the nationality concept and without the full assimilation of ODAS to ships. Moreover, they argued, such a provision would prejudge the outcome of the UNCLOS III, in particular with regard to bottom bearing fixed ODAS. Accordingly these delegates were in favour of deleting Article 6 altogether (19).

As regards the question of jurisdiction, the relevant provisions of Article 6 read as follows :

"1.....
2. The Registry State shall exercise effective jurisdiction and control in all matters concerning ODAS registerd in such State in the same manner and to the same degree as provided in the case of vessels by the norms of international law, except as modified in this Convention.

3......
4. Parties may exercise jurisdiction in all matters concerning ODAS registered in another State in the same manner and to the same degree as provided in the case of vessels of another nationality by the norms of international law, except as modified in this Convention."

The purpose of the second paragraph is to place an obligation upon the Registry State to exercise its jurisdiction

with regard to ODAS to the same degree as in the case of
vessels.   The question of the required degree of jurisdiction
exercised upon vessels naturally arises.   Under Article 5 (1)
of the Geneva Convention on the High Seas:
"Each State shall fix the conditions for the grant of
its nationality to ships, for the registration of ships in its
territory, and for the right to fly its flag.   Ships have
the nationality of the State whose flag they are entitled to
fly.   There must exist a genuine link between the State and
the ships;   in particular, the State must effectively exercise
its jurisdiction and control in administrative, technical
and social matters over ships flying its flag."
International law has traditionally left each State
free to determine under what conditions it will register and
thereby confer its nationality upon a ship, and this liberty is
confirmed by the above Article.   This freedom has, however,
been abused by certain States, in particular Panama, Honduras,
Liberia and Costa Rica (sometimes referred to as 'Panholibco'),
which allow the use of their flags by foreign shipping by
a simple administrative formality - Flags of Convenience System
(20).
It is exactly because of this practice that the International
Law Commission, in recognising the freedom of each State to fix
the conditions of registration, formulated a rule limiting
the scope of this freedom - by introducing the 'genuine link'
principle.   According to the ILC's Commentary to draft
Article 29 (now Article 5):
"Obviously the State enjoys complete liberty in the case
of ships owned by it or ships which are the property of a
nationalized company.   With regard to other ships, the
State must accept certain restrictions.   As in the case of the
grant of nationality to persons (21), national legislation on
the subject must not depart too far from the principles adopted
by the majority of States, which may be regarded as forming
part of international law..... The Commission accordingly
thought it best to..... enunciating the guiding principle that,
before the grant of nationality is generally recognized, there
must be a genuine link between the ship and the State granting
permission to fly its flag" (22).
The Commission made no attempt, however, to define a
'genuine link'.   It felt, - as did the Geneva Conference later
- that the legislation of traditionally maritime States was
too divergent to permit any internationally binding definition.
Nevertheless, "the majority of the Commission preferred a vague
criterion to no criterion at all.   While leaving States a
wide latitude in this respect, the Commission wished to make
it clear that the grant of its flag to a ship cannot be a
mere administrative formality, with no accompanying guarantee
that the ship possess a real link with its new State" (23).
Undoubtedly the determination of the genuineness of

existing links in many individual cases will prove a haphazard business involving a lot of casuistry. However, it is felt that among the criteria that may be used are nationality or domicile of the owner, his principal place of business, nationality of officers and crew and the location of the immediate effective control (24).

As regards ODAS it will be remembered that an ODAS has the nationality of the Registry State, whose flag it is entitled to display, and that, according to Article 5 (1), special registers are established by State Parties "deploying or authorizing the deployment of ODAS within the scope of the present Convention..." Prima facie, Article 5 (1) imposes no restrictions whatsoever on a State Party for the authorization for deployment of ODAS, whereas a previous draft provided that, "Each Party shall establish a special register for ODAS and shall require the entry therein..... of any ODAS to be deployed by itself or any person permanently resident in its territory" (25).

With respect to ODAS owned and deployed by a State, the latter obviously enjoys complete liberty to fix the conditions of registration. In the case of other ODAS, however, and in view of the provisions contained in Article 6 (2) of the Draft Convention on ODAS States must accept certain restrictions as with ships (26).

Thus, the Registry State must effectively exercise its jurisdiction and control in administrative, technical and social matters over ODAS displaying its flag. It is not anticipated, in any case, that in relation to ODAS the 'flags of convenience' phenomenon would ever assume the proportions and significance it has assumed with ships. The reasons that gave rise to this phenomenon do not apply as regards ODAS. As has been pointed out, this is a problem of international competition in a very important industry rather than a legal problem, and the ODAS is nowhere near becoming such an enterprise like shipping. Nevertheless, a link between the ODAS owner and the Registry State should be established according to the principles applying to persons and ships and adopted by the majority of States, forming part of international law.

Certain delegations believed that the recognition of jurisdiction was the necessary legal basis for the protection of ODAS against illegal interference, the substance of draft Article 7 (27). Indeed, the draft Convention has opted for the system of exclusive jurisdiction of the Registry State of the ODAS in the same way as a State has rights and obligations in respect of ships sailing under its flag, (Article 6 (1), (2) and (4) and Article 7 (1)).

A number of delegations, on the other hand, questioned the granting of exclusive jurisdiction to the Registry State of the ODAS. They believed that the doctrine of exclusive jurisdiction of the flag State should not apply to ODAS (28).

The Legal Committee of IMCO has also expressed a similar view (29). The last paragraph (5) of Article 6 provides that, "in the case of deployment of any ODAS, the Registry State shall not thereby claim or have any jurisdiction in the adjacent or underlying sea-bed, subsoil or water column and such ODAS shall not possess the status of an island." Of similar scope is also Article 71 of the Revised Single Negotiating Text, Part III, which lays down that scientific research installations and equipment "shall not have the status of islands or possess their own territorial waters, and their presence shall not affect the delimitation of the territorial sea, continental shelf or economic zone of the coastal State" (30).

The logic of such a provision is obvious. Deployment of ODAS, and in particular emplacement of bottom-bearing ODAS, should not give rise to any claim concerning jurisdiction over the sea-bed or the superjacent waters in the vicinity of the device. In fact, this paragraph adopts for ODAS the provisions of the Convention on the Continental Shelf 1958 (Article 5 (4)) dealing with the jurisdictional aspects of installations and other devices necessary for the exploration and exploitation of the shelf resources.

IV. LIABILITY FOR UNAUTHORIZED INTERFERENCE WITH ODAS

1. Intentional Illegal Interference

Many ODAS are unmanned and are not under the constant supervision of the owner, operator or any other person. This fact raises particularly difficult problems in relation to unauthorized interference. These problems are very serious at the present time and "have made it highly undesirable to leave unmanned surface ODAS unattended in certain waters. Numerous cases have been reported in the last few years of interference with ODAS or equipment thereon.....Often the theft is of a minor portion only of the ODAS (such as part of the mooring rope) but leads inevitably to the total loss of the ODAS, together with very valuable equipment; the operator is then obliged to spend a great deal of money replacing equivalent equipment on station and repeating the data collection" (31).

It is accordingly the purpose of draft Article 7 to offer a considerable degree of protection to ODAS by creating civil remedies and penal sanctions. Paragraph 1 of Article 7, entitled "Illegal Acts", provides that State Parties and persons must refrain from interference with or removal of registered ODAS or its appurtenant equipment in areas outside national jurisdiction.

This paragraph essentially confirms the exclusive juris-diction of the Registry State of ODAS. On the other hand, it is clear that not any interference with or removal of ODAS is

illegal (32).   Thus Article 7 (5) lays down that a coastal
State may take, with respect to an ODAS within the sphere of
its jurisdiction the necessary measures to prevent any activity
likely to jeopardize the peace, order or security of that
State.

(a)   Criminal Liability

It is clear that in cases where interference amounts to
an illegal act such as theft, damage or endangering of life, it
should be liable to punishment as a criminal offence.   Moreover,
"the penalty should be set at a level designed to discourage
the offence" (33).

As matters stand now, ODAS would not appear to be
completely without protection and liability for piracy or
intentional illegal interference with ODAS can be established
in certain cases.   Benedict says, for example:

"Conversion, if committed on navigable waters, is a tort
of which Admiralty has jurisdiction....   (34).

Cases of spoiliation and damage are of Admiralty and
maritime jurisdiction.   They include illegal seizure, or
depredation of vessels or goods afloat, embracing the civil
injury called piracy, which consists in an unwarranted violation
of property, committed on the high seas.   The injured party
may proceed against the property, or its proceeds, for a
recovery thereof or against the person of the wrong-doer for
the damage.   Every violent dispossession of property on the
ocean is prima facie a maritime tort and as such subject to
the maritime jurisdiction" (35).

Furthermore, according to Article 15 of the 1958 High
Seas Convention, the crime of piracy consists of any illegal
acts of violence, detention or any act of depredation, committed for private ends by the crew or the passengers of a
private ship or a private aircraft, and directed against a ship,
aircraft, persons or property in a place outside the jurisdiction
of any State.

With regard to ODAS the following acts fall under the
provisions of the said Article 15:

(i)   An act of piracy directed on the high seas against
        an ODAS which is a ship (As has been seen, however,
        these ODAS are not covered by the draft Convention).
        It is also clear that an ODAS-ship may commit the
        crime of piracy as defined above;   and

(ii)   An act of piracy committed by the crew or passengers
        of a private ship, private aircraft or an ODAS-ship
        and directed against an ODAS in a place outside the
        jurisdiction of any State.

On the other hand, it is equally clear that the following
acts cannot constitute the crime of piracy under international
customary law: Any illegal acts of violence, detention or any

act of depredation, even if committed for private ends by any person on board an ODAS not being a ship, an installation for the exploration and exploitation of the sea-bed, or any other artificial structure on the seas, not being a ship, and directed against an ODAS, or for that matter against a ship, aircraft or any artificial structure on the high seas.

The necessity thus arises for the adoption of new provisions to cover all these illegal acts of interference by and/or against an ODAS on the high seas. According to the IOC Group of Experts on ODAS:

"Under a Convention governing the legal status of ODAS, States should undertake to extend their penal legislation so as to cover any criminal interference by their nationals on the high seas. This will only partially solve the problem, as the punishment of offenders by their own Government may not always be assured.

As matters stand at present, a jurisdictional void exists with regard to activities on the high seas committed against ODAS, in that a State has no right in international law to assert jurisdiction over such acts committed in this area by the nationals of another State.

Prosecution for offences on the high seas can only be urged through diplomatic channels and this may be ineffective in its results and in terms of discouraging the commission of such offences. The analogy of maritime acts of depredation against property is satisfactory in cases of seizure and similar acts committed against manned ODAS (cf. Articles 14-22 of the Convention on the High Seas); however, depredations committed for private ends against unmanned ODAS often take place in conditions where concurrent jurisdiction is denied because the acts are attributable to a ship flying a flag other than that of the detecting vessel. Present international law allows the exercise of powers of detection, apprehension or sanction over ships of foreign flag in but few situations which are carefully specified and regulated by that law.

It may seem desirable therefore to devise some concept according to which more than one State could legitimately apprehend on the high seas persons who have committed such offences. It also might be made possible under carefully circumscribed conditions for States to board vessels carrying the flag of another State, for the purposes of investigating the commission of such offences" (36).

Similar proposals were submitted by one delegation during the discussions of the IMCO Legal Committee on the legal status of ODAS in 1970. It was then suggested that, "a provision authorizing the officers of any Contracting State to board a ship which it reasonably suspects of having committed an offence against ODAS," be inserted in the Article under consideration. Many delegations, however, felt that this "would constitute a radical departure from international law. They felt that the right of action proposed to be granted to States was so likely to abuse and that it should be approached with extreme caution. It was suggested that, if a provision of this sort was thought necessary, it might be sufficient to have one along the lines of the provision in the International Convention on Prevention of Pollution of the Sea by Oil, 1954, as amended in 1962" (37).

Further difficulties were emphasized by the IOC Group of Experts in relation to the effective punishment of criminal offences against ODAS. In the case of theft or damage of an unmanned ODAS, for example, the criminal is virtually always able to carry out his activity without any possiblity of being detected. It was suggested, therefore, that a possible solution to this problem "will be to provide that a person found in the possession of identifiable ODAS or parts of an ODAS, in circumstances that suggest the commission of a criminal offence, bears the burden of proving that his possession is lawful. For the purpose of any such action, the entry in an ODAS register should be regarded as presumptive proof of the ownership of an ODAS or any part of its equipment, bearing the specified marking" (38).

With respect to the draft Convention on ODAS, paragraph 3 of Article 7, which deals with criminal offences committed by and/or against ODAS, reads as follows :

"Any illegal act of violence, damage, detention or any act of depredation committed (for private ends) (on the high seas) (outside national jurisdiction) :
  (a) by any person against a registered ODAS or against persons or property on board an ODAS, or
  (b) by any person on board an ODAS, and directed against a ship, aircraft, installation for the exploration or exploitation of the sea-bed, or against persons or property on board such ship, aircraft or installation shall be a punishable offence.

These offences shall be punishable by the State that has jurisdiction over the ODAS, ship, aircraft or installation or by the State of nationality of the persons committing the act."

Originally, the definition of punishable offences was much similar to the wording and structure of Article 15 on piracy in the Geneva Convention on the High Seas, 1958. In the words of the Rapporteur the Article was "intended to assimilate, where this may not already be the case, any act which would be piracy if committed with regard to vessels, aircraft, etc., committed or directed against a manned ODAS. The practical consequences of this is that any State has jurisdiction to punish the acts in question" (39). The phrase "for private ends" has been retained in the final draft in brackets as several delegations objected to it on the basis that it was too limiting and that the acts should be illegal regardless of the end for which they are committed.

It will be noticed that the perpetrator of acts against ODAS is not specified in sub-paragraph (a) as it was in the original draft or in Article 15 of the Convention on the High Seas, 1958. Thus the offender may be anyone committing an illegal act against a registered ODAS and being on board a ship, an aircraft, the ODAS itself or another ODAS, an artificial island or any artificial structure on the seas – and not only the crew or the passengers of a ship or an aircraft.

Sub-paragraph (b) provides that a punishable offence may be committed not only against a registered ODAS but also by an ODAS, and directed against a ship, aircraft, installation for the exploration and exploitation of the sea-bed or against persons or property on board such structures. No reason is given for the restrictive enumeration of the structures against which the punishable offence may be committed.

The provision for the protection of the aforesaid installations was added at the proposal of the French delegation, but it is not only these installations which need protection on the high seas. Other artificial structures such as buoys, floating buoy terminals, floating stations, etc., need also be protected on the high seas. It is accordingly submitted that a provision covering any artificial structures deployed on the high seas for peaceful purposes, be added to sub-paragraph (b),

In conclusion, the following salient points concerning the essential features of punishable offences under Article 7, should be emphasized (40):

(i) The intention to rob (animus furandi) is not required. Illegal acts may be "prompted by feelings of hatred or revenge, and not merely by the desire for gain,";

(ii) It is undecided whether the acts must be committed for private ends only or not;

(iii) It is equally undecided whether a punishable offence can be committed only on the high seas or in a place situated outside the territorial jurisdiction of any State, and/or within a zone under the jurisdiction of a coastal State;

(iv) The acts can be committed by anyone on board a ship, an aircraft, an ODAS and an artificial island or structure on the seas and directed against a registered ODAS or against persons or property on board an ODAS;

(v) The acts can also be committed by any person on board an ODAS, and directed against a ship, aircraft, installation for the exploration or exploitation of the sea-bed, and, it is submitted, any artificial structures deployed for peaceful purposes, or against persons or property on board such ship, aircraft, installation and artificial structures.

(vi) The illegal acts include, further, acts committed by any person on board an ODAS and directed against the ODAS itself;

(vii) No special provision is made for, and no distinction is made between, warships, government ships, government aircraft and government ODAS on the one hand, and private ships, private aircraft and private ODAS on the other.

(b)   Civil Liability

Under most existing systems of municipal law, the owner or operator of an ODAS would have a civil action to recover possession of any part of it from an unauthorized possessor. This rule should be made universal and the owner or operator of an ODAS should be entitled to obtain compensation for any loss or damage he has suffered.   Article 7, paragraph 4, is intended, in the words of the Rapporteur, "to assure the ODAS owner of a civil remedy to provide compensation from the wrongdoer for any losses suffered" (41):

"The owner or operator of a registered ODAS shall have an enforceable legal right to recover possession of such ODAS or any part thereof which has been the object of any act specified in paragraph 3 of this Article subject to the rights of third parties according to the law of the State where recovery is claimed and to obtain compensation for the loss or damage arising directly from such act from the person having committed the act."

The qualification that recovery of possession is subject to the rights of third parties according to the law of the State where recovery is claimed, would appear to be in accordance with the fundamental principle of law, that third parties entering transactions in good faith must be protected.

A small problem arises with regard to the compensation due for loss or damage suffered by an ODAS owner.   Originally the draft made a reference to a "right to compensation for any consequential damage" (42).   However, during the discussions of the IMCO Legal Committee on ODAS it was pointed out that the inclusion of the duty to pay compensation for "consequential damage" was likely to create serious difficulties since that notion is related to the problem of "remoteness of damage." Since, moreover, this problem is treated differently under different municipal systems of law, it was suggested that the question might be resolved by merely referring to the right to compensation for any loss or damage arising from unauthorized interference with ODAS (43).

Fortunately, Article 7, paragraph 4, by providing that compensation is due "for the loss or damage arising directly from such act", is wiser in its precision than the above suggestion. It would appear that all direct losses will be compensated,

while damages should be assessed in accordance with factors
such as the value of the equipment, additional costs such
as the ship time of the ODAS tender, the expense of personnel
time due to loss of data and replacement of the equipment.

Finally, according to the IOC Group of Experts, it may
be desirable to introduce provisions similar to those laid
down in the Geneva Convention on the High Seas 1958, and
the International Convention on the Protection of Submarine
Telegraph Cables 1884, which provide that vessels and persons
causing damage to cables shall be responsible for making good
the damage if it can be shown that the damage has been done
wilfully or through culpable negligence (44). An additional
argument might be the fact that the Convention on ODAS includes
a provision under the heading "Compensation for expenses,"
to the effect that :

"The owner of a vessel who can prove that he has
sacrificed an anchor, fishing gear or any other property in
order to avoid injuring or destroying an ODAS shall be
indemnified by the owner or operator of the ODAS, provided
the vessel had taken all reasonable precautionary measures
beforehand" (45).

2. Salvage

Draft Article 14 attempts to deal with the difficult
problem of salvage. It is designed mainly to avoid unwarranted
salvage and discourage fraudulent salvage of ODAS.

Salvage has been generally described as the right to
a reward for rescuing maritime property from peril at sea (46).
With regard to ODAS which are vessels or are manned, no
particular difficulties arise and the normal rules of salvage
most probably apply. The presence of witnesses on the ODAS
assures that both sides of the case will be heard in the event
of controversy. Thus, paragraph 1 of Article 14 simply assim-
ilates existing salvage law to manned ODAS: The norms of
international law regarding matters of salvage and assistance
which are applicable to vessels shall be applied to registered
manned ODAS as if they were vessels.

Since paragraph 1 refers to "the norms of international
law," a brief reference to the Brussels Convention on assistance and salvage at sea (1910) will be made in this context (47).
The Convention recognizes the fundamental rule that every
act of assistance or salvage which has had a useful result
gives rise to a claim to equitable remuneration (48), but in
no case is the salvage reward to exceed the value of the
property salved, (Article 2) (49). Persons who have taken
part in salvage operations in spite of the express and
reasonable prohibition of the vessel assisted, have no right
to any remuneration, (Article 3). No remuneration is due
from persons whose lives are saved, but nothing in the Convention

is to affect the provisions of national laws on the subject,
(Article 9) (50). Article 8 lays down general principles
to guide the Court in fixing the remuneration for salvage,
and actions for such remunerations are, as a rule, barred
after two years, from the date when the salvage services were
rendered, (Article 10).

Article 11 provides further that "every master is bound,
so far as he can do so without serious danger to his ship,
her crew and passengers, to render assistance to every person,
even if he is an enemy, found at sea in danger of being lost"
(51). Although the Article does not apply to warships or
government vessels on public service, (Article 14), "several
States make it incumbent on their warships, under their
municipal legislation, to render such assistance to vessels
in distress" (52).

With regard to unmanned ODAS a number of difficulties
arise. In view of the fact that there will probably be no
witnesses to testify on behalf of the unmanned ODAS, "should
salvage rules be applied to normally operating unmanned ODAS,
there could be a serious threat to their physical security" (53).
Indeed, salvage rules might encourage the intentional interference with, and further tampering and theft of, normally
operating systems and equipment. On the other hand, the
adoption of the easy solution – that of prohibiting the
award of salvage in all cases of unmanned ODAS – " would
prevent the operation of this otherwise salutory provision
of marine law even where the ODAS operator in a given case
might very much want to have his ODAS salvaged" (54). This
view of indiscriminate prohibition was adopted, for instance,
by the United Kingdom Government in its reply to the UNESCO/IOC
circular letter of 23 November 1962 (55). However, the IOC
Group of Experts rejected the view for an outright prohibition
and it introduced the element of agreement: "The case is
strongly put that no claim should ever be allowed for the
salvage of unmanned ODAS whether moored or free-floating, unless
there is an agreement between the owner and the salvor.....
This proposal was made in the belief that it is better to
forego the occasional benefits of legitimate salvage operations
in which property is genuinely imperilled in order to reduce
the number of cases of false salvage and loss of equipment,
data, etc. The only action proposed is to rescind any legal
right accorded or implied in the law of the sea by which a
salvor is entitled to an award. A special rule of this
kind for ODAS would not preclude the voluntary giving of a
reward, nor, as stated above, interfere with agreed salvage
operations" (56).

According to the present formulation of Article 14 (2),
the general rule is that salvage awards for unmanned ODAS
will not be allowed. If, however, an ODAS owner or operator
desires salvage, either permanently or for a stated period
of time, he shall give due notice to the Registry State or

enter a contractual arrangement with a salvor.   Paragraph 3
provides further that in the case of controversy over
salvage of unmanned ODAS, the burden of proving that notice
under paragraph 2 was given shall be upon the salvor.

There is little doubt that Article 14 tends to discourage
salvage efforts concerning unmanned ODAS, even where an ODAS
owner has advertised to the contrary.   As the Rapporteur
has pointed out, however, the general experience of ODAS
operators concerning fraudulent or unnecessary salvage
would indicate that this is the preferable attitude which
the law should take (57).

Under customary law ODAS would not probably be considered
subject to salvage because they would not be classed
technically as "maritime property" (58).   The right to
salvage arises, as has already been seen, only if maritime
property is saved, that is ship, her apparel, cargo or
wreckage.   In the United Kingdom, for instance, "until the
enactment of legislation relating to salvage of aircraft (59)
the only property which could become the subject of salvage
was a vessel, her apparel, cargo, or wreck and, so far as
it may be called property, freight at risk.   Apart from
such legislation, this is still the case.   The saving of
other kinds of property such as a buoy adrfit from its
moorings or goods in a house or fire does not give rise
to any right to salvage reward" (60).   And again, "it should
be noted that not every property in tidal waters is maritime
property.   This quality does not extend to buoys or other
like structures, but only to vessels used in navigation...(61).

Thus, in The Gas Float Whitton No. 2 (62), salvage
reward was claimed for services rendered in saving a gas-float
which was adrift in the River Humber (63).   The Court of
Appeal, reversing the decision of the Divisional Court of
Admiralty, held that the gas-float was not a subject matter
in respect of which a salvage claim would be maintained.   Lord
Esher delivering the judgment of the Court of Appeal after
an exhaustive review of Admiralty law came to the conclusion
that the only subjects in respect of the saving of which a
claim for salvage reward could have been maintained in that
court were a ship, her apparel and cargo, including flotsam,
jetsam and lagam, the wreck of these and freight (64).   This
view was upheld on appeal in the House of Lords.

3.   Collision

The consequences of accidental interference with property
at sea, particularly as a result of collisions, have been
from early times the subject of legal regulation.   However,
the law governing such accidental interference with property
at sea is extremely complicated, and it often turns out, in
practice, to vary considerably from one country to another.

For example, when considering the question of liability for
damage caused accidentally by vessels to ODAS, "there is
found to be no uniform pattern as to whether the Admiralty
rules or the ordinary rules for delict or tort should apply"
(65). The following examples confirm this conclusion of
the IOC Group of Experts.

In France, "the word, 'abordage' (collision), as used
in the Commercial Code, means the striking together of two
ships underway... Two characteristics are essential for
an 'abordage':

(i) the collision must involve ships; (ii) the
collision between the two ships must itself give rise to
damage.....If a ship strikes a floating object which is
not legally considered a ship," no 'abordage' has taken place
(66).

According to the American maritime expert Benedict, on
the other hand, "The word collision, in its ordinary
Admiralty significance, means the striking together of two
vessels. But is also used in a broader or looser sense of
a vessel striking some other object: the Admiralty takes
jurisdiction where the ship owner sues in personam for
damages to his vessel by contact with a non-maritime structure
...."(67).

The English Authority Marsden states that: "Where
damage is done to persons or to property of any kind on land
or on water, owing to the negligent navigation or management
of a vessel, a course of action arises against those who,
by their own negligence or by the negligence of their servants
or agents, caused such damage to be done" (68).

In so far as collision results from negligent navigation
this has been defined by Lord Stowell in The Dundee as (69):
"A want of that attention and vigilance which is due to the
security of other vessels that are navigating on the same
seas, and which if so far neglected as to become, however
unintentionally, the cause of damage of any extent to such
other vessels, the maritime law considers as a dereliction
of bounden duty, entitling the sufferer to reparation in
damages..."

It follows that, although, as the IOC Group of Experts
has pointed out, both the Admiralty system and the ordinary
system of delict or tort in any given country would probably
require some form of negligence in order to found liability,
there are important differences - notably the admiralty rules
as regards the limitation of liability. These differences
would make it extremely difficult, if not impossible, to
state accurately the legal consequences of a collision
between a vessel and an ODAS. This area, therefore, concluded the IOC Group of Experts, "may best commend itself
for clarification by international convention for the
establishment of fixed and readily determinable rules to

apply in all national courts" (70).

The IOC Group of Experts in formulating Draft Article 13 on Collision Liability worked on the basis that in cases of collision between a vessel and an ODAS, liability ought, in accordance with existing principles, to be based on the concept of fault. "This would regulate whether the vessel or the ODAS is to be held liable for resultant damage and would also enable account to be taken of cases of shared responsibility" (71). The Rapporteur explained further that the aim of the Article is to alleviate the problem of gathering evidence: "The crux of the legal problems in collision cases is the gathering of evidence. The bulk of Admiralty law assumes the presence of witnesses on both vessels and paragraph (1) is intended to assimilate the general rules of law relating to vessels to the case of ODAS. However, with regard to the unmanned ODAS, it would seem that certain additional provisions are necessary to place the ODAS on a reasonable parity with the manned vessel" (72).

Thus, in terms of collision liability a fundamental distinction has to be made between manned (paragraph 1) and unmanned (paragraphs 2-4) ODAS.

(a) Manned ODAS

Article 13 (1) reads as follows :

"Except as otherwise provided in this Convention, in the event of a collision involving a registered ODAS and a vessel, aircraft or another ODAS, liability shall be determined on the basis of fault and the loss or damage shall be apportioned in accordance with the norms of international law or national legislation. If the collision is accidental, or if it is due to force majeure, or if there is doubt as to the cause of the collision, the damages shall be borne by those who have suffered them."

Because of the numerous difficulties that were identified during the preliminary discussion, a number of delegations were of the opinion that Article 13 requires to be reconsidered with a view to reformulation. The need for any treaty regulation on this matter was even questioned (73). In the words of the Swedish delegation, for example, "The expresssion 'in accordance with the norms of international law or national legislation' provides little guidance as to which law shall furnish the basis for the distribution of the liability. There is reason to fear lest the provision will be differently applied in various countries. It should be considered instead to include in the Convention provisions of substance corresponding to those which apply to collisions between ships" (74). Indeed, it is clear that if a uniform application of this provision is desired throughout the world, reference should be made only to international law. Furthermore, provisions of substance should also be included, as the Swedish delegation has proposed.

The following Conventions which apply to collisions between ships would seem to be particularly relevant in the present context:

(i) The International Convention for the Unification of Certain Rules of Law in Regard to Collisions, Brussels, 23 September 1910 (75).   The main provisions concerning liability and damage are as follows :

Article 2: If the collision is accidental, or it is caused by force majeure, or if the cause of the collision is left in doubt, the damages are borne by those who have suffered them;

Article 3: It provides that the liability to pay damages for a collision attaches to the vessel whose fault caused the collision;

Article 4: If two or more vessels are at fault, the liability of each vessel is in proportion to the degree of the faults respectively committed. If, however, having regard to the circumstances, it is not possible to establish the degree of the respective faults, or if it appears that the faults are equal, the liability is apportioned equally;

Article 7: Actions for the recovery of damages are barred after two years from the date of the casualty.

(ii) International Convention on Certain Rules Concerning Civil Jurisdiction in Matters of Collision, Brussels, 10 May 1952 (76).

Under the Convention considerable latitude remains in the choice of jurisdiction by the parties, which may agree on the court of their choice or go to arbitration.   In case of no agreement, the plaintiff may bring his action either (a) before the Court where the defendant has his habitual residence or a place of business; or (b) before the Court of the place where arrest has been effected of the defendant ship or of any other ship belonging to the defendant which can be lawfully arrested, or where arrest could have been effected and bail or other security has been furnished; or (c) before the Court of the place of collision when the collision has occurred within the limits of a port or in inland waters.

(iii) International Convention for the Unification of Certain Rules Relating to Penal Jurisdiction In Matters of Collision or Other Incidents of Navigation, Brussels, 10 May 1952 (77).

The Convention applies only to collisions or other incidents of navigation occurring in the territorial sea and the high seas, (Article 4).

The right to institute criminal or disciplinary

proceedings in relation to a collision or any other incident
of navigation concerning a sea-going ship and involving the
penal or disciplinary responsibility of the master or
of any other person in the service of the ship, or to order
the arrest or detention of a vessel, is limited only to the
State whose flag the ship was flying at the time of the
collision, (Articles 1 and 2).

(iv) The Geneva Convention on the High Seas, 1958.

The same provision as above is made, in relation
only to the high seas, by Article 11 of this Convention.

(b) Unmanned ODAS

The IOC Group of Experts considered that certain
additional provisions are necessary to place unmanned ODAS
on a reasonable parity with the manned vessel. The underlying idea is that since the available testimony about the
circumstances of collisions involving unmanned ODAS would
be from one side only, it seems necessary to establish a series
of presumptions about the incidence of fault.

Paragraph 2 of draft Article 13 provides that :

"In the case of a controversy arising out of
collision or other incident involving unmanned registered
surface-penetrating bottom bearing or anchored ODAS and a
vessel, the burden of providing compliance on the part of
the ODAS with Article 8 shall be upon the ODAS owner and
the burden of proving non-compliance on the part of the
ODAS with Article 9 shall be upon the vessel owner (78).
However, the provisions of this section shall not apply in
the case where an anchored ODAS has come adrift or broken
free of its anchor or mooring prior to the collision or other
incident."

Thus, whereas the ODAS owner will have to prove that
he has complied with the notification procedure, the burden
of proving that the lights and other signals of an anchored
or bottom bearing ODAS were not being properly displayed is
upon the colliding vessel. Otherwise the ODAS owner would
have a heavy burden of proof, with a great likelihood of
no eye-witness available to testify on his behalf.

In the case of collision or other incident involving
unmanned drifting ODAS which are surface penetrating, in view
of the somewhat higher risks which this type of ODAS creates,
the burden of proving compliance with notification procedures
and marking and signal requirements, shall be upon the ODAS
owner, (paragraph 3). However, with regard to unmanned
sub-surface ODAS, paragraph 4 deals with these as dangerous
devices, if some sort of surface signal is not provided.
Thus, it is provided that in the case of collision involving
such ODAS that does not display a signal as required, and
a vessel, the ODAS shall be solely liable for the damages

which may have been incurred   (paragraph 4).

Draft Article 13, far from being complete, leaves outside its scope many contingencies, such as a collision between ODAS and some other structure, which is neither a ship nor an ODAS.   This is not to say, however, that the IOC Group of Experts or the Preparatory Conference were not aware of the complexity of the problem and the difficulties involved (79).   Simply, collision liability still requires a considerable amount of work and it is currently being studied by the Group of Experts on private law aspects of ODAS (80).

In view of the fact that the Draft Convention on ODAS will take a few years to materialise, it would seem advisable to describe the jurisdictional principles that would be applied, and the scope of liability prescribed, by courts, in cases of collisions involving ships and ODAS, under existing law.   In this respect, the conclusions reached by the IOC Group of Experts best summarise the position under customary law:

"In cases of damage to vessels caused by the presence of ODAS on the high seas, it might be expected that courts would apply jurisdictional principles similar to those applicable to collisions of vessels or collisions of vessels with non-maritime objects.... Thus the place of the accident, the place of seizure, the nationality and the domicile of the parties involved would be important factors in determining jurisdiction but it is possible that any State in which an action is brought might consider itself competent to hear the case.

Cases involving the liability for ODAS would probably be decided in accordance with principles of maritime or general liability applicable in the jurisdiction where a case is heard.   Where all the parties involved are nationals of another State, the court might apply the law of the other State in accordance with its conflict of law rules.

Since there are no known cases where liability has been imposed upon those responsible for ODAS, it is difficult to anticipate precisely the scope of that liability.   Yet it would seem likely that a court would apply at least a minimum theory of negligence in determining liability.   The person responsible might thus be held to a general standard of care that a reasonably prudent man would exercise under all the circumstances.   If courts should apply such a principle it may be seen that a number of factors would affect the finding of liability, including size, weight and character of the equipment, its location in or near recognized sea lanes, the giving of notice, type of notice,

use of warning devices, such as bells, horns, lights
and radar reflectors, visibility, colour, the number
and distribution of devices and so forth.   It is
impossible to determine abstractly, in advance, what
combination of these and other possible factors would
be sufficient to find or avoid liability.   This
uncertainty is further complicated by the possibility
that a court would consider the conduct of the Master
of the damaged vessel in determining the question of
liability or in apportioning it " (81).

Indeed, two known municipal court decisions of some
pertinence, reported by the United States authorities, would
appear to confirm the present state of affairs, as described
above by the IOC Group of Experts.   These cases which deal with
collisions between vessels and off-shore structures (fixed
oil-well platforms) are :

Continental Oil Co. v M.S. GLENVILLE, D.C.S.D., Texas
1962, 210 F. Supp. 865, and Placid Oil Company v s.s. WILLOWPOOL,
D.C.E.D. Terms 1963, 214 F. Supp.449, (82).

Both collisions occurred on the high seas and both
vessels were flying foreign flags.   Both platforms were lighted
in accordance with United States regulations and there was no
impairment of visibility.   Both courts held the vessels solely
at fault.   The courts treated the cases under the rules
governing collision between a moving vessel and a vessel at
anchor, holding that there was a presumption of fault which
the moving vessel would have to (but could not) overcome.
Referring to these decisions the United States Government
has commented that :

"There is no reason to believe that the character of a
structure as oil-exploitation or oceanographic makes
any difference as to the treatment it would be
accorded in the courts" (83).

NOTES

1.   See the Rapporteur's comment to Draft Article 6 of
the Proposed Articles, SC/IOC. WG-4/INF.-1 in IMCO DOC. LEG
VIII/2/Add.1, 1 April 1970, at p.5.
2.   IMCO DOC.LEG VIII/WP.3, 23 April, 1970, at p.9.
3.   See the Rapporteur's comment to draft Article 6, supra.
4.   Annex to U.N. General Assembly Resolution 2345 (XXII),
Dec.19, 1967.   General Assembly, 22nd. Session, Official Records,
Suppl. No.16 (A/6716), p.6; T.I.A.S. No.6599; reproduced in
7 I.L.M. (1968), p.151; and 63 A.J.I.L. (1969), pp.382-385.
For an analysis of this Agreement see M. Lachs, The Law of

Outer Space, 1972, Chapter VII; and B. Cheng, The 1968 Astronauts Agreement or How not to Make a Treaty, 23 Y.B.W.A. (1969),
pp.185-208.

    5.   See also Article V of the Treaty on Principles
Governing the Activities of States in the Exploration and Use
of Outer Space, Including the Moon and Other Celestial Bodies,
27 January 1967, which contains a similar provision; for the
text of this treaty see in 6 I.L.M. (1967), pp.386-390.

    6.   See also Article VIII of the Treaty Governing
Activities in Outer Space, supra.

    7.   See the Rapporteur's comment to draft Article 6,
supra.

    8.   In this context it is interesting to note that the
IMCO Maritime Safety Committee decided at its twenty-fourth
session to establish a Group of Experts for the preparation
of a Draft Agreement on a Search and Rescue System. See the
relevant IMCO Docs. MSC XXVIII/12, 16 June 1973; MSC XXXII/14,
31 December 1974; and MSC XXXIV/9, 29 January 1976 (containing a report of the Group of Experts as well as a draft of
the future SAR Convention, 1978, Doc. SAR III/9, 5 January 1976).

    9.   See also Article 86 (Duty to render assistance)
of R.S.N.T., Part II.

    10.   Comment on draft Article 7 of the Proposed Articles
for the Preliminary Draft Convention, SC/IOC. WG-4/INF-1, see
in IMCO DOC. LEG VII/2/Add.1, 1 April, 1970, at p.6.

    11.   Lord Chorley and O.C. Giles, Shipping Law, 6th ed.,
1970, at p.5. Subject to registration are also hovercraft
or air-cushion vehicles, which can operate on the water or be
airborne over water or land; see the United Kingdom Hovercraft
Act, 1968, S.I.

    12.   DOC.SC-72/CONF.85/8, Summary Report at pp. 7-8.

    13.   Paragraph 2 of draft Article 7 of the Proposed Articles
for the Preliminary Draft Convention provided that a State
could register only an ODAS deployed either by itself or by
a person permanently resident in its territory. It was
thought that the introduction of the permanent residence link
would help avoiding some of the difficulties which have been
experienced in the parallel situation involving vessels, that is
the "flag of convenience" phenomenon.

    14.   See, for instance, the United Kingdom Merchant
Shipping Act, 1894, Sections 2 (Obligation to register British
Ships) and 3, (Exemptions from registry).

    15.   See the Comment to Draft Article 7 of the Proposed
Articles, supra.

    16.   See DOC.SC-72/CONF.85/8, Annex III, at pp.8 and 17.

    17.   As regards ships, see the corresponding Article 5
of the Geneva Convention on the High Seas, 1958.

    18.   SC/IOC.EG-1 (IV)/12, 17 September 1970, Annex III,
Comment on Article 6 at p.17.

    19.   DOC.SC-72/CONF.85/8, Summary Report, at pp.8-9.

20.   Shipowners register their ships in such flags of
convenience States for various reasons.   Taxation is very low
and operating cots are lower because the legislation and
collective agreements on wages, labour conditions and social
security of the traditionally maritime countries do not apply.
Lack of substantive maritime legislation in these States also
means that there are no stringent provisions in relation to
safety requirements, accommodation and protection of crews,
and so forth.   Finally, shipowners wish to avoid the possibility of their vessels being requisitioned by their national
States in the event of war, and the consequences of political
unrest where a change of government might result in confiscation
of property.   See in general, "Study on the Expansion of the
Flags of Convenience Fleets and Various Aspects Thereof,"
Organization for European Economic Co-operation, DOC.C/(57) 246,
28 January 1958; B.A. Boczek, Flags of Convenience, 1962;
and S.G. Sturmey, British Shipping and World Competition, 1962,
at pp.210-233.
21.   The principle upon which the International Court
of Justice acted in the Nottebohm Case, was that only if the
grant of nationality is based upon a genuine connection between
the State and the individuals, and is thus the legal expression
of a real and effective nationality corresponding with the
factual situation, can it be invoked against foreign States
as a valid legal act, Judgment of 6 April 1955,(second phase)
I.C.J. Reports, 1955, p.4.
22.   II ILC Yearbook 1956, atpp.278-279.
23.   Ibid., at p.279.
24.   It is generally agreed that the problem of flags
of convenience has not been solved by the Geneva Convention.
Indeed unless the flags of convenience States are prepared to
modify their legislation and practice, and unless traditional
maritime countries discourage their capital and shipping
interests from resorting to this means of competition in international shipping, there is no real hope of solving this problem.
But this then is a problem of international competition in a
hugely important industry rather than a problem of the law of
the sea.
25.   See Paragraph 2 of draft Article 7 of the Proposed
Articles for the Preliminary Draft Convention, DOC.SC/IOC.
EG-1/7, Annex IV, p.5.
26.   See the ILC's Commentary to draft Article 29 (now
Article 5). II ILC Yearbook 1956, at p.278.
27.   DOC.SC-72/CONF.85/8, Summary Report, p.8.
28.   See, for example, the position taken by the
Netherlands delegation, DOC.SC-72/CONF.85/8, Annex III, at
pp.12-13.
29.   IMCO DOC. LEG VIII/WP.3, 23 April 1970, at p.11.
30.   See further Article 52 of R.S.N.T., Part III:
"Marine scientific research activities shall not form the
legal basis for any claim whatsoever to any part of the

marine environment or its resources."

31.   DOC.SC/IOC.EG-1/7, Annex III, at p.6; see also
DOC.SC/IOC-VI/INF.142, Annex I, at p.4.

32.   From that point of view perhaps the word 'interference'
should consequently be qualified by an appropriate word such
as 'undue' or 'unjustified,' even though the paragraph starts
with "Except as otherwise provided in this Convention.....".

33.   DOC.SC/IOC.EG-1/7, Annex III, at p.6.

34.   Knauth's Benedict on Admiralty 358 (1958).

35.   Ibid., at p.371.

36.   DOC.SC/IOC.EG-1/7, Annex III, at p.7.

37.   IMCO DOC. LEG. VIII/WP.3, 23 April 1970, at p.12.
The above mentioned Convention lays down that inspection of
the Oil Record Book, which is carried by every ship to which
the Convention applies, may take place on board any such ship
by the competent authorities of any Contracting State - but only
while the ship is within a port in any of that State's territories.   The Netherlands delegation has also suggested during
the discussions of the IMCO Legal Committee on the Legal Status
of ODAS, that the system adopted in the Convention for the
Protection of Submarine Telegraph Cables, 1884, may well
deserve consideration in this context.   Under that system,
investigation and prosecution can be undertaken by all Contracting States but trials can be conducted only by the State to
which the ship having caused the damage belongs, (Articles 8
and 9), IMCO DOC. LEG VIII/2/Add.2, 15 April 1970 at p.3.

38.   DOC/SC/IOC.EG-1/7, Annex III, at p.7, According to
the draft Article concerning penal responsibility, prepared
by the Group of Experts on private law aspects of ODAS, "States
Parties undertake to make it.... (e) a serious offence to
possess, sell or arrange to sell an unlawfully obtained ODAS
or any part thereof"; see DOC IOC/ODAS-LEG/3, 10 June 1974,
Annex II, Appendix I.

39.   DOC.SC/IOC.EG-1(IV)/12, Annex III, at p.19.

40.   See the corresponding comments of the ILC on draft
Article 39 (now Article 15), on Piracy, II ILC Yearbook 1956,
at p.282.

41.   DOC.SC/IOC.EG-1(IV)/12, 17 September 1970, Annex III,
at p.19.   See also the draft Article on civil liability for
interference with an ODAS, prepared by the Group of Experts on
private law aspects of ODAS, DOC. IOC/ODAS-LEG/3, Annex II, at p.3.

42.   Article 9 (3) of the Proposed Articles for the
Preliminary Draft Convention, DOC.SC/IOC.EG-1/7, Annex IV, at p.6.

43.   IMCO DOC.LEG.VIII/WP.3, 23 April 1970, at p.13.

44.   See Articles 27-28 of the Convention on the High
Seas, and Articles 2 and 4 of the 1884 Submarine Telegraph
Cables Convention.

45.   Article 15 of the draft Convention on ODAS.   This
Article adopts the provisions concerning submarine cables to
the case of ODAS, see Article 29 of the Geneva Convention on

the High Seas, 1958.

46.   Salvage originates in a sort of maritime equity and it is of very ancient date.   For practical purposes a salvor's service has been defined as a "service which saves or helps to save maritime property - a vessel, its apparel, cargo, or wreck - or lives of persons belonging to any vessel, when in danger, either at sea or on the shore of the sea, or in tidal waters, if and so far as the rendering of such service is voluntary, and attributable neither to legal obligation, nor to the interest of self-preservation, nor to the stress of official duty," Kennedy, Civil Salvage, 4th edition, 1958, at pp.4-5; Lord Chorley, O.C. Giles, Shipping Law, 6th edition 1970, at pp.273-274.

47.   Convention for the Unification of Certain Rules of Law Respecting Assistance and Salvage at Sea, Brussels, 23 September 1910; see in N. Singh, International Conventions of Merchant Shipping, second edition, 1973, at pp.1422-1426. See further the Protocol to Amend the Convention for the Unification of Certain Rules of Law relating to Assistance and Salvage at Sea, signed at Brussels, September 23, 1910, done at Brussels, 27 May 1967, also in N. Singh, at pp.1426-1428.

48.   Success of the salvage operations is one of the three conditions necessary to secure a reward, S.S. Melanie v. S.S San Onofre, 1925, A.C.246, at 262 per Lord Phillimore; The Cheerful, 1885, II P.D. 3; The Marguerite Molinos, 1903, P.160.   The other two conditions are : (i) the existence of danger, and (ii) the voluntary character of the service.

49.   It is a fundamental rule of the law relating to salvage that no award may be higher than the value of the salved property, see The Tarbert, 1921, P.372.

50.   In the United Kingdom the common law position is that where a salvor saves both life and property the amount he will recover will probably be higher than if he had only saved property; yet if he saves life alone he will have no right to reward, The Renpor, 1883, 8 P.D., 115, p.117 per M.R. Brett; The Cargo ex Sarpedon, 1877, 3 P.D.28; The Medina, 1876, 1 P.D.272; 2 P.D.5.   Today the situation in regard to life salvage is to some extent regulated by Statute. If salvage services are rendered to a British ship anywhere or to a foreign ship in British waters, and no or insufficient property is saved, the Board of Trade may in its discretion award a sum out of the Mercantile Marine Fund; Merchant Shipping Act, 1894, S.544 (3); Merchant Shipping (Mercantile Marine Fund) Act, 1898, S.I. (1) (b).

51.   See the corresponding Articles 8 of the 1910 Brussels Convention on collisions, and 12 of the Geneva Convention on the High Seas, 1958.

52.   Colombos, International Law of the Sea, sixth edition, 1967, at pp.341, 348-349.

53.   IOC, Techn. Ser., No. 5, at p.14.

54, DOC.SC/IOC.EG-1(IV)/12, 17 September 1970, Annex III, at pp.32-33.

55. IOC, Techn. Ser., No. 5, at p.26.

56. DOC.SC/IOC.EG-1/7, Annex III, at pp.7-8.

57. DOC.SC/IOC.EG-1(IV)/12, 17 September 1970, Annex III, at p.33.

58. A similar view has also been expressed by the IOC Group of Experts as regards unmanned ODAS, IOC, Techn. Ser., No. 5, at p.14.

59. See the Air Navigation Act, 1920, section 11 and the Civil Aviation Act, 1949, section 51(1).

60. Kennedy, Civil Salvage, fourth edition, 1958, at p.4.

61. Lord Chorley and O.C. Giles, Shipping Law, sixth edition, 1970, at p.274.

62. 1895, P.301; 1896 P.42 C.A; 1897 A.C.337.

63. The gas-float was like a ship but had no rudder, sails or engines; it was constructed and used solely to provide a lighted aid to navigation such as is provided by lightships or lighted buoys.

64. 1896, P.42, 63.

65. IOC, Techn. Ser., No. 5, at p.13.

66. 3 Rippert, Droit Maritime, 1953, at pp.11, 13-14, cited in IOC, Techn. Ser., No. 5, at pp.13-14.

67. 1 Knauth's Benedict on Admiralty 364 (New York 1958), cited in IOC, Techn. Ser., No. 5, at p.14.

68. Marsden, Collisions at Sea, Eleventh Edition, 1961, at p.1. See further The Tolten, 1946, P.135 at 147 per L.J. Scott.

69. 1823, 1 Hag. Ad., 109 at 120.

70. IOC, Techn. Ser., No. 5, at p.14.

71 DOC.SC/IOC.EG-1/7, Annex III, at p.8.

72. DOC.SC/IOC.EG-1(IV)/12, 17 September 1970 Annex III, at p.31.

73. DOC.SC-72/CONF.85/8, Summary Report, at p.14.

74. Ibid., Annex III, at p.23.

75. For the text of the Convention see in Marsden, Collisions at Sea, 11th ed., 1961, at pp.891-894, and also in N. Singh, International Conventions of Merchant Shipping, 2nd ed., 1973, at pp 1337-1341.

76. For the text of the Convention see in Marsden, supra, at pp. 900-902, and also in N. Singh, supra, at pp.1444-1447.

77. See Marsden, supra, at pp.902-903, and N. Singh, supra, at pp.1447-1450.

78. Draft Article 8 deals with notification of deployment, activities and information concerning ODAS, while draft Article 9 deals with marking and signals.

79. See, for example, the list of problems that were encountered in formulating the Preliminary Draft at the Preparatory Conference, DOC.SC-72/CONF.85/8, Summary Report, at p.14.

80. See DOC. IOC/ODAS-LEG/3, 10 June 1974, Annex II, Arts. I and XI.

81. IOC, Techn. Ser., No. 5, at p.15.

82. These cases are cited in IOC, Techn. Ser., No.5, at p.28.

83. Ibid.

Chapter 9

SAFETY RULES COVERING ODAS: ACCOMMODATION
OF CONFLICTING USES

INTRODUCTION

Safe navigation requires the orderly movement of
maritime transport and gradually a body of rules for preventing
collisions at sea has evolved, both by independent national
enactment and by international act.   On the international
level, a number of Conferences have resulted in a series of
Collision Regulations.
The last system to enter into force was the International
Regulations for Preventing Collisions at sea (1), approved
by, and annexed to the Final Act of, the International
Conference on Safety of Life at Sea (SOLAS), London 17 June 1960
(2).
Measures for safety at sea are also provided for in the
Geneva Convention on the High Seas 1958.   According to
Article 10 of the Convention, every State shall take such
measures for ships under its flag as are necessary to ensure
safety at sea with regard, inter alia, to: (a)   the use of
signals, the maintenance of communications and the prevention
of collisions;   (b)   the manning of ships and labour conditions
for crews;   and (c)   the construction, equipment and seaworthi-
ness of ships.   In taking such measures States are required
to conform to generally accepted international standards and
also ensure their observance.
Just as the safety of navigation involves common action
and adoption of uniform rules on the part of maritime States,
so the protection of both ODAS and other maritime uses might
be best served by uniform and widely promulgated rules.   The
two objectives are clearly related.   Adequate safety measures
must be provided to ensure that ODAS do not become a hazard to

navigation and fishing (fishing vessels). Certain of these
devices could also be used as navigational aids both to
vessels and to aircraft.

Presently, of course, there is no international Convention
in force regulating the deployment and use of ODAS or
navigational buoys (3). However, there have certainly been
individual national enactments which have led to diversity
of usage throughout the world (4).

IMCO, being particularly keen in matters affecting
maritime safety, is especially aware that consideration must
be given to the hazard which special craft, such as ODAS,
drilling rigs, production platforms and other devices, may
present to navigation. The Convention on IMCO has established
the Maritime Safety Committee to deal with a variety of respon-
sibilities including rules for the prevention of collisions,
hydrographic information, aids to navigation, maritime safety
procedures and requirements, and in general any matters directly
affecting maritime safety. The Committee has the duty to
maintain such close relationship with other intergovernmental
organizations concerned with transport and communications as
may further the purpose of IMCO in promoting maritime safety.
In this respect the Committee has maintained a close working
relationship with IOC regarding the safety aspects of the
operation of ODAS. For example, the development and application of a scheme of distinctive marking and identification
of ODAS is of continuing concern to the Maritime Safety
Committee of IMCO, which has drawn up certain drafts on
safety requirements.

Measures for ensuring safety in navigation and protecting
ODAS are, in summary, susceptible to treatment in both
domestic and international law. The task ahead is to decide
the appropriate course of action in both areas. The problem
is, of course, primarily an administrative one within the
ambit of the technical expert. However, the contribution
of the lawyer may be considerable in this context, since the
measures chosen may involve extension of existing legal concepts and the amendment of rules currently in force on both
the national and international planes.

The draft Convention on ODAS contains a number of Articles
dealing with the problem of safety measures and the protection
of navigation. The main provisions are to be found in
the following Articles : Article 8 - Notification;
Article 9 - Marking and Signals; Article 10 - ODAS used as
aids to navigation; Article 11 - Construction Arrangements
and other safety provisions; and Article 12 - Requirements in
matters of safety of deployment.

Of direct interest in the present context are also the
three, out of four, Annexes attached to the draft Convention,
dealing with technical matters. These Annexes are: Annex I
entitled 'Notification'; Annex II entitled 'Marking and Signals';

and Annex III entitled 'Construction Arrangements and other Safety Provisions' (5).

I.   NOTIFICATION

With Article 8 the ODAS Convention attempts to promote safety at sea by requiring notice of deployment and information concerning ODAS.   It provides that member States shall require ODAS operators to give notice to the appropriate authorities of the Registry State of deployment, activities and information concerning ODAS, for promulgation in accordance with the provisions of Annex I.

In the words of the Rapporteur, "it is absolutely essential that mariners be apprised of the location of ODAS, the signal characteristics and other information which will assist in the prevention of collisions and will also preclude unintentional interference with ODAS - a passing uninformed mariner might retrieve an ODAS under the misapprehension that the device was abandoned, unintentionally adrift, and so forth" (6).

A number of delegations felt that the Article had an essential defect, in that provision had not been made for any sanction in cases where an ODAS deployer or the Registry State did not give notification (7).   The Article does not specify the particular methods to be employed in notification and dissemination of information.   It was intended that the traditional methods of exchange and publication of such information be utilised.   This would certainly include notices to mariners, radio navigational warnings, hydrographic bulletins and sailing directions.   Detailed provisions concerning notices of activities, information and details related to ODAS, advance notice and danger messages, are incorporated in Annex I, which is expressly referred to in Article 8 (8).

II.   MARKING AND SIGNALS

Whether deployed in internal waters, in the territorial sea or on the high seas, a strong case exists for uniformity in marking and signal requirements for ODAS, so that mariners have only one set of rules to apply in all areas.   Standard markings (colours, lighting, etc.) for ODAS have been approved by IMCO and recommended by IOC for adoption by Member States (9).

Article 74 of the Revised Single Negotiating Text, Part III, lays down that scientific research installations or equipment "shall bear identification markings indicating the State or international organization where they are registered and shall have adequate internationally agreed warning signals to ensure the safety of sea and air navigation, taking into account the principles established by competent international organizations."

Article 9 and Annex II of the ODAS Convention are designed to fulfil the need for uniformity in marking and signals. Article 9 provides that all (registered) ODAS shall comply with the marking and signal requirements prescribed in Annex II.

There was some discussion as to whether this Article should apply only to registered ODAS, hence the brackets, but surely in the interests of safety it should apply to all ODAS and not only to registered ones. Doubts were also expressed as to whether a distinction should be made between ODAS-vessels and any other ODAS. The International Rules for Preventing Collisions at Sea 1960, do not cover such devices as aids to navigation, offshore drilling platforms, or ODAS. In the words of the Rapporteur, "these rules contemplate either an ability to manoeuvre or at least to transmit human intelligence (such as the breakdown or not under-command signal) which ability is not a characteristic of the bulk of ODAS" (10).

III. ODAS USED AS AIDS TO NAVIGATION

Draft Article 10 of the ODAS Convention was introduced to cover the situation where an ODAS, normally an anchored, moored or bottom bearing type, is used as an aid to navigation. The Article was put in brackets since a number of delegations considered it undesirable and beyond the competence of the Conference to adopt. However, it was pointed out that to deploy and maintain a device of any kind at sea was highly costly and it was thereforevery desirable to allow for the use of multi-purpose systems (11).

Paragraph 1 provides that in areas in which aids to navigation are provided, an anchored or bottom bearing ODAS may, with the consent of the owner and the agreement of the Registry State, be designated as an aid to navigation by the State providing aids to navigation in the area concerned, in conformity with the lighting and marking regulations for aids to navigation prevailing in that area. In that case, and not withstanding the provisions of Articles 8 and 9 of the Convention (concerning notification and marking and signals), the ODAS which has been designated as an aid to navigation shall no longer be required to conform to those provisions of Annexes I and II which conflict with the requirements for aids to navigation in the area.

The Rapporteur had commented on an earlier draft that ODAS may be designated as aids to navigation provided that certain tests are met: permanency, charting, standard signal characteristics and reliability standards (12).

It should be noted that in some States buoyage is entirely a governmental matter, in certain others, at least technically, a private matter and in others it is a combination of both (13). In the first case, it is, in the words of the Rapporteur," common sense that if the ODAS is to be

designated an aid to navigation, it should conform to the
scheme in force in the area," and the Article so provides (14).
However, on the high seas where no Buoyage State is operating
a system of aids to navigation and in the absence of any
international standardization of aids to navigation, signal
characteristics, marking etc., the Registry State appears
to be the logical State to make the designation (15).

In the United States, for example, establishment of aids
to navigation is provided for by statute and is regulated by
the provisions of Title 33 of the Code of Federal Regulations
which is concerned with navigation and navigable waters
generally (16). Establishment of aids to navigation by a
federal agency of the United States is provided for and
protected by regulation, and it is generally required that
such establishment be co-ordinated with the Coast Guard.
Private individuals or groups may establish aids to navigation
in the navigable waters of the United States, and these are
protected from interference or obstruction in the same manner
as government maintained aids (17).

Paragraph 2 is intended to cover the situation where
an ODAS is no longer employed as such. It provides that:
"An ODAS once designated as an aid to navigation
shall retain that designation and function, with the
agreement of the Registry State until properly
terminated by the designating State even though it
may, for any reason, no longer function as an ODAS."
In the words of the Rapporteur, "from the view-point of the
ODAS operator, its mission can be terminated promptly. However,
the interests of the mariner lie in a good degree of permanence
for aids to navigation. Accordingly, the proper disestablishment
of an aid to navigation, entailing adequate advance notice to
the mariner, may take a longer period of time. This paragraph
precludes abrupt termination of the responsibility to maintain
the device as an aid to navigation" (18).

In this context, therefore, the requirement for the
agreement of the Registry State is questionable. Earlier
drafts did not contain such a provision. However, in the
interests of navigation the agreement of the Registry State
should not be withheld in normal circumstances.

Paragraph 3 attempts to settle the difficult question
of liability in the special case of ODAS designated as aids
to navigation: "Liability for damage caused to or by ODAS
designated as an aid to navigation shall be governed by the
law of the designating State."

IV. CONSTRUCTION ARRANGEMENTS AND OTHER SAFETY PROVISIONS

According to Article 11 of the ODAS Convention all
(registered) ODAS shall comply with the provisions of Annex III

relating to construction arrangements and other safety
provisions.

The safety requirements are designed to apply
essentially to manned ODAS and, according to Annex III, they
do not apply to an installation, which has primarily been designed and deployed for purposes other than ocean data acquisition, e.g. off-shore drilling rigs, production platforms,
navigational aids, submersibles, etc., even if it is used for
ocean data acquisition (19). Article 11 and technical
Annex III are intended to provide for regulatory measures
covering such matters as the use of explosive, flammable,
toxic or radio-active substances, fire protection, ventilation
systems, life-saving appliances, distress signals, radio
communication, machinery and electrical installations, pressure
vessels, high voltage equipment, automatically operated rocket
propelled radio-sondes, and so forth. The same Annex provides
further that the Registry State shall establish and maintain
an effective system of inspection in order to ensure compliance
with the requirements of this Annex.

In the words of the Rapporteur, "perhaps in this area
more than any other, the need for a technical annex incorporating
all provisions which are susceptible to modification to maintain
currency with technological developments, is clear. Further,
it is recognized that this annex would need to be capable of
ready amendment as new devices are developed and as experience
dictates the need for control or regulation in a particular
area" (20).

The Sub-Committee on Safety of Navigation of the IMCO
Maritime Safety Committee has also considered the problem of
safety requirements on construction and equipment. In its
view the Registry State in promulgating the safety and other
standards in relation to deployment, equipment, operation
and manning of ODAS, should be guided by relevant requirements
of current International Conventions and appropriate Codes
and Recommendations. The Registry State should further
establish and maintain an effective system of inspecting ODAS
from the point of view of construction, marking, signals and
safety equipment. Machinery should finally be established
to allow for the necessary amendment and up-dating of these
requirements of the ODAS Convention which may depend on other
relevant international instruments in cases where the latter
are changed (21).

V. REQUIREMENTS IN MATTERS OF
SAFETY OF DEPLOYMENT

Article 12, of the ODAS Convention, which remains rather
unfinished and confusing and is, perhaps, exceedingly long,
deals with the problems involved in the safety of deployment
of ODAS. Clearly, this Article has been modelled on the

provisions contained in Article 5 of the Geneva Convention
on the Continental Shelf 1958, dealing with the construction
and maintenance on the continental shelf of installations
and other devices necessary for the exploration and exploitation
of its natural resources.

Paragraph 1 provides that a Registry State may establish
safety zones around anchored, bottom bearing or nuclear, surface-
penetrating ODAS, the size of which shall take due account
of the location of the ODAS and of the nature of the hazard
involved.   These safety zones shall not interfere with the
freedom of navigation in the area concerned, and will only
be established with the agreement of the State providing aids
to navigation in the area, if such exists.   All ships must
respect these safety zones in so far as practicable.

It will be noted that safety zones may be established
only around certain types of ODAS: anchored, bottom bearing
and nuclear, surface-penetrating ODAS.   Secondly, the
breadth of the safety zones is not defined in Article 12.
According to Article 72 of the Revised Single Negotiating Text,
Part III, on the other hand, "safety zones of a reasonable
width not exceeding a distance of 500 meters may be created
around scientific research installations...   All States shall
ensure that such safety zones are respected by their vessels."

The discussion on Article 12 focussed on the establishment of these safety zones, which proved quite controversial.
Several delegations considered that safety zones could imply
an appropriation of stretches of the high seas.   Consequently,
this Article did not cover solely technical aspects but
raised a serious question of international law which would
be considered by the United Nations Sea-Bed Committee.   Other
delegations, however, opposed this view.   According to them,
safety zones did not imply such appropriation.   The purpose
of safety zones is solely to protect both the interests of
shipping and safe navigation and also the ODAS and, further,
to safeguard the collection of ocean data.   The object, thus,
is merely to avoid conflict with other legitimate uses (22).
Following the doubts expressed as to the desirability or
necessity of safety zones, and the recommendation of a working
group of the Conference that they should not be permitted (23),
all provisions concerning the establishment of safety zones
have been placed in brackets.

Assuming, however, that the establishment of safety
zones around ODAS will be deemed desirable or necessary, the
problem of jurisdiction exercised within these zones will have
to be faced.   It will be remembered that under Article 6,
ODAS are subject to the "effective jurisdiction and control"
of the Registry State.   Thus, any act or omission which
takes place on, under or above them will be under the competence
of the Registry State's courts.   They are subject to any
regulations and orders issued by the Registry State authorities,

such as those concerning maintenance of order on ODAS, safety measures, registration, etc. There is not, however, a comparable provision for safety zones, where the position is not at all clear and a number of questions arise. Article 5 (2) of the Geneva Convention on the Continental Shelf, 1958, provides that the coastal State may "establish safety zones around installations and devices and to take in those zones measures necessary for their protection."

Even though draft Article 12 does not contain a similar provision, the Registry State must surely be able to take within the safety zones the measures necessary for the protection and normal function of ODAS. The kind of measures which could be taken in that case should be clearly defined, and in this respect the experience gained from the analogous situation concerning installations established on the continental shelf for exploration and exploitation purposes can be very useful.

Paragraph 2, in conjunction with paragraph 5, provides further that safety zones shall not be established in certain areas. According to paragraph 5 ODAS should not ordinarily be deployed in straits, fairways, approaches to ports, converging areas where traffic separation schemes are in force, fishing ground or other areas of congested marine traffic.

However, the same paragraph 5 provides also that where it is necessary or useful to acquire data from such areas, particularly data of value to fishing, navigation or pollution control, the deployment of ODAS in such areas of congested marine traffic shall be subject to a number of conditions.

Paragraph 6 deals with the sub-surface ODAS. It provides that a sub-surface ODAS which, due to the depth at which it is deployed may constitute a danger to shipping and safe navigation, shall either be escorted by a vessel capable of giving due warning of its presence to passing marine traffic, or else be provided with signals as set forth in Annex II.

As the Rapporteur has observed, "because of the technical problems involved, it is unlikely that unmanned, sub-surface drifting ODAS of any size will be deployed. In the case of manned, sub-surface, drifting ODAS, an attending vessel on the surface is necessary for many other reasons and the obligation that this vessel give warning to passing mariners seems appropriate. Sub-surface anchored or bottom-bearing ODAS which may constitute a danger to shipping and safe navigation can however be covered by the requirement for effective signal characteristics on or above the surface, i.e. on a marker buoy of some kind" (24).

Finally, paragraphs 3 and 4 deal with the removal of abandoned or disused ODAS. The underlying idea is that all such ODAS must be removed, and all costs for such removals should be borne, by the owner. Paragraph 3 provides that if an ODAS is abandoned or disused, it shall be removed, when the Registry State considers it necessary or upon the request

of the State which provides aids to navigation in the area,
if such exists.   The owner is required to remove the ODAS
entirely, if it is a bottom-bearing or anchored ODAS not gone
adrift;   in other cases the owner shall be required to make
every practicable effort to remove the ODAS.   Paragraph 4
provides further that in the event of abandoned or disused
ODAS, or an ODAS which has been sunk, constituting a danger
to shipping and safe navigation, or fishing operations, the
State, or where appropriate the designated authority,
providing the aids to navigation in the area, may mark and/or
remove it with due notification to the Registry State and
recover the cost from the owner.

The Preparatory Conference on ODAS adopted a Resolution
on the Advance Implementation of Safety Provisions, urging
the member States of UNESCO, IMCO and IOC to use voluntarily
the provisions of the technical Annexes I, II and III, prior
to the possible entry into force of any eventual ODAS
Convention.   Indeed, the IMCO Maritime Safety Committee and
the Executive Council of IOC agreed to publish the technical
Annexes, with a view to recommending their voluntary use by
member States as provisional guidelines for national measures.
IMCO has now published, on behalf of the two Agencies, the
Annexes as a composite document under the title "Safety
Provisions of Ocean Data Acquisition Systems, Aids and
Devices, (ODAS)."

NOTES

1.   1966 U.K.T.S. 23.   The Regulations entered into
force on September 1, 1965 and they have been accepted or
followed by States representing almost the whole of the
world's tonnage.   The new Convention on the International
Regulations for Preventing Collisions at Sea, London, October
1972, is not in force yet (May 1976).

2.536 U.N.T.S. 271;   1965 U.K.T.S.65.   The SOLAS Convention
came into force on 26 May 1965.   A new International Convention
for the Safety of Life at Sea, intended to replace the 1960
SOLAS Convention, was concluded in London on November 1 1974.
The texts of the final Act of the Conference (October 21-
November 1, 1974) and the Convention, appeared at 14 I.L.M. 1975,
at p.959.

3.   An unsuccessful attempt to conclude one was made at the
Conference for the Unification of Buoyage and Lighting of Coasts,
Lisbon, 1930.   At a later date, an agreement for a uniform
system of buoyage was opened for signature by the League of
Nations, but did not enter into force.   However, certain of the

Buoyage Rules annexed to the agreement are in current use in some maritime States by provision of domestic law, IOC. Techn. Ser., No. 5 at p.12.

 4. The International Hydrographic Bureau lists information on the systems of Maritime Buoyage and Beaconage adopted by various countries in its special publication No.38.

 5. Annex IV is entitled 'Recommended Standard Form for Registration of ODAS.' These technical Annexes are contained in Annex IV of the Document SC-72/CONF.85/8.

 6. DOC.SC/IOC.EG-1(IV)/12, Annex III, at p.20.

 7. DOC.SC-72/CONF.85/8, Summary Report, at p.11.

 8. DOC.SC-72/CONF.85/8, Annex IV, at pp. 1-3.

 9. See Annex XI-A to the Report of the IOC Third Session - UNESCO/NS/191, dated 29 October 1964, and Annex III to IOC. Techn. Ser., No.5.

 10. DOC.SC/IOC.EG-1(IV)/12, 17 September 1970, Annex III, at p.22.

 11. DOC.SC-72/CONF.85/8, Summary Report, at pp.11 and 18.

 12. DOC.SC/IOC.EG-1(IV)/12, 17 September 1970, Annex III, at p.24; DOC/SC/IOC.WG-4/INF-1, see in IMCO DOC.LEG.VIII/2/Add.1, 1 April 1970, at p.9.

 13. Ibid.

 14. Ibid.

 15. DOC.SC/IOC.WG-4/INF-1, in IMCO DOC.LEG.VIII/2/Add.1, 1 April, 1970, at p.9.

 16. See the United States Report to IOC on the Legal Status of Fixed Oceanographic Stations, IOC. Techn. Ser., No.5, p.26 at p.27.

 17. Ibid.

 18. DOC.SC/IOC.EG-1/IV)/12, 17 September 1970, Annex III at p.24.

 19. Technical Annex III, 1.1.1. and 1.1.2., DOC.SC-72/CONF. 85/8, Annex IV, at p.6.

 20. DOC.SC/IOC.EG-1(IV)/12, 17 September 1970, Annex III, at p.25.

 21. IMCO DOCS. LEG VIII/2/Add.3, 20 April 1970, at p.10 and LEG VIII/WP.3, 23 April 1970, at p.15.

 22. DOC.SC-72/CONF.85/8, Summary Report, at p.12.

 23. Ibid., Annex III, at p.19.

 24. DOC.SC/IOC.EG-1(IV)/12, 17 September 1970, Annex III, at p.29.

INDEX OF PERSONS

Alexander, L.M., 41
Andrassy, J., 40
Askevold, G., 186
Auburn, F.M., 7,40,48

Baker, A.A.L., 18
Bankes, L.J., 118
Bardarch, J.E., 42
Benedict, 236,244,252,254
Bernfeld, 120
Beynon, L.R., 45
Boczek, B.A., 251
Bonasia, J., 6
Brett, M.R., 253
Brierly, J.L., 124,153
Briggs, H.W., 80
Brown, E.D., 41,47,79,80,81
  83,85,86,116,155,169,187,
  188,189,224,225,226
Brownlie, I., 121
Burke, W.T., 12,39,47,57,70
  79,81,84,85,94,116,154,
  186,224,225,226

Cheng, B., 57,81,117,118,153
  250
Chorley, Lord, 250,253,254
Christy, F.T., 156
Churchill, R., 40,43,83,191
Clark, B.L., 18
Colombos, C.J., 59,82,83,85,
  119,154,155,156,189,253
Craven, J.P., 38,40,41,49

Dixit, R.K., 225
Dollar, A.T.J., 118
Dyer, I., 41

Eckhardt, S., 48,86
Eisemann, P.M., 85
Ely, N., 156
Emde Boas, M.J. van, 47,81,
  82,84,147,154,155,157
Finlay, Lord, 97
Finlay, L.W., 187
Fitzmaurice, Sir Gerald, 116
Flipse, J.E., 187

Ford, G., 28,76
Francois, J.P.A., 82,98,129
Fricke, P., 41
Friedmann, W., 40,80,83

Gamble, J.K., 45, 157
Gauthier, M., 187'
Gibson, A.E., 44
Gibson, R.S., 81
Gidel, G., 39,82,90,115,116
Giles, O.C., 250,253,254
Glaser, P.E., 43
Glassner, M.I., 186
Goldie, L.F.E., 81, 187
Gombos, L., 189
Graham, M., 46
Grotius, H., 58
Guilcher, A., 40
Gutteridge, J.A.C., 80

Hackworth, G.H., 120, 154
Hall, W.E., 120, 127,154
Hammet, D.S., 6
Hammond, Dr., 3
Henkin, L., 157, 187
Heydte, F.A. von der, 120
Hildreth, R.G., 45
Hirsch, A., 45
Hodgson, R.D., 116
Hoffman, J.F., 49
Huber, M., 130
Hudson, M.O., 121
Hughes, H., 164
Hunnings, N.M., 153,154,155,156

Jaffe, A., 187
Jessup, P.C., 90, 115
Johnson, D.H.N., 82,115,128,154,
  155,157
Johnston, D.M., 43,45,46,47,49,
  156
Judy, J., 40,41,45,46,47,48,80,
  84

Kalinkin, G.F., 81
Keaton, S.K., 40,41,45,46,47,48
  80,84

Kennedy, W.R., 253,254
Kennett, Lord, 46
Knight, H.G., 44,82,83,119, 157
Koers, A.W., 157
Krueger, R.B., 86,190

Lachs, M., 249
Lauterpacht, Sir Hersch, 63, 84,115
Lawrence, W.H., 44,46
Lay, S.H., 191
Lazaratos, G., 116,117
Lerner, L., 46
Loftas, T., 186
Luard, E., 47

McDougal, M.S., 12,39,47, 57,70,79,81,84,85,94,116, 154,225
McKee, A., 42,43
McQuade, Mr., 41
Margue, M., 59,82,112,147
Marsden, 244,254
Marvaldi, J., 187
Meyers, H., 99,117,118
Moody, J.D., 186
Moore, J.B., 115,120
Morris, J.W., 190
Mouton, M.W., 58,65,69,82,84 85,91,141,155,156
Murty, B.S., 156

Nastin, P., 225
Nelson, L.D.M., 86
Newton, L.K., 43
Nordquist, M., 191

O'Connell, D.P., 121
Oda, Sh., 42,169,187
Oppenheim, L., 90,115,126
Oxman, B.H., 87,117,187,224

Padilla Nervo, L., 76,86
Panhuys, H.F. van, 47,48,81,82, 84,147,154,155,157
Pauw, F. de., 82
Pearcy, G.E., 39
Petrowski, L.C., 47
Phillimore, Lord, 253

Pontecorvo, G., 45, 157
Pot, J.J., 6,41,44

Richardson, I.D., 43,58,138
Ripert, G., 254
Riphagen, W., 12,39,40,82,84, 144,156
Roberts, W.O., 201
Rolin, H., 82
Rosa, Mr., 4
Rousseau, Ch., 82
Russel, Sir Charles, 89,90
Ryther, J.H., 42

Samuels, A., 189,190
Schwarzenberger, G., 114,120,121, 153
Scott, L.J., 254
Scott, Sir William, 69,70
Scrutton, L.J., 118
Seabrook Hull, E.W., 14,42
Sibthorp, M.M., 47,187
Simmonds, K.R., 40,43,83
Singh, N., 188,253,254
Skinner, D.J., 6
Smedal, G., 120
Smith, R.W., 116
Soons, A.H.A., 45,80,84,157
Spiropoulos, J., 82
Stevenson, J.R., 87,117,224
Stowell, Lord, 244
Sturmey, S.G., 251
Szasz, P.C., 47

Tammes, A.J.P., 59
Tamrazyan, G.P., 118
Thornberry, C., 189

Vysotsky, A., 225

Waldock, Sir Humphrey, 58,68 82,83,84,85,120,127,138,153, 154,155,156,157
Walker, C.W., 44,46,82,84,119, 152,154,156,157
Warbrick, C.,83
Waugh, G.D., 43
Welch, J., 40,43,83
Westlake, J., 90,115
Whiteman, M.M., 39,154

Woodliffe, J.G., 47,155,
    189,190
Wooster, W.S,224

Yeich, B., 41
Young, E., 41
Young, R., 188

Zourek, J., 82

***   ***   ***   ***

SUBJECT INDEX

"Abalonia", 36
Aquaculture, 20-21
"Aquapolis", 3
Archipelagos, 94
Artificial Extension of Land Into the Sea, 11-13
Artificial Islands and Installations,
    Conflict With Other Users, 4,61,84,110-112,257-265
    Defined, 6
    Economic Use, 17-24
    Feasibility and Implications, 37-39
    Japan, 2
    Juridical Status of Artificial Islands, q.v.
    Jurisdiction Over Artificial Islands, q.v.
    Legal Problems Created, 3-5
    North Sea, 2, 17
    Right to Construct Artificial Islands, q.v.
    Scientific Investigation, 31-32
    Set up as "New Sovereign States", 4,36-37,112-115
    Types, 11-37
    U.S. Atlantic and Gulf Coasts, 2
ASW Sonar Systems, 33-34
"Atlantis, City of Gold", 4,74,86,115

Belgium,
    Act on "Pirate" Broadcasting, 134
    Continental Shelf Practice, 146
    Working Paper Concerning Artificial Islands, 53-54,64,72,
                                  141,148-149
Bos Kalis Westminster Dredging Group, 18

Cobb Seamount, 2,14,31
Collision, Maritime, 243-244
Communication Stations, 30-31
Conservation of the Living Resources of the Sea, 172,173
Contiguous Zone, 54,80,123,131,210
Continental Shelf,
    Installations, 170-186
    Outer Limit, 168
    Resources, 161-165
    Sovereign Rights, 22,66-67,83,85,130,144,168-169
    Technology, 165-167
    Tunnelling from Terra Firma, 175
Council of Europe,
    Agreement on "Pirate" Broadcasting, 35-36,135-136
    Recommendation on Artificial Islands, 61-62

Declaration of Principles Governing the Sea-Bed, etc., (1970)
                          56,81

Deep-Sea Mining, 56,80,81,167
Deepsea Ventures Inc., 164,167
Deep Water Ports. See Off-Shore Terminals
Deepwater Port Act 1974 (U.S.), 28,109
                              See also under United States
Deployment of ODAS, 205-224
   Contiguous Zone, 210
   Continental Shelf, 216-219
   Exclusive Economic Zone, 220-221
   High Seas, 212-215
   Internal Waters, 207-208
   International Co-operation, 222-224
   International Organizations, 221-222
   Territorial Sea, 208-209

European Agreement on "Pirate" Broadcasting, 35-36, 135-136
Exclusive Economic Zone, 51,76-78.
   See also under Revised Single Negotiating Text

Fish, As a Sea Resource,18-19
Fisheries,
   Conducted by Means of Equipment Embedded in the Sea Floor, 19-20
   Sedentary, 19
Fish Farming
   See Aquaculture
Flags of Convenience, 233,251
Floating Docks, 29
France,
   Continental Shelf Act (1968), 182
   Decree on "Pirate" Broadcasting, 133-134
Freedom of Fishing, 172
Freedom of High Seas, 55, 57-59,81,82,211
Freedom to Construct Artificial Islands in the High Seas, 58-66
Freedom to Lay Submarine Cables and Pipelines, 174
Freedom of Navigation, 172,173,209

"Genuine Link" Concept, 233-234,251
"Glomar Challenger", 1,166
"Grand Capri Republic", 4,74,115
Group of Experts on Private Law Aspects of ODAS, 197

IMCO
   Attitude to "Pirate" Broadcasting, 136
   Maritime Safety Committee, 258
   Work on ODAS, 195-197
Individuals in International Law, 114-115
Industrial Artificial Islands, 17-18
"Industrial Vessels and Personnel", 177-178
Informal Working Paper No. 12 on Artificial Islands (UNCLOS III,
   Caracas Session) 52,65,71,141-142

Installations for the Exploration and Exploitation of the
    Natural Resources of the Continental Shelf, 104,120,144,145,
                            161-191
        Jurisdiction, 120,144,145,178-186
            State Practice, 179-186
        Legal Status, 104,174-178
        Notice of Construction, 171
        Reconciliation With Other User, 172-174
        Removal, 171
        Right to Construct, 144,170
        Safety Zones, 144,171,179
        Technology, 165-167
Installations Relating to the Conduct of Activities in the
    International Sea-Bed Area, 108,143,172
Intergovernmental Oceanographic Commission, 195
Internal Waters, 51-52,123,207-208
International Co-operation in Deployment of ODAS, 222-224

Juridical Status of Artificial Islands, 89-121
    Artificial Islands Other Than Sea-Cities, 108-112
    Sea-Cities, 104-107
Jurisdiction Over Artificial Islands and Installations,
    Continental Shelf, 144-150,152,178-186
        Artificial Islands, 146-149
        Floating Installations, 145
    Exclusive Economic Zone, 151,152
    High Seas, 127-144,151-152
        "Flag-State" Jurisdiction, 138-140,142
        International Supervision and Control, 141-143
        Personal Jurisdiction, 127-129,137
        U.N. Report on International Machinery, 139-140
    Internal Waters, 123,151
    Territorial Sea, 123,151
Jurisdiction over ODAS, 232-235
Jurisdiction Over Ships, 124-127,145,154,176
    Exclusive Jurisdiction of Flag-State, 125
    Stateless Ships, 125-126
Jurisdictional Matters Concerning ODAS, 227-255
    Jurisdiction, 232-235
    Liability for Unauthorized Interference with ODAS, q.v.
    Recovery and Return, 227-229
    Registration, 229-231

Legal Vacuum Theory, 129-130
Liability for Unauthorized Interference with ODAS, 235-249
    Collision, 243-249
        Manned ODAS, 245-247
        Unmanned ODAS, 247-249
    Intentional Illegal Interference, 235-241
        Civil Liability, 240-241

Criminal Liability, 236-240
Salvage, 241-243
Lighthouses, Legal Status of, 89-90
Low-Tide Elevations, 92,93,96,97

Manganese Nodules, 163-164
See also under Natural Resources
Man-Made Islands. See Artificial Islands and Installations
Marine and Broadcasting (Offences) Act 1967 (U.K.), 132-133
Marine Hydrocarbons, 162. See also under Natural Resources
Marine Pollution, 111-112
Military Installations, 33-35
Minerals Extracted from Sea Water, 164-165
"Minerva Republic", 36-37, 115
Moratorium Resolution, 56
Multi-Purpose Artificial Islands, 17-18
See also under Artificial Islands and Installations

Natural Islands, Legal Status of, 91-97
Geneva Convention on the Territorial Sea and the
Contiguous Zone 1958, 92-94
International Customary Law, 91-92
Hague Codification Conference 1930, 91-92
Harvard Research, 92
UNCLOS III, 94-96
Natural Resources, 161-165. See also under Continental Shelf
Defined, 161-162
Marine Hydrocarbons, 162
Minerals Extracted from Sea Water, 164-165
Superficial Deposits, 162-164
Negligent Navigation, Defined, 244
North Sea,
Oil Storage Tanks, 28-29
Oil Technology, 1
North Sea Installations Act 1965 (Netherlands), 101,147,150
North Sea Island Group, 2,17-18
Nuclear Power Stations, 3,24. See also under Power Stations

Objective Territorial Jurisdiction, 124,153
Ocean Fish Traps, 20
Oceanography, 193-194
Ocean Thermal Energy Conversion Plants, 23
See also under Power Plants
ODAS
Definition, 104,198-200
Deployment of ODAS, q.v.
Jurisdictional Matters Concerning ODAS, q.v.
Preparatory Conference, 3, 196-197
Safety Rules Covering ODAS, q.v.
Work by IOC/IMCO, 195-197

Off-Shore Airports, 2,29-30,109
    Safety Zones, 109
Off-Shore Storage Facilities, 28-29
Off-Shore Terminals, 2,12,25-28,83,109
    Part of the Harbour System, 12
    Safety Zones, 109
Oil and Gas Industry, 1-2, 162

Patrimonial Sea. See Exclusive Economic Zone
Personal Jurisdiction, 124,127,137
Pilkington Glass Age Development Committee, 3,16
Piracy, 236-237
"Pirate" Broadcasting Stations, 3,35-36,131-137
    IMCO Attitude, 136
    ITU Attitude, 136-137
    Legislation Enacted by European States, 131-136
Ports, 11-13
Power Stations, 22-24
    Nuclear, 24
    OTEC Plants, 23
    Tidal, 22-23

Recovery and Return of ODAS, 227-229
Recreational Facilities, 3,32-33
Registration of ODAS, 229-231
R.E.M.Station,35-36,101,129
Revised Single Negotiating Text,
    Archaeological and Historical Objects 22
    Continental Shelf,
        Artificial Islands and Installations, 71,149
        Outer Limit, 168
    Exclusive Economic Zone,
        Artificial Islands and Installations, 77,108,111,151,172
        Notice of Construction, 110
        Outer Limit, 76
        Safety Zones, 109-110
        Sovereign Rights, 76,165,169
    Freedom to Construct Artificial Islands in the High Seas, 60
    High Seas, Defined, 83,210
    International Sea-Bed Area,
        Installations, 108,143,172
        Prohibition of Appropriation, 107
        Safety Zones, 110,171
    Marine Pollution, 111-112
    Natural Islands, 96
    Ports, 13
    Scientific Research, 206,208,212,259
    Territorial Sea Breadth, 52

Right to Conduct Scientific Research,
   Contiguous Zone, 210
   Continental Shelf, 206,215-216
   Exclusive Economic Zone, 206,220-221
   High Seas, 55,173-174,207,210-212,214
   Internal Waters, 207
   Territorial Sea, 208
Right to Construct Artificial Islands, 51-87
   Contiguous Zone, 54
   Continental Shelf, 66-75
   Exclusive Economic Zone, 76-78
   High Seas, 54-66
   Internal Waters, 51-52
   Territorial Sea, 52-54

Safety Rules Covering ODAS, 257-265
   Construction Arrangements, 261-262
   Liability, 261
   Marking and Signals, 259-260
   Notification of Deployment, 259
   ODAS Used as Aids to Navigation, 260-261
   Safety Requirements, 262-265
Safety Zones, 108,109-110,143-144,179,263-264
Salvage of ODAS, 241-243
San Marco Launching Facility, 2
Scandinavian Legislation on "Pirate" Broadcasting Stations,134-135
Scientific Research. See also under Revised Single Negotiating
   Text
      Defined, 205-206
Scripps Institute of Oceanography, 31
Sea-Bed, Legal Status of, 55-57, 68-69
Sea-Bed Committee, Establishment of, 94
Sea-Cities
   Fixed on the Sea-Bed, 16,104-107
   Floating, 17,107
   Juridical Status, 104-107
   Off the Norfolk Coast (U.K.), 3,16
   Technology, 16-17
Sealab Programme, 3,31
"Sealand, Independent State of", 36
Seamounts,
   Communication Stations on Seamounts, 30
   Economic, Political and Military Significance, 4,13-16
   Legal Status, 55-56,65-66
Sedentary Fisheries, 19
Ships, Legal Status of, 97-103
Soviet Decree on Continental Shelf, 72-73,171,182,190-191
States, Criteria of Independent Statehood, 114-115
State Jurisdiction Under International Customary Law, 124,153
Stateless Ships, 125-126

Subsea Production Systems, 1-2, 166. See also under
    Continental Shelf
Subsoil of Sea-Bed, Legal Status of, 56-57
Superficial Deposits, 162-164
Superports. See Off-Shore Terminals
Surtsey Island, 105

Tektite Experiments, 3,31
Territorial Jurisdiction, 123,124
Territorial Sea, 52-54,123
Territory, Title by Occupation, 113-114,120
Theory of Contiguity, 69,130
Tunnelling from Terra Firma, 175

Underwater Habitats, 3
Unilateral Declarations of Jurisdiction, 147
United Kingdom,
    Attitude to "Pirate" Broadcasting Stations, 131-133
    Continental Shelf Act 1964, 170,179-181,190
    Report on Automatic Data-Gathering Stations 1972, 2-3
    Report on Off-Shore Airports 1970, 2
United Nations,
    General Assembly, Resolutions, Legal Significance of, 56-57
    Secretary-General's Report on International Machinery, 21-22
                        139-140
United States,
    Aids to Navigation, 261
    Deepwater Port Act 1974, 28,109
    Outer Continental Shelf Lands Act 1953, 73-75,171,181-182
    Sea Use Programme, 31
Universal Theory of Crime, 124

"Veronica", Radio-Ship, 101,118